PANEL DATA ECONOMETRICS

METHODS-OF-MOMENTS AND LIMITED DEPENDENT VARIABLES

PANEL DATA ECONOMETRICS

METHODS-OF-MOMENTS AND LIMITED DEPENDENT VARIABLES

Myoung-jae Lee

Department of Economics
Sungkyunkwan University
Seoul Korea

ACADEMIC PRESS
An Elsevier Science Imprint

San Diego   San Francisco   New York   Boston   London   Sydney   Tokyo

Academic Press
An Elsevier Science Imprint
525 B Street, Suite 1900, San Diego, California 92101-4495, USA
http://www.academicpress.com

Academic Press
32 Jamestown Road, London NW1 7BY, UK
http://www.academicpress.com

Library of Congress Catalog Card Number: 2002100863

International Standard Book Number: 0-12-440656-4
International Standard Book Number: 0-12-440657-2(diskette)

PRINTED IN THE UNITED STATES OF AMERICA
02 03 04 05 06   EB 9 8 7 6 5 4 3 2 1

*To my wife, Hyun-sook,
and two children,
Joung-woo and Eugene*

CONTENTS

3

TOPICS FOR PANEL LINEAR MODELS

4

PANEL DATA ESTIMATORS
FOR BINARY RESPONSES

5

PANEL DATA ESTIMATORS
FOR LIMITED RESPONSES

6

PANEL DATA AND
SAMPLE SELECTION MODELS

PREFACE

A search in the *Journal of Economic Literature* using the key words *panel data* yields 1063 entries for journal articles over the 1983 to 1999 period, and 1867 entries when books and others papers are included. This shows well how popular panel data research has become over the years.

Compared with cross-section data, the number of panel data observations is "T-times" greater than that for the single cross-section (the single "wave"). More important than the bigger sample size, panel data provide better ways to control for unobserved individual heterogeneity than cross-section data. With these advantages in hand, one can afford to do away with the strong parametric assumptions often used in cross-section and time-series data.

With easy access to many panel data sets these days, particularly on the Internet, one needs a fairly good excuse to use a single wave rather than panel data. Also, because panel data show the history of individuals, researchers often want to (and can) do far more with panel data than with cross-section data.

As a result, there has been a high demand for econometric knowledge about handling panel data. There are some textbooks (Hsiao, 1986, and Baltagi, 1995) and chapters in edited volumes (Chamberlain, 1984, Mátyás and Sevestre, 1992, and Arellano and Honoré, 2001), but books on *recent advances in panel data econometrics with emphasis on weak model assumptions* ("semiparametric") are not available. The goal of this book is to fill this void in the literature. The book is divided into two parts: the first part, Chapters 1 to 3, introduces panel data and panel linear models, and the second part, Chapters 4 to 6, examines limited response models.

Chapter 1 introduces issues in panel data to give the reader an idea about what is to come in the other chapters. Chapter 2 examines the basics of methods-of-moment estimation for linear panel data models. Chapter 3, continuing the Chapter 2 discussion, explores various topics for linear panel data models. Chapter 4 reviews estimators for panel binary response models. Chapter 5 discusses panel estimators for count, censored, and multinomial response models. Finally, Chapter 6 examines panel sample selection and attrition models. The second halves of Chapters 3 and 4 and all of Chapter 6 may be skipped if the reader is time-constrained; Chapter 3 and 5 also can be read selectively.

Numerous empirical examples are included at different levels, ranging from a simple description of the result to a full-scale analysis; some carry explicit subsection titles and some are buried in sections. GAUSS programs and the data used in some empirical examples are provided. To make this book self-contained, background materials are provided whenever necessary, assuming that the reader has some exposure to cross-section (and basic time-series) models.

It seems inevitable that, as in any book, the choice of topics and references reflect the author's own interest and taste; the original manuscript for this book carried a qualifier "a course" in the title, which was subsequently dropped, however, at the recommendation of a referee. My apology goes to the authors who made contributions to the literature of panel data but are not given credit in this book.

The title carries also a qualifier, "econometrics": the statistical literature on panel data ("longitudinal data" or "repeated measurements") is not covered. One reason is that the statistical literature deals mostly with data collected at varying intervals over (almost) continuous calendar time (in days or weeks), whereas most econometric panel data are collected at regular intervals over discrete time (often yearly). Another reason is that econometricians emphasize individual heterogeneity and endogeneity problems far more than statisticians do; this stems from concerns about causality and structural models from which statisticians often stay away. The reader interested in the statistical literature should search recent issues of major statistics journals using the key words *longitudinal data*. Also, within econometrics, macropanels with nonstationary time-series are not treated in this book; interested readers should have no difficulty finding papers on macropanels in recent issues of major econometrics journals.

This manuscript is based on lecture notes for the last couple of years and can be taught in one quarter or semester course. The target audience is master's or Ph.D-level students who have taken one or two econometrics courses. In view of the fact that available econometric packages are not flexible enough for the recent methods in panel data analysis, the computational steps as well as the main theoretical ideas are presented so that the reader can analyze panel data on his or her own.

Over the past couple of years, a number of students have provided me with feedback on this book; one of them, Jin-beom Kim, helped me prepare T_EX files for the book. I am especially grateful to two friends of mine, Bertrand Melenberg and Juao Santos Silva, who read the entire manuscript and gave me valuable comments; I am also grateful to the anonymous referees from Academic Press. Finally, continuous help througout the publication process from the editor, Scott Bentley, his assistant, Kirsten Funk, and Jocelyn Lofstrom, production manager, at Academic Press, and Amy Hendrickson at T_EXnology Inc. is much appreciated.

1

INTRODUCTION TO PANEL
DATA ISSUES

1.1 INTRODUCTION

This chapter is a "gentle" introduction to panel data issues that will give an idea of what is to come in the following chapters. Almost all of the issues discussed in this chapter will reappear in later chapters; those readers in a hurry may skip this chapter, although this is not recommended. To keep the reader focused, this chapter will not include long empirical examples or references; these will be provided in later chapters at the appropriate places.

Suppose we are interested in the effect of schooling on wage—that is, what happens to one's wage if an individual changes his or her schooling by, say, one year from 10 to 11? In cross-section data with N individuals, we will be comparing people with different levels of schooling; for example, person 1 with 10 years of schooling and person 2 with 11. The wage difference between person 1 and 2 is then taken as the effect of schooling on wage, but the problem is that the wage difference may be due to differences in variables other than schooling (for example, ability or residential location). In cross-section data, the interpersonal differences of many people are used for the intertemporal difference of a single individual, which can result in misleading conclusions.

1

Suppose we use time-series data of T periods on a single person to remedy the shortcoming of cross-section data. Clearly, we can get the intertemporal difference of the individual. But then, there is no reason to believe that the effect of schooling on wage for this particular individual will hold for other individuals; here, we need an average effect, average over many people. This is essentially what panel data deliver that neither cross-section nor time-series data alone can: the average of the intertemporal differences of many people.

As there are time series of an individual ("micro time series") and times series of an aggregate entity ("macro time series"), there are micropanel data (panel of individuals) and macropanel data (panel of aggregate entities such as countries or regions). The two panel types differ much in terms of the techniques required to analyze them: micropanel data can be analyzed with the usual cross-section data methods, whereas macropanel data may require special time-series methods. They also differ in terms of N and T: micropanel data typically have a large N (and a small T), whereas macropanel data have a small N (and a large T, or $T \cong N$).

Our goal is studying micropanel (or longitudinal) data with a large N (and a small T). Our analysis may be applicable to some macropanels if the condition on N is met. For this, we will start with a cross-section data model in Section 1.2, and then introduce the extra time dimension for panel data. As the time dimension is added, new features not available in cross-section arise: temporal moment conditions in Section 1.3 and time-varying parameters in Section 1.4. Section 1.5 introduces a time-invariant error, say δ_i, allowed to be related to regressors in arbitrary ways, which is an important advantage of panel data as will be seen later. The error term δ_i is removed in a number of different ways in Sections 1.5 and 1.6; δ_i also brings in a dynamic feature for it represents "inertia," which is seen in Section 1.7. Finally, δ_i combined with a time-variant error gives an error-term structure, which leads to some interesting observations in Section 1.8.

1.2   EXTRA TIME DIMENSION

In a typical cross-section model, we have

$$y_i = x_i'\beta + u_i, \quad i = 1, ..., N, \tag{2.1}$$

where $\{(y_i, x_i)\}_{i=1}^{N}$ is observed, $x_i = (1, x_{i2}, ..., x_{ik})'$ is a $k \times 1$ regressor vector, β is the parameter to estimate, and u_i is an error term with

$$E(xu) = (E(u), E(x_2 u), ..., E(x_k u))' = 0;$$

the subscript i is omitted, as will be done often in the following as well. This $k \times 1$ vector moment condition is equivalent to $COV(u, x_j) = 0$, $j = 2, ..., k$, because $E(u) = 0$ (the first component of $E(xu) = 0$) and

$$0 = E(ux_j) = E(ux_j) - E(u) \cdot E(x_j) = COV(u, x_j). \tag{2.2}$$

From $E(xu) = 0$, we get, assuming $\{E(xx')\}^{-1}$ exists,

$$0 = E\{x(y - x'\beta)\} \Rightarrow \beta = \{E(xx')\}^{-1}E(xy) \qquad (2.3)$$

Defining $Y = (y_1, ..., y_N)'$ and $X = (x_1, ..., x_N)'$, which is an $N \times k$ matrix, the least squares estimator (LSE) b_{lse} is just a "sample analog" for β in (2.3):

$$b_{lse} = (X'X)^{-1}(X'Y) = (\sum_i x_i x_i'/N)^{-1} \sum_i x_i y_i/N. \qquad (2.4)$$

Note that the outer product $x_i x_i'$ in the first sum is

$$x_i x_i' = \begin{bmatrix} 1 \\ \vdots \\ x_{ik} \end{bmatrix} \cdot [\ 1\ \cdots\ x_{ik}\ ] = \begin{bmatrix} 1 & x_{i2} & \cdots & x_{ik} \\ \vdots & \vdots & & \vdots \\ x_{ik} & x_{ik}x_{i2} & \cdots & x_{ik}^2 \end{bmatrix}. \qquad (2.5)$$

More generally, suppose we have an $m \times 1$ $(m \geq k)$ instrument vector z_i such that $E(zu) = 0$, $\text{rank}\{E(zz')\} = m$, and $\text{rank}\{E(zx')\} = k$. Here, the question is how to combine m-many (more than enough) instruments to come up with k-many (just enough) instruments. Observe

$$0 = E\{z(y - x'\beta)\} \Rightarrow E(zy) = E(zx') \cdot \beta.$$

The matrix $E(zx')$ is not invertible when $m > k$; we need an invertible matrix next to β. For this, multiply both sides of $E(zy) = E(zx')\beta$ by $E(xz')\{E(zz')\}^{-1}$ to get

$$E(xz')\{E(zz')\}^{-1}E(zy) = E(xz')\{E(zz')\}^{-1}E(zx') \cdot \beta$$
$$\Rightarrow \beta = [E(xz')\{E(zz')\}^{-1}E(zx')]^{-1}E(xz')\{E(zz')\}^{-1}E(zy).$$

A sample analog for this is the following instrumental variable estimator (IVE):

$$b_{ive} \equiv \{\sum_i x_i z_i'(\sum_i z_i z_i')^{-1}\sum_i z_i x_i'\}^{-1} \cdot \sum_i x_i z_i'(\sum_i z_i z_i')^{-1}\sum_i z_i y_i. \qquad (2.6)$$

Pay attention to the dimensions in $\sum_i x_i z_i'(\sum_i z_i z_i')^{-1}\sum_i z_i x_i'$, which can be viewed as a "dimension reduction device" from m to k:

$$\{(k \times 1) \cdot (1 \times m)\} \cdot \{(m \times 1) \cdot (1 \times m)\} \cdot \{(m \times 1) \cdot (1 \times k)\} = k \times k. \qquad (2.7)$$

The IVE includes the LSE as a special case when $z_i = x_i$. In the IVE, the moment conditions used can be seen by replacing y_i in the last sum $\sum_i z_i y_i$ with u_i: $(1/N) \sum_i z_i u_i = 0 \Rightarrow E(zu) = 0$.

In panel data, we observe the same N subjects over T years; each cross section is called a "wave." A typical model is

$$y_{it} = x_{it}'\beta + u_{it}, \quad i = 1, ..., N, \quad t = 1, ..., T, \qquad (2.8)$$

where now all variables carry the extra time subscript t. In X, we stacked the N individuals' $k \times 1$ regressors into the $N \times k$ matrix X. With the extra time dimension T, can we have an expression analogous to the cross section b_{lse}? For this, $(X'X)^{-1}(X'Y)$ is not good; rather, we use $(\sum_i x_i x_i'/N)^{-1}$ $\sum_i x_i y_i/N$. In $x_i x_i'$ with the dimension $k \times k = (k \times 1) \cdot (1 \times k)$, we "sneak" the time dimension T in the middle to get the same $k \times k = (k \times T) \cdot (T \times k)$. That is, we use matrices now to stack the data over time for each individual: define y_i ($T \times 1$ vector), x_i ($k \times T$ matrix), and u_i ($T \times 1$ vector) now as

$$
y_i \equiv \begin{bmatrix} y_{i1} \\ \vdots \\ y_{iT} \end{bmatrix}, \quad x_i' \equiv \begin{bmatrix} x_{i1}' \\ \vdots \\ x_{iT}' \end{bmatrix}, \quad \text{and} \quad u_i \equiv \begin{bmatrix} u_{i1} \\ \vdots \\ u_{iT} \end{bmatrix}. \tag{2.9}
$$

With these, analogously to (2.1), we get,

$$
y_i = x_i'\beta + u_i, \quad i = 1, ..., N, \tag{2.10}
$$

and a panel version of LSE is

$$
b_{lse} = (\sum_i x_i x_i')^{-1} \sum_i x_i y_i \tag{2.11}
$$

which looks just like the cross section LSE. The following section will show, however, that there is a better panel LSE than this.

1.3   TEMPORAL MOMENT CONDITIONS

Although (2.10) looks the same as (2.1), putting the extra time dimension T in $x_i x_i'$ leads to attaching $\sum_t$ to each component of (2.5): denoting person i's j-th regressor at time t as x_{itj}, we get

$$
x_i x_i' = \begin{bmatrix} 1 & \cdots & 1 \\ x_{i12} & \cdots & x_{iT2} \\ \vdots & & \vdots \\ x_{i1k} & \cdots & x_{iTk} \end{bmatrix} \begin{bmatrix} 1 & x_{i12} & \cdots & x_{i1k} \\ \vdots & \vdots & & \vdots \\ 1 & x_{iT2} & \cdots & x_{iTk} \end{bmatrix}
$$

$$
= \begin{bmatrix} \sum_t 1 & \sum_t x_{it2} & \cdots & \sum_t x_{itk} \\ \vdots & \vdots & & \vdots \\ \sum_t x_{itk} & \sum_t x_{itk} x_{it2} & \cdots & \sum_t x_{itk}^2 \end{bmatrix}.
$$

This shows that the panel LSE (2.11) can be written as

$$
b_{lse} = (\sum_i \sum_t x_{it} x_{it}')^{-1} \sum_i \sum_t x_{it} y_{it} : \tag{3.1}
$$

if we pull all waves together ignoring the panel nature to apply LSE as in a cross section, then the LSE is as shown in (2.11).

To see the moment condition implicit in (3.1), replace y_{it} in $\sum_i \sum_t x_{it} y_{it} / N$ with u_{it} and observe

$$\sum_t \left(\sum_i x_{it} u_{it} / N \right) \cong \sum_t E(x_{it} u_{it}) = 0; \tag{3.2}$$

only the sum $\sum_t E(x_{it} u_{it})$ is zero, not necessarily the individual terms. This does not really make sense, for there is no reason to use less than the usual cross-sectional moment condition $E(x_{it} u_{it}) = 0$ for all t; in total, we get $k \cdot T$ moment conditions, more than the number of parameters. The panel LSE will be an inefficient estimator; a more efficient panel LSE will take a form of IVE.

One way to use all the cross-section moment conditions is to estimate each cross section separately and then combine the T-many estimators. Suppose we apply LSE to each wave to get the LSE b_t for t. How do we combine them? A crude way is to calculate a simple average $(1/T) \sum_t b_t$, but a better method is to use an weighted average $\sum_t w_t b_t$, where $\sum_t w_t = 1$ and $w_t \geq 0$ for all t. For example, consider the following two estimates with $T = 2$ years (this example is actually taken from a nonlinear model):

Effect of schooling on joining a union: -0.24 ($t = 1$), -0.43 ($t = 2$). (3.3)

The simple average is $(-0.24 - 0.43)/2 = -0.335$, whereas a weighted average is a number between -0.24 and -0.43, depending on the weights. The weights w_t's can be chosen optimally using "minimum distance estimation" (MDE); essentially, the less variance the estimator has, the higher weight it gets. MDE will play an important role in panel data.

Although the idea of MDE is important, it is somewhat cumbersome due to its two stage nature; the first stage (for example, cross-section LSE) is usually simple, but the second is not. Another way to use all of the cross-section moment conditions is by utilizing the IVE, which can be done in one step (but we have to toil more at the single step). As with the LSE, the panel IVE takes the same form as the cross-section IVE except that the time dimension T replaces 1 in (2.7).

To be specific, z_i becomes diagonal for panel data: for example, with $T = 3$,

$$z_i = \text{diag}(z_{i1}, z_{i2}, z_{i3}),$$

where z_{it} is a $k_t \times 1$ instrument vector for time t. This leads to

$$z_i u_i = \begin{bmatrix} z_{i1} & 0 & 0 \\ 0 & z_{i2} & 0 \\ 0 & 0 & z_{i3} \end{bmatrix} \begin{bmatrix} u_{i1} \\ u_{i2} \\ u_{i3} \end{bmatrix} = \begin{bmatrix} z_{i1} u_{i1} \\ z_{i2} u_{i2} \\ z_{i3} u_{i3} \end{bmatrix}, \tag{3.4}$$

where 0's are the null vectors to make the matrix conformable. Taking $(1/N) \sum_t$ on (3.4), we can see that the moment conditions used are $E(z_{it} u_{it}) = 0$ for all t.

Note that z_i is $(\sum_t k_t) \times T$, whereas x_i is only $k \times T$. A panel LSE better than (3.1) is the panel IVE with

$$z_i = \mathrm{diag}(x_{i1}, \ldots, x_{iT}), \tag{3.5}$$

for this makes use of $E(x_{it}u_{it}) = 0$ for all t.

From (3.4), we can see that $\sum_t k_t$ moment conditions are in use in $E(z_i u_i) = 0$ for the panel IVE. Typically, k_t is much bigger than k (for example, $k_t = tk$), which means that $\sum_t k_t$ is much greater than $k \cdot T$, the number of moment conditions when all cross-section moment conditions are put together. We can be even more imaginative:

$$E(x_{is}u_{it}) = 0, \quad \text{for all } s \text{ and } t, \tag{3.6}$$

which yields $k \cdot T^2$ many conditions; for this case, $z_{it} = (x'_{i1}, \ldots, x'_{iT})'$ for all t in (3.4). Equation (3.2) with k moment conditions and (3.6) with $k \cdot T^2$ moment conditions are two extremes; in practice, the number of moment conditions for a panel IVE falls between these two extremes. If $k = 10$ and $T = 3$, then (3.2) renders 10 moment conditions, whereas (3.6) renders 90; the difference can have a substantial implication for the IVE's efficiency.

Four types of temporal moment conditions ["summation" in (3.2), "contemporary" in (3.5), "strict exogeneity" in (3.6), and "predeterminedness," a variation of which appears later in (6.9)] will provide a uniform platform on which panel methods-of-moment estimation can be discussed.

1.4   TIME-VARYING PARAMETERS

We saw the idea of estimating each wave separately and then combining the T-many estimators. But what if the parameter vector β varies over time? In this case, there will be no need to combine the estimators $b_1, \ldots, b_T$; rather, they will show the time-varying pattern of the parameters. In (3.3), the effect of schooling may vary over time, and the two estimates may be indeed for two different parameters. But allowing all components of β to time-vary may be too burdensome because there will be too many parameters to estimate. A sensible compromise is to let only the intercept (β_1 for the regressor 1) vary over time, while keeping all slope coefficients $\beta_s \equiv (\beta_2, \ldots, \beta_k)'$ constant.

Suppose we follow the MDE idea of estimating each wave one by one and then combining only the slope estimates, say $b_{s1}, \ldots, b_{sT}$. Again, the simple average $(1/T) \sum_t b_{st}$ will do, but it is better to use a weighted average $\sum_t w_t b_{st}$. Differently from $\sum_t w_t b_t$, however, finding the optimal weight becomes cumbersome, for we cannot use the variance of b_t right away: the part relevant only for b_{st} should be pulled out.

Suppose we go for a single step method, not the MDE. We should use then

$$y_{it} = \tau_t \cdot 1 + x'_{it}\beta + u_{it}, \tag{4.1}$$

where x_{it} is redefined as the old x_{it} without 1, and β is the time-invariant slope parameters; the time-variant intercept is τ_t, which is to be estimated (the regressor 1 is attached). The intercept τ_t can be thought of as a macroeconomic shock that works the same for all i. If the macroshock varies across individuals, then we may assume $\tau_{it} = \tau_t + \varepsilon_{it}$ and absorb ε_{it} into u_{it}, which takes us back to (4.1).

Stacking (4.1) over time to get an expression analogous to (2.10) becomes slightly more involved: with $T = 3$,

$$
\begin{bmatrix} y_{i1} \\ y_{i2} \\ y_{i3} \end{bmatrix} = \begin{bmatrix} 1 & 0 & 0 \\ 0 & 1 & 0 \\ 0 & 0 & 1 \end{bmatrix} \begin{bmatrix} \tau_1 \\ \tau_2 \\ \tau_3 \end{bmatrix} + \begin{bmatrix} x'_{i1} \\ x'_{i2} \\ x'_{i3} \end{bmatrix} \cdot \beta + \begin{bmatrix} u_{i1} \\ u_{i2} \\ u_{i3} \end{bmatrix}; \quad (4.2)
$$

"time dummies" appear, say d_t for $t = 1, 2, 3$, that takes 1 at time t and 0 otherwise. The parameters and the data can be put together:

$$
\begin{bmatrix} 1 & 0 & 0 \\ 0 & 1 & 0 \\ 0 & 0 & 1 \end{bmatrix} \begin{bmatrix} \tau_1 \\ \tau_2 \\ \tau_3 \end{bmatrix} + \begin{bmatrix} x'_{i1} \\ x'_{i2} \\ x'_{i3} \end{bmatrix} \cdot \beta = \begin{bmatrix} 1 & 0 & 0 & x'_{i1} \\ 0 & 1 & 0 & x'_{i2} \\ 0 & 0 & 1 & x'_{i3} \end{bmatrix} \begin{bmatrix} \tau_1 \\ \tau_2 \\ \tau_3 \\ \beta \end{bmatrix}.
$$

$$(4.3)$$

The product of the two matrices on the right-hand side can be denoted as, say, $w'_i \gamma$ to yield

$$y_i = w'_i \gamma + u_i. \quad (4.4)$$

For γ, the aforementioned LSE or IVE can be applied. It should be clear by now that a generalization as simple as the time-varying intercept requires some care. For the example (3.3), the intercept estimates are $\hat{\tau}_1 = 3.591$ and $\hat{\tau}_2 = 3.523$; it seems $\tau_1 = \tau_2$.

The diagonal matrix consisting of the three time dummies in (4.3) in fact shows what it takes to allow all components of β to time-vary: put 1 back into x_{it} and use the following matrix product instead of (4.3):

$$
\begin{bmatrix} x'_{i1} & 0 & 0 \\ 0 & x'_{i2} & 0 \\ 0 & 0 & x'_{i3} \end{bmatrix} \begin{bmatrix} \beta_1 \\ \beta_2 \\ \beta_3 \end{bmatrix}. \quad (4.5)
$$

Defining the matrix as w'_i and the vector as γ, we get $y_i = w'_i \gamma + u_i$, which can be then estimated by LSE or IVE. In principle, this does not pose any problem; in practice, however, the temporal variation of x_{it} can be rather small, leading to a singular matrix problem.

In general, whether a parameter is time variant or not depends on the time span between periods and how volatile the periods are. If the time span is short, say a month, then we would not expect much change in the parameters describing the subjects' behavior. On the other hand, if the span is long, say several years, then time-variation of parameters is certainly possible. Even when the span is short, if the periods are volatile, then the parameters can still vary. Unlike panel data, time-series data cannot afford time-varying parameters in an arbitrary way.

1.5   THE UNIT-SPECIFIC TERM AND ITS REMOVAL BY DIFFERENCING

One of the main (in fact, probably the most important) attraction of panel data is allowing for a time-invariant error (or unit-specific term), say δ_i, that is possibly related to some regressors; those regressors are then "endogenous" to the error term. With society shifting away from responsibility taking toward responsibility passing, our behavior is more and more claimed to be determined by "endowments" such as genes, IQ, parents, and so on. Other than endowments, there is often substantial inertia in our behavior ("habit persistence," for example). Many variables in economic models are governed by and linked through those endowments or inertia, the unobserved part of which is represented by δ_i.

Consider

$$y_{it} = x_{it}'\beta + \delta_i + u_{it} \tag{5.1}$$

where $v_{it} \equiv \delta_i + u_{it}$ is the composite error term. Suppose, for instance, that

$$
\begin{aligned}
&y_{it} \text{ is calorie intake per day,} \\
&x_{it} \text{ is observable factors (weight, income, age, sex,...),} \\
&u_{it} \text{ is unobservable time-varying factors (stress, busy,...),} \\
&\delta_i \text{ is unobservable time-invariant factors (genes,...);}
\end{aligned}
\tag{5.2}
$$

genes may be related to weight in x_{it}. Due to endogeneity, the LSE is not valid. Although the IVE can be applied, finding an instrument is not easy: a variable related to weight but not to δ_i nor to u_{it}. For instance, if the time spent on exercises is related to weight but not to δ_i, it may be used as an instrument. But one may object to this, on the ground that exercise is also affected by the same genes affecting weight: some people may be genetically programmed to be overweight and lazy (thus no exercise). Instead of the hard task of finding an instrument, we can purge δ_i from the model.

First-difference the model (5.1) to get

$$\Delta y_{it} = \Delta x_{it}'\beta + \Delta u_{it}, \tag{5.3}$$

where $\Delta y_{it} \equiv y_{it} - y_{i,t-1}$. Define Δy_i as the stacked version of Δy_{it}'s over t (if $T = 2$, $\Delta y_{i2} = \Delta y_i$), and define Δx_i and Δu_i analogously. LSE (or IVE) can be applied to (5.3). With δ_i gone, we do not have to worry about the endogeneity of regressors caused by the relationship with δ_i anymore.

Although differencing sounds straightforward, it is not always so. For instance, all time invariants should be removed from x_{it} before differencing (for example, $\Delta sex_{it} = 0$); otherwise, Δx_i will contain zero columns and $\sum_i \Delta x_i \Delta x_i'$ becomes singular. Although many panel models are routinely written as (5.1) with x_{it} containing both time-invariant and variant regressors, it is better to treat them separately. Some variables are time variant, but in a deterministic manner: a well-known example is age: $\Delta age_{it} = 1$ always for yearly data. That is, age_{it} becomes the column of T-many 1's in Δx_i. With age_{it} in x_{it}, 1 should not be in Δx_{it} to prevent singularity; when $T = 2$, the coefficient of 1 (or Δage_{it}) in Δx_{it} is $\tau_2 - \tau_1$.

Although differencing is beneficial in taking care of the relation between x_{it} and δ_i, it has some shortcomings. First, we lose all time invariants while our main interest may very well be on the coefficient of a time-invariant variable; a well-known example is "returns to schooling," where the main interest is on the coefficient of schooling, but schooling is time invariant for most adults. Second, differencing does not take care of the endogeneity due to the relation between x_{it} and u_{it}. Third, the temporal variation of x_{it} can be rather small; with little variation in Δx_{it}, we get to estimate β with low precision in the differenced model.

Panel IVE can overcome these shortcomings. First, time-invariant variables are not lost because the model equation is not differenced; instead, the relation between x_{it} and δ_i is handled with instruments. For instance, suppose $x_{it} = \delta_i + \tilde{x}_{it}$ and $\tilde{x}_{it}$ is unrelated to u_{it}. Then $\Delta x_{it} = \Delta \tilde{x}_{it}$ can be used as an instrument for x_{it}. Second, a relation between x_{it} and u_{it} is allowed. For instance, suppose $\{x_{i1}, ..., x_{iT}\}$ is unrelated to δ_i but related to u_{it} only through x_{it}. Then $x_{i,t-1}$ (and many others) can be used as an instrument for x_{it}. Third, as these examples show, some elements of x_{it} are used in level rather than in increment. The weakness of panel IVE is that it relies on an assumption about the relationship between $\{x_{i1}, ..., x_{iT}\}$ and $\{v_{i1}, ..., v_{iT}\}$, whereas differencing does not need any assumption on the relationship between $\{x_{i1}, ..., x_{iT}\}$ and δ_i.

1.6   OTHER WAYS TO REMOVE UNIT-SPECIFIC TERM

So far we have been dealing with linear models with a continuously distributed response y_{it}. In the linear models, differencing takes care of δ_i. But in nonlinear models (for example, y_{it} is a limited dependent variable), we need other ways to remove δ_i. This section presents ideas for removing δ_i in nonlinear models. Instead of removing δ_i, another way to deal with δ_i is to spell out the exact relationship between δ_i and x_{it}; this requires rather strong assumptions and will appear only once in a later chapter.

Suppose y_{it} is a count response taking $0, 1, 2, ...$ (number of shopping or recreational trips per year, number of visits to doctors per year, etc.). Because $y_{it} \geq 0$, we want to have its regression function to be positive always, and for this purpose, suppose

$$E(y_{it}|x_{it}, \delta_i) = \exp(x_{it}'\beta + \delta_i) = \exp(x_{it}'\beta) \cdot \exp(\delta_i); \qquad (6.1)$$

the unit-specific effect $\exp(\delta_i)$ appears multiplicatively. This implies

$$E(y_{it}|x_{it}) = \exp(x_{it}'\beta) \cdot E(\exp(\delta_i)|x_{it}). \qquad (6.2)$$

If δ_i is independent of x_{it}, then $E(\exp(\delta_i)|x_{it})$ is a constant, say σ. In this case

$$E(y_{it}|x_{it}) = \exp(x_{it}'\beta + \ln(\sigma)); \qquad (6.3)$$

$\ln(\sigma)$ is absorbed into the intercept in β to accord the familiar model

$$E(y_{it}|x_{it}) = \exp(x_{it}'\beta). \qquad (6.4)$$

β can be estimated easily by, for example, a nonlinear LSE minimizing $\sum_i \sum_t \{y_{it} - \exp(x'_{it}\beta)\}^2$ for β. If δ_i is related to x_{it}, however, in general $E(\exp(\delta_i)|x_{it})$ is a function of x_{it}, and the nonlinear LSE is inconsistent.

Much like differencing in the additive linear model, the multiplicative unit-specific term can be removed by dividing. The idea goes like this: divide $\exp(x'_{is}\beta + \delta_i)$ by $\exp(x'_{it}\beta + \delta_i)$ to get, $\exp((x_{is} - x_{it})'\beta)$, but because δ_i and β are not observed, we can think of dividing y_{is} by y_{it}. This method does not work exactly (y_{it} can take 0), but the following method does.

Strengthen the assumption (6.1) into

$$E(y_{it}|x_{i1}, ..., x_{it}, \delta_i) = E(y_{it}|x_{it}, \delta_i) = \exp(x'_{it}\beta + \delta_i); \tag{6.5}$$

the first equality is an assumption that, with x_{it} and δ_i given (or "known"), the old regressors are not informative; without the equality, the following moment condition does not hold. Observe, with $s = t - 1$,

$$E\{y_{is} - y_{it}\exp(x'_{is}\beta)/\exp(x'_{it}\beta)|x_{i1}, ..., x_{is}\} \tag{6.6}$$
$$= E[\{E(y_{is}|x_{i1}, ..., x_{is}, \delta_i) - E(y_{it}\exp(x'_{is}\beta)/$$
$$\exp(x'_{it}\beta)|x_{i1}, ..., x_{it}, \delta_i)\}|x_{i1}, ..., x_{is}]$$
$$= E[\exp(x'_{is}\beta + \delta_i) - \exp(x'_{it}\beta + \delta_i) \cdot \exp(x'_{is}\beta)/$$
$$\exp(x'_{it}\beta)|x_{i1}, ..., x_{is}] = 0. \tag{6.7}$$

Thus we get

$$E(\varepsilon_{it}|x_{i1}, ..., x_{i,t-1}) = 0 \quad \text{where } \varepsilon_{it} \equiv y_{i,t-1} - y_{it}\exp((x_{i,t-1} - x_{it})'\beta). \tag{6.8}$$

β can be estimated with a nonlinear IVE using, for example,

$$E(\varepsilon_{it}x_{iq}) = 0, \quad q = 1, ..., t - 1, \quad t = 2, ..., T. \tag{6.9}$$

The moment conditions in (6.9) fall in between the two cases $E(\varepsilon_{it}x_{it}) = 0$ for all t (zero contemporary correlation) and $E(\varepsilon_{is}x_{it}) = 0$ for all s and t (strict exogeneity, ε_{is} being orthogonal to x_{it} at all leads and lags). In (6.9), ε_{it} is orthogonal only to past regressors. This allows individual i to choose the future regressors after observing ε_{it}. For instance, suppose y_{it} is a farm output, x_{it} is production factors including fertilizer, and ε_{it} is rainfall. A farmer can adjust his or her future fertilizer after observing ε_{it} (for example, less rain, more fertilizer). This results in a negative relationship between $x_{i,t+1}$ and ε_{it}. The strict exogeneity does not allow for this, although (6.9) does. It is important to know that whether a moment condition is appropriate or not depends on the problem at hand.

It is also possible to remove δ_i by "conditioning," which is related to division. Let $T = 2$, and consider, instead of $\exp(x'_{i2}\beta + \delta_i)$,

$$\exp(x'_{i2}\beta + \delta_i)/\{\exp(x'_{i1}\beta + \delta_i) + \exp(x'_{i2}\beta + \delta_i)\}. \tag{6.10}$$

Dividing the numerator and denominator by $\exp(x_{i1}'\beta + \delta_i)$, we get

$$\exp(\Delta x_i'\beta)/\{1 + \exp(\Delta x_i'\beta)\}$$

which is free of δ_i. With this, a maximum likelihood estimation (MLE) is possible for β as shown in the following.

Suppose $T = 2$, and y_{it} is binary such that

$$y_{it} = 1[x_{it}'\beta + \delta_i + u_{it} > 0], \tag{6.11}$$

u_{it} follows the logistic distribution independently of $(\delta_i, x_{i1}, x_{i2})$, and

u_{it}'s are iid across i and t,

where $1[A] = 1$ if A holds and 0 otherwise, and v is logistic if $P(v \le c) = e^c/(1 + e^c)$ for all c. There are many examples for binary y_{it}: a labor-union member or not, giving a birth or not, working or not, and so on.

If $y_{i1} + y_{i2} = 1$, then there are only two possibilities: $y_{i1} = 0$, $y_{i2} = 1 (\Leftrightarrow \Delta y_i = 1)$ and $y_{i1} = 1$, $y_{i2} = 0 (\Leftrightarrow \Delta y_i = -1)$. In (6.10), $\exp(x_{i2}'\beta + \delta_i)$ in the numerator is for $(y_{i1} = 0, y_{i2} = 1)$ (the denominator is a normalizing term for $y_{i1} + y_{i2} = 1$), which leads to

$$P(\Delta y_i = 1|y_{i1} + y_{i2} = 1, \delta_i, x_{i1}, x_{i2}) = \exp(\Delta x_i'\beta)/$$
$$\{1 + \exp(\Delta x_i'\beta)\}, \tag{6.12}$$
$$P(\Delta y_i = -1|y_{i1} + y_{i2} = 1, \delta_i, x_{i1}, x_{i2}) = 1/\{1 + \exp(\Delta x_i'\beta)\}.$$

β can be estimated by the cross-section logit using the subsample with $\Delta y_i \ne 0$. The key point is that conditioning on the nonzero temporal variation of y_{it} removes δ_i.

This "conditional logit" is an analog for LSE on the differenced linear model, because only Δy_i and Δx_i appear in (6.12). In contrast, for ε_{it} in (6.8) with $t = 2$,

$$\varepsilon_{i2} = y_{i1} - y_{i2}\exp(-\Delta x_i'\beta) :$$

whereas x_{i1} and x_{i2} appear only in Δx_i, y_{i1} and y_{i2} appear separately. The conditional logit for binary choice can be extended to multiple choices. Other than dividing or conditioning, certain "stationarity" assumptions also yield consistent estimators for β using only Δy_i and Δx_i in some limited response models, as will be shown in a later chapter.

1.7 DYNAMIC FEATURES AND RESTRICTIONS ON PARAMETERS

Unlike cross section, the time dimension of panel data enables us to assess dynamic features. A familiar dynamic model is

$$y_{it} = \alpha y_{i,t-1} + x_{it}'\beta + u_{it}, \quad |\alpha| < 1, \tag{7.1}$$
$$u_{it} = \rho u_{i,t-1} + \varepsilon_{it}, \quad |\rho| < 1 \quad \{\varepsilon_{it}\} \text{ is iid across } i \text{ and } t. \tag{7.2}$$

If $\rho = 0$ and $\alpha \neq 0$ ($\alpha = 0$ and $\rho \neq 0$), then the dynamic features operate only through the (un)observed "carry-overs." If $\alpha \neq 0$, u_{it} cannot be strictly exogenous to the regressors:

$$E\{u_{it} \cdot (\text{regressors at } t+1 \text{ including } y_{it})\} \neq 0$$

because y_{it} depends on u_{it}. Another familiar form of dynamics is lagged regressors in x_{it}. Rational expectation models include $E(y_{i,t+1}|I_t)$ or $E(x_{i,t+1}|I_t)$ as regressors, where I_t is the information available at t.

The preceding forms of dynamics are all relevant in panel data as much as they are in time series. But panel data has a unique dynamic feature: the unit-specific effect δ_i. It appears in all time-period equations, and through δ_i, over-time behaviors are related. This presence of δ_i is felt regardless of its relation to x_{it}.

In (7.2), $E(u_{it}u_{is})$ approaches zero at the exponential rate $\rho^{|t-s|}$ due to $|\rho| < 1$. Suppose $\rho = 0$; then $\{u_{it}\}$ are independent and identically distributed (iid) across i and t with $V(u_{it}) \equiv \sigma_u^2$. Also suppose $\{u_{it}\}$ is uncorrelated with δ_i with $V(\delta_i) = \sigma_\delta^2$. Defining $v_{it} \equiv \delta_i + u_{it}$, we get

$$
\begin{aligned}
V(v_{it}) &= E\{(\delta_i + u_{it})^2\} = E(\delta_i^2 + 2\delta_i u_{it} + u_{it}^2) \\
&= \sigma_\delta^2 + \sigma_u^2, \quad \text{for all } t; \quad (7.3) \\
COV(v_{is}, v_{it}) &= E\{(\delta_i + u_{is})(\delta_i + u_{it})\} \\
&= E(\delta_i^2 + \delta_i u_{is} + \delta_i u_{it} + u_{is}u_{it}) = \sigma_\delta^2, \quad \text{for all } s \neq t.
\end{aligned}
$$

If $T = 3$, the error term covariance matrix is, with $v_i \equiv (v_{i1}, v_{i2}, v_{i3})'$,

$$
\begin{aligned}
E(v_i v_i') &= \begin{bmatrix} E(v_{i1}^2) & E(v_{i1}v_{i2}) & E(v_{i1}v_{i3}) \\ E(v_{i2}v_{i1}) & E(v_{i2}^2) & E(v_{i2}v_{i3}) \\ E(v_{i3}v_{i1}) & E(v_{i3}v_{i2}) & E(v_{i3}^2) \end{bmatrix} \\
&= \begin{bmatrix} \sigma_\delta^2 + \sigma_u^2 & \sigma_\delta^2 & \sigma_\delta^2 \\ \sigma_\delta^2 & \sigma_\delta^2 + \sigma_u^2 & \sigma_\delta^2 \\ \sigma_\delta^2 & \sigma_\delta^2 & \sigma_\delta^2 + \sigma_u^2 \end{bmatrix}. \quad (7.4)
\end{aligned}
$$

Note $E(v_{i1}v_{i2}) = E(v_{i1}v_{i3})$ ($\Leftrightarrow COR(v_{i1}, v_{i2}) = COR(v_{i1}, v_{i3})$) despite the time differences being different. In an empirical example to explain ln(wage), the residuals $\hat{v}_{it}$ for v_{it} yield $COR(\hat{v}_{i1}, \hat{v}_{i2}) = 0.730$, and $COR(\hat{v}_{i1}, \hat{v}_{i3}) = 0.665$, not too far away from 0.730.

Suppose δ_i is related to x_{it}. Because δ_i is time invariant, it is likely that δ_i is related to $x_{i1}, ..., x_{iT}$, not just to x_{it}. Thus, suppose

$$\delta_i = x_{i1}'\eta_1 + \cdots + x_{iT}'\eta_T + v_i, \quad COR(v_i, x_{it}) = 0 \text{ for all } t. \quad (7.5)$$

Then

$$
\begin{aligned}
y_{it} &= x_{it}'\beta + x_{i1}'\eta_1 + \cdots + x_{iT}'\eta_T + v_i + u_{it} \quad (7.6) \\
&= x_{it}'(\beta + \eta_t) + \sum_{s, s \neq t} x_{is}'\eta_s + e_{it}, \quad \text{where } e_{it} \equiv v_i + u_{it};
\end{aligned}
$$

y_{it} seems to be "affected" by $x_{i1}, ..., x_{iT}$. This should not be construed as x_{iT} really acting upon y_{it}; x_{iT} is simply associated or related to y_{it} in a certain way. Noteworthy here is that seemingly different dynamic features (δ_i vs. $x_{i1}, ..., x_{iT}$) can have the same source. Also notable is that (7.5) is not really an assumption, for we can always decompose δ_i as in (7.5) using "linear projection," as will be shown in the following chapter.

Suppose $T = 2$ for (7.6):

$$y_{i1} = x_{i1}(\beta + \eta_1) + x_{i2}\eta_2 + e_{i1} \quad \text{and} \quad y_{i2} = x_{i1}\eta_1 + x_{i2}(\beta + \eta_2) + e_{i2}. \quad (7.7)$$

If we apply LSE to each wave, we will be estimating $(\gamma_{11}, \gamma_{12}, \gamma_{21}, \gamma_{22})$ in

$$y_{i1} = x_{i1}\gamma_{11} + x_{i2}\gamma_{12} + e_{i1} \quad \text{and} \quad y_{i2} = x_{i1}\gamma_{21} + x_{i2}\gamma_{22} + e_{i2} \quad (7.8)$$

to get estimates $(\hat{\gamma}_{11}, \hat{\gamma}_{12}, \hat{\gamma}_{21}, \hat{\gamma}_{22})$. Comparing (7.7) to (7.8), we have

$$\gamma_{11} = \beta + \eta_1, \quad \gamma_{12} = \eta_2, \quad \gamma_{21} = \eta_1, \quad \gamma_{22} = \beta + \eta_2. \quad (7.9)$$

Whereas there are four γ's on the left-hand side, there are three parameters (β, η_1, η_2) on the right. We can take two types of action with (7.9). First, replace γ's in (7.9) with $\hat{\gamma}$:

$$\hat{\gamma}_{11} = \beta + \eta_1, \quad \hat{\gamma}_{12} = \eta_2, \quad \hat{\gamma}_{21} = \eta_1, \quad \hat{\gamma}_{22} = \beta + \eta_2, \quad (7.10)$$

and see if there exists a solution $(\hat{\beta}, \hat{\eta}_1, \hat{\eta}_2)$ for these four equations; if not, (7.9) is rejected. Second, if (7.9) is not rejected, the solution is an estimator for (β, η_1, η_2). In fact, these two things can be done with the MDE. Essentially, the MDE combines more than enough information (four $\hat{\gamma}$'s) to get three estimates.

In an empirical example explaining ln(wage), the estimate $\hat{\gamma}$'s for union membership (x_{it})'s effect are

	x_{i1}	x_{i2}
$t = 1$:	0.171 (for $\beta + \eta_1$)	0.042 (for η_2)
$t = 2$:	0.048 (for η_1)	0.150 (for $\beta + \eta_2$)

(7.11)

From $\gamma_{12} = \eta_2$ and $\gamma_{21} = \eta_1$, $\hat{\eta}_1 = 0.048$ and $\hat{\eta}_2 = 0.042$. From $\gamma_{11} = \beta + \eta_1$ and $\gamma_{22} = \beta + \eta_2$, $\hat{\beta}$ is $0.171 - 0.048 = 0.123$ or $0.150 - 0.042 = 0.108$; either way, the effect of union membership on ln(wage) is positive. If the difference $0.123 - 0.108$ between the two estimates for β is statistically significant, then (7.9) is rejected; otherwise, combining 0.123 and 0.108 will give a single $\hat{\beta}$.

1.8 ERROR TERM STRUCTURE

We stated that the main attraction of panel data is to allow regressors to be related with the error term $v_{it} = \delta_i + u_{it}$ through δ_i. But this is not always possible in nonlinear models, despite some successes shown already for count response and panel logit. Even when δ_i is independent of x_{it}, δ_i can still play an informative role, one of which is the dynamics described in the preceding section. Because the case of δ_i being independent of x_{it} will not receive much attention in the other chapters, in this section, we consider this case in some detail.

In $y_{it} = x'_{it}\beta + \delta_i + u_{it}$, the error term $v_{it} = \delta_i + u_{it}$ has a structure, consisting of two terms. In fact, we can also think of three-term structure $\delta_i + \tau_t + u_{it}$, but τ_t is easily estimable as a time-varying intercept. With both δ_i and u_{it} unrelated to x_{it}, β can be estimated consistently with ease, for example, by LSE. Now the question is this: Can we make any good use out of the known error term structure? The answer is yes for two reasons; one is efficiency and the other is a better understanding of the source of errors as shown in the following.

First, recall (7.4):

$$E(v_i v'_i) = \sigma_u^2 \cdot I_3 + \sigma_\delta^2 \cdot 1_3 1'_3 \qquad (8.1)$$

where $1_3 \equiv (1, 1, 1)'$, and $1_3 1'_3$ is the 3×3 matrix with 1's. Under the homoskedasticity assumption

$$E(v_i v'_i | x_{i1}, ..., x_{iT}) = E(v_i v'_i), \qquad (8.2)$$

one can easily do a generalized LSE because $E(v_i v'_i)$ can be estimated replacing σ_u^2 and σ_δ^2 with some estimates. Because $E(v_i v'_i)$ can be estimated consistently by $(1/N) \sum_i \hat{v}_i \hat{v}'_i$, (7.4) shows many ways to estimate σ_u^2 and σ_δ^2: there are only two parameters but six nonredundant equations ($E(v_i v'_i)$ is symmetric). The resulting generalized LSE is more efficient than the simple LSE.

Second, with $\{u_{it}\}$ iid across i and t, σ_u^2 shows the variation across time within an individual ("within-group" variation, with group meaning one person), whereas σ_δ^2 shows the interpersonal ("between-group") variation. The ratio

$$\sigma_\delta^2 / (\sigma_\delta^2 + \sigma_u^2) \qquad (8.3)$$

is informative, being the proportion of the interpersonal variation relative to the total variation. For instance, if the ratio is almost one ($\Leftrightarrow \sigma_u^2 \cong 0$), then almost all temporal variation of y_{it} is due to observed time-variant regressors.

Being able to get (8.3) is another advantage of panel data, not available in cross-section data. In the so-called mover-stayer problem, suppose we have only cross-section data in which 50% of the people are working whereas the other 50% are not. There are two diametrically different scenarios for this. First, the population consists of two groups, one group working always, and the other always not. Second, there is only one group in the population, but everybody works 50% of the times (imagine that everybody flips a coin each period and decides whether or not to work). Which is the case can be easily determined by panel data. If the first is the case, the same people are seen to work all periods [all stayers and (8.3) $= 1$]. If the latter is the case, eventually everybody will move in and out of the labor force [all movers and (8.3) $= 0$].

2

METHODS-OF-MOMENTS FOR PANEL LINEAR MODELS

2.1 INTRODUCTION

In the preceding chapter, we introduced a simple panel data model

$$y_{it} = x'_{it}\beta + \delta_i + u_{it}, \quad i = 1, ..., N, \quad t = 1, ..., T, \quad (1.1)$$

and various panel data features not found in cross-section nor in time-series data, where y_{it} is a response variable, x_{it} is a regressor vector, β is a parameter of interest, and $\delta_i + u_{it}$ is a composite error term. In this and the following chapters, more general panel linear models and panel methods-of-moments are examined in detail. For the reader who might have skipped Chapter 1, part of Chapter 1 is repeated in this chapter. In the following, we examine panel data advantages over time-series and cross-section data, and then introduce terminologies frequently used for panel data.

A common advantage of panel data over cross-section and time-series data is that panel data use both interpersonal and intertemporal variations of variables, whereas cross-section and time-series data use only one of them. Consequently, model parameters can be estimated more precisely in panel data. This advantage is more than simply increasing the sample size in cross section or time series; for example, price variables usually have little variation across individuals, whereas they have substantial variation across time, and increasing N does not change this.

15

Compared with cross-section data, panel data hold a number of advantages. First, whereas cross-section data have difficulty controlling for unobserved variables, panel data can control for them much better either by removing them or by providing more instruments; the ability to remove time-invariant unobservable δ_i can be the single most important advantage of panel data. Second, panel data allow dynamic models with lagged response variables and regressors; with this, short-run effects and short-run dynamic features can be found, whereas cross-section data show mostly long-run effects; this point is discussed further in the next chapter. Third, whereas a cross-section data provides only a snapshot at a given time, panel data can show whether the cross-section image is stable or not over time by allowing time-varying parameters.

Compared with time-series data, panel data have a number of advantages. First, whereas it is difficult to allow for time-varying parameters in time series (imagine T-many parameters for T-many observations), panel can allow for time-varying parameters easily (imagine T-many parameters for TN-many observations). Second, an arbitrary form of temporal correlations can be allowed for the error terms; this task, although possible, requires more assumptions in time-series. Third, economic theories are developed usually at the individual level (an economic agent optimizing some function), not at the aggregate level, and with panel data, we can test for the theories, which is difficult to do with aggregate time-series data: restrictions at the individual level do not necessarily hold at the aggregate level, nor is what holds at the aggregate level true at the individual level.

Turning to panel data terminologies, if δ_i is related with components of x_{it}, then we will call the model a "related-effect" model; otherwise, it is called an "unrelated-effect" model. In the literature, the former is often called "fixed effect" and the latter is called "random effect." Although these are what most people use "fixed effect" and "random effect" for, there are a couple of other cases where the term "fixed effect" might be appropriate:

(a) δ_i is estimated along with β.
(b) a likelihood function conditional on δ_i is used.   (1.2)
(c) the sample is equal to the population.

In (a), δ_i is treated as a parameter; in (b), δ_i is conditioned upon, and thus fixed; in (c), there is no sampling error to make δ_i random. In our approach with a large N and weak model assumptions, however, (a) and (b) will not be seen; for (c), we can think of a "grand experiment" in which the population is one realization, and thus δ_i is random.

What the preceding paragraph shows is that δ_i is random in most cases, and the terms "fixed effect" and "random effect" are misleading. We will use the term "related effect" when δ_i is allowed to be related to components of x_{it}, and "unrelated effect" otherwise; these terms have not been rooted in the literature, but at least they stand for what they really are. Because related effect is something cross-section data have difficulty dealing with, *our focus will be on related-effect models*, which include unrelated-effect models as special cases.

Sometimes the number of observations for individual i varies across i: that is, T_i instead of T. Then the panel is called an "unbalanced panel," whereas a panel with the same T for all i is called a "balanced panel." An unbalanced panel is often turned into a "rectangular panel" by trimming the data so that T becomes a number between $\min_i T_i$ or $\max_i T_i$. Some people call it a "square panel," but this name suits better when $N \cong T$. A rectangular panel may not be representative of the population. For example, for a panel data spanning over 30 years, those remaining until the end can be special; for one thing, they may be patient (or disciplined) filling out the survey questionnaire every year, and for another, they are healthy surviving 30 years from period 1. This is a "sample-selection problem," which may be also called a "survivorship-bias problem" in this context.

Another example of unbalanced panel is cross-section data with a "group structure" where i indexes household, town, city, or whatever can be called a group, and there are T_i members in each group; δ_i represents the common unobserved characteristics of group i. In fact, groups can be formed at multiple levels (household to town to city, etc.); see, for example, Rice and Jones (1997) and the references therein. One critical difference from unbalanced panel is that, within each group, there is no temporal ordering of the observations. Despite this difference, however, panel data techniques can be applied fruitfully to group structure data.

If each wave is drawn anew from the population, then we get "repeated cross-sections" or a "time-series of (independent) cross-sections." Under some conditions, an artificial panel data with its variables measured with errors can be created using repeated cross-sections, and such a panel is called a "pseudo panel." Deaton (1985) initiated this approach; see Collado (1997) and the references therein for the development since then. Pseudo panels will not be discussed in this book.

In a "rotated panel," the subjects are rotated for two reasons: one is to replace voluntary dropouts and the other is to keep people fresh (not tired of filling out the questionnaire every period). Because T_i varies across i, a rotated panel is unbalanced, but the difference is that an unbalanced panel can occur when everybody starts at period 1 and then some people drop out later (return after a dropout is rare), whereas a rotated panel necessarily has people starting (rotation-in) at different periods and staying for different durations until rotation-out or dropout. We will deal with balanced panels mainly, but when appropriate, we will note how unbalanced panels can be accommodated.

The rest of this chapter is organized as follows. Section 2.2 reviews the least squares estimator (LSE), the instrumental variable estimator (IVE), and the generalized method of moment (GMM) for cross-section data. Section 2.3 presents our main linear panel data model; differently from (1.1), time-invariant and variant regressors will be separated, which is convenient for programming panel estimators in practice. Section 2.4 lists four types of temporal moment conditions and then presents panel IVE and GMM. Because moment conditions used in practice may not exactly fit one of the four types, Section 2.5 shows through an example how to construct instruments (with transformed regressors); to aid in this explanation, "linear projection" is introduced in this section. Instead of IVE for the model with the error term $\delta_i + u_{it}$, Section 2.6 first-differences the panel linear model to remove δ_i; this is closely related to the "within group estimator," which is reviewed in this section along with the "between group estimator.". Finally, Section 2.7 provides an empirical example on a production function for panel IVE and panel GMM. In Sections 2.2 through 2.5, we will be fully occupied with building up the basics of panel IVE and panel GMM, and thus the empirical examples there will be pedagogical; more interesting ones will be given in Sections 2.6 and 2.7 and the following chapters.

Throughout this chapter, $T = 3$ cases will be often used as examples. As for notations, we use $a_N =^P b_N$ for convergence in probability ($P(|a_N - b_N| < \varepsilon) \to 1$ as $N \to \infty$ for any positive constant ε), and $=^d$ or $\Longrightarrow$ for convergence in distribution. If $\sqrt{N}(b_N - \beta) =^d N(0, \Omega)$ for an estimator b_N for β and $\Omega_N \overset{p}{=} \Omega$, then we may denote this simply as $\sqrt{N}(b_N - \beta) =^d N(0, \Omega_N)$; almost always, Ω and Ω_N take the form, respectively, $E\{\theta_i(\beta)\}$ and $(1/N)\sum_{i=1}^{N} \theta_i(b_N)$ for some function $\theta_i(\cdot)$. Zero vectors and matrices may be denoted simply as 0 if the dimension is clear from the context. Denote the correlation and covariance for λ_1 and λ_2 as $COR(\lambda_1, \lambda_2)$ and $COV(\lambda_1, \lambda_2)$, respectively; the standard deviation of λ_1 will be denoted as $SD(\lambda_1)$.

2.2 REVIEW OF CROSS-SECTION IVE AND GMM

Most econometric estimators are method-of-moment estimators (MME); this also holds for panel data estimators. In this section, we review IVE and GMM for linear cross-section models to pave the way to panel IVE and GMM in the next section. Nonlinear IVE and GMM will be reviewed in a later chapter.

Consider a typical cross-section linear regression model:

$$y_i = x_i'\beta + u_i, \quad x_i = (1, x_{i2}, ..., x_{ik})',$$

$E(x_i x_i')$ is positive definite (p.d.), and (x_i', y_i), $i = 1, ..., N$, are

observed and iid (independent and identically distributed), $E(u_i x_i) = 0$,

$$(2.1)$$

where y_i is a response variable, x_i is a $k \times 1$ regressor vector, u_i is an error term, and β is a parameter of interest. We will often drop the subscript i in view of the iid assumption.

Under $E(ux) = 0$, LSE for β is

$$b_{lse} \equiv \{\sum_i x_i x_i'\}^{-1} \sum_i x_i y_i,$$

$$(2.2)$$

and the asymptotic distribution of $\sqrt{N}(b_{lse} - \beta)$ is

$$N(0, \ E^{-1}(xx') \cdot E(xx'u^2) \cdot E^{-1}(xx')), \tag{2.3}$$

where $E^{-1}(\cdot)$ means $\{E(\cdot)\}^{-1}$. A consistent estimator for the asymptotic variance matrix is, with the residual $\hat{u}_i \equiv y_i - x_i'b_{lse}$,

$$\{(1/N) \sum_i x_i x_i'\}^{-1} \cdot (1/N) \sum_i x_i x_i' \hat{u}_i^2 \cdot \{(1/N) \sum_i x_i x_i'\}^{-1}.$$

Sometimes, the condition $E(ux) = 0$ for LSE does not hold, but an alternative moment condition does. Consider two equations for y_i and d_i :

$$
\begin{aligned}
y_i &= \beta_1 + \beta_2 d_i + \beta_3 x_{i3} + \beta_4 x_{i4} + u_i = x_i'\beta + u_i, \\
d_i &= \alpha_1 + \alpha_2 w_i + \varepsilon_i, \quad \alpha_2 \neq 0, \\
E(u) &= E(\varepsilon) = E(x_3 u) = E(x_4 u) = 0, \ \text{but}, \ E(\varepsilon u) \neq 0
\end{aligned}
$$

where $x_i = (1, d_i, x_{i3}, x_{i4})'$, $\beta \equiv (\beta_1, \beta_2, \beta_3, \beta_4)'$, and (x_i', y_i, w_i) is observed. This model contains an "exclusion restriction" that w does not appear in the y-equation. For instance, y is health, d is the dummy for smoking, x_3 is age, x_4 is gender, w is the dummy for being in an education program on the harms of smoking, and both ε and u include a gene responsible for both health and smoking propensity. Here the interest is on the effect of smoking on health, but $COR(d, u) \neq 0$ due to $COR(\varepsilon, u) \neq 0$, and as a result, the LSE of y on x is inconsistent. Suppose w is randomly assinged to the subjects. Then w becomes an "instrument" for d (and u), because w satisfies

$$
\begin{aligned}
COR(w, d) &\neq 0 \quad \text{due to the "inclusion restriction" } \alpha_2 \neq 0, \\
COR(w, u) &= 0 \quad \text{due to the randomization.}
\end{aligned}
$$

Defining an instrument vector $z_i = (1, w_i, x_{i3}, x_{i4})'$, $E(uz) = 0$ holds, which is the aforementioned alternative moment condition; the dimension of $E(uz) = 0$ is the same as that of $E(ux) = 0$. Because $COR(x_3, x_3) \neq 0$ and $COR(x_3, u) = 0$ analogously to $COR(w, d) \neq 0$ and $COR(w, u) = 0$, we may call x_3 a "self-instrument"; the same can be said of 1 and x_4.

More generally, consider a $K \times 1$ instrument vector z, where $E(zu) = 0$, $K \geq k$, rank$(E(zz')) = K$, and rank$(E(xz')) = k$; in the previous example, z can be $(1, w, x_3, x_4)'$ with $K = 4$, or $(1, w, m, x_3, x_4)'$ with $K = 5$ where m is the dummy for another educational program on the benefits of healthy lifestyle. Then an IVE is (see, for example, Lee, 1996)

$$b_{ive} \equiv \{\sum_i x_i z_i' (\sum_i z_i z_i')^{-1} \sum_i z_i x_i'\}^{-1} \cdot \sum_i x_i z_i' (\sum_i z_i z_i')^{-1} \sum_i z_i y_i. \tag{2.4}$$

A motivation for this formula is the desire to solve for β:

$$E(zy) = E(zx') \cdot \beta \quad (\Leftarrow 0 = E\{z(y - x'\beta)\}). \tag{2.5}$$

For this, multiply both sides by the $k \times K$ matrix $E(xz')\{E(zz')\}^{-1}$ and solve the equation for β, which is the "population analog" for b_{ive}. The asymptotic distribution of $\sqrt{N}(b_{ive} - \beta)$ is

$$N(0, \ A \cdot E(zz'u^2) \cdot A')$$

where

$$A \equiv \{E(xz') \cdot E^{-1}(zz') \cdot E(zx')\}^{-1} E(xz') \cdot E^{-1}(zz').$$

A consistent estimator for the asymptotic variance is

$$A_N \cdot (1/N) \sum_i z_i z_i' r_i^2 \cdot A_N,$$

where $r_i \equiv y_i - x_i' b_{ive}$, and

$$A_N \equiv [(1/N) \sum_i x_i z_i' \cdot \{(1/N) \sum_i z_i z_i'\}^{-1} \cdot (1/N) \sum_i z_i x_i']^{-1}$$
$$\cdot (1/N) \sum_i x_i z_i' \cdot \{(1/N) \sum_i z_i z_i'\}^{-1}.$$

The term IVE will be used in two senses: estimators specifically taking the form (2.4) in the narrower sense and estimators based on a moment condition in the form of orthogonality $E(\mu) = 0$ in the broader sense, where μ consists of products of error terms and instruments, with $E(uz) = 0$ being an example.

There exists a (broad-sense) IVE at least as efficient as b_{ive} under $E(zu) = 0$; it is the GMM (Hansen, 1982):

$$b_{gmm} = (\sum_i x_i z_i' \cdot C_N^{-1} \cdot \sum_i z_i x_i')^{-1} \cdot \sum_i x_i z_i' \cdot C_N^{-1} \cdot \sum_i z_i y_i, \qquad (2.6)$$

where C_N is a consistent estimator for $C \equiv E(zz'u^2)$; for example,

$$C_N = (1/N) \sum_i z_i z_i' r_i^2.$$

In IVE, we multiplied (2.5) by the $k \times K$ matrix $E(xz')\{E(zz')\}^{-1}$ and solved the equation for β, but, in fact, any other matrix of the same dimension will do, so long as the resulting equation can be solved for β. The best choice turns out to be $E(xz')\{E(zz'u^2)\}^{-1}$, which is used in GMM. $E(zu) = 0$ is a vector, and $E(zz'u^2) = V(zu)$ is used as a weighting (or normalizing) matrix to prevent only a few components of $E(zu) = 0$ from dominating all the other components.

The asymptotic distribution of $\sqrt{N}(b_{gmm} - \beta)$ is

$$N(0, \{E(xz') \cdot E^{-1}(zz'u^2) \cdot E(zx')\}^{-1}); \qquad (2.7)$$

the asymptotic variance matrix can be consistently estimated by

$$\{(\sum_i x_i z_i'/N) \cdot C_N^{-1} \cdot (\sum_i z_i x_i'/N)\}^{-1}.$$

It is known that, for $K > k$ and $u_{Ni} \equiv y_i - x_i' b_{gmm}$,

$$(1/\sqrt{N}) \sum_i z_i' u_{Ni} \cdot \{(1/N) \sum_i z_i z_i' u_{Ni}^2\}^{-1} \cdot (1/\sqrt{N}) \sum_i z_i u_{Ni} \Rightarrow \chi_{K-k}^2,$$

(2.8)

which can be used as a test statistic for $H_o : E(zu) = 0$. This test is called the "GMM overidentification test."

Later, we will see that almost the same formulas as (2.2) to (2.8) hold for panel IVE and GMM. Although GMM is more efficient than IVE, the small sample performance of b_{gmm} can be worse than that of b_{ive} if C_N is not a good estimator for C; more discussion and references on GMM are presented in Section 5.2 when nonlinear GMM is reviewed; b_{ive} is sometimes called the "equally weighted GMM."

GMM is efficient under the given *unconditional* moment condition $E(zu) = 0$. If we have $E(u|z) = 0$, which is stronger than $E(zu) = 0$, the GMM for $E(zu) = 0$ is not efficient. There is, however, a GMM that is efficient once $E(zu) = 0$ is expanded to incorporate the extra information due to the stronger $E(u|z) = 0$; for example, $E(wu) = 0$ is used in addition to $E(zu) = 0$ where w consists of polynomial functions of components of z. For this reason, we will consider mostly only unconditional moment conditions. See, for example, Lee (1996) and the references therein for more on GMM.

As an example of IVE, Angrist and Krueger (1991) considered ln(wage) equation with education as a regressor; its coefficient is called "returns to education." The problem is that ability is usually not observed and thus becomes part of the error term; through ability, the error is related with education. Angrist and Krueger used the quarter for birth date as an instrument. Under a compulsory school attendance law, one has to attend school until the 16th or 17th birth date; those born early in the year attend school shorter than those born later, for the former group wait longer until the school starts. Thus birth quarter is related with education (but not with ability). If the law requires education until a certain grade as in some countries, then birth quarter will be unrelated with education. This example shows that finding an instrument is not easy; it often takes a good deal of ingenuity. Using census data ($N = 329, 509$), the LSE (SD) for returns to education in Angrist and Krueger (1991) is 0.063 (0.0003), whereas their IVE (SD) is 0.081(0.016). The estimates are close, but the SD of IVE is far much greater (these number are taken from Angrist and Krueger, 1995).

As in IVE for cross-section models, there are two issues for panel IVE: finding instruments and getting an efficient IVE under the given moment conditions. The second issue has been resolved by GMM, and hence the first is the main concern in IVE for panel data models. For the equation at time t, regressors at different times are often used as instruments. Panel data also offer a unique "constant instrument" that amounts to differencing the model. Moreover, differenced regressors or other transformations of the regressors can be used as instruments. The preceding IVE was feasible because $y_i = x_i'\beta + u_i$ was solvable for u_i, which renders $E(zu) = 0 \Leftrightarrow E\{z(y - x'\beta)\} = 0$, a moment condition expressed in terms of observed variables and the parameter of interest. In models nonlinear in u_i, usually it is impossible to express $E(zu) = 0$ into a moment condition involving only observed variables and the parameter of interest; for example, a binary response model $y_i = 1[x_i'\beta + u_i > 0]$ is not solvable for u_i where $1[A] = 1$ if A holds and 0 otherwise. This is the case in general for panel limited dependent variable models. For those panel nonlinear models that will appear later, IVE is not feasible.

2.3 PANEL LINEAR MODEL

This section introduces our main panel linear model. We will make special efforts to make the panel model look analogous to the cross-section linear model in (2.1). This will alleviate the extra burden of considering the time dimension T not present in cross section; the panel model, given in (3.7), will reduce to the cross-section model when $T = 1$. Suppose we observe N units (subjects, individuals, or firms) over T periods, and assume that N is large so that we can apply asymptotic theory with respect to (wrt) N.

Our main model is, for $i = 1, ..., N$ and $t = 1, ..., T$,

$$y_{it} = \underset{1 \times 1}{\tau_t} + \underset{1 \times k_{\tilde{c}}}{\tilde{c}_i'\,\tilde{\alpha}} + \underset{1 \times k_x}{x_{it}'\,\beta} + \delta_i + u_{it} \tag{3.1}$$

where τ_t, $\tilde{\alpha}$ and β are the parameters of interest, $\tilde{c}_i$ is a time-invariant regressor vector, x_{it} is a time-variant regressor vector, $\delta_i + u_{it}$ is the error term, and the expression "$a \times b$" denotes the dimension of the matrix (or vector) right above the $a \times b$. Define further

$$\tilde{k} \equiv k_{\tilde{c}} + k_x, \quad \tilde{\gamma} \equiv (\tilde{\alpha}', \beta')', \quad \tilde{w}_{it} \equiv (\tilde{c}_i', x_{it}')', \quad v_{it} \equiv \delta_i + u_{it},$$

to compactly rewrite the model as

$$y_{it} = \tau_t + \underset{1 \times \tilde{k}}{\tilde{w}_{it}'\tilde{\gamma}} + v_{it}. \tag{3.2}$$

An example for (3.1) is

y_{it} : Hourly ln(wage) of married men of age 40 to 60
τ_t : Effect of the economy on y_{it} common to all i
$\tilde{c}_i$: Race, schooling years
x_{it} : Work hours, local unemployment rate, self-employment dummy
δ_i : Ability, IQ, or productivity
u_{it} : Unobserved time variants such as detailed residential location
    information (3.3)

The variables and error terms are classified depending on observability and variation across i or t:

τ_t : Unobservable, time variant, unit invariant
$\tilde{c}_i$: Observable, time invariant, unit variant
x_{it} : Observable, time variant, unit variant
δ_i : Unobservable, time invariant, unit variant
u_{it} : Unobservable, time variant, unit variant.

Although τ_t is an unobservable variable, because there are only T-many of them, τ_t's are taken as parameters and will be estimated along with $\tilde{\gamma}$.

One category missing in the classification is "observable, time variant and unit invariant" (for example, inflation rate or a macropolicy common to all individuals). They are excluded because they do not appear often in micro-panels; once τ_t's are estimated, however, we can regress τ_t on those variables to estimate the coefficients, if necessary. Another category we can think of is "time invariant and unit invariant" (observable or unobservable). This is in essence the intercept in (3.1): τ_1 is the ("baseline") intercept, whereas $\tau_2, \tau_3, ..., \tau_T$ reflect changing intercepts due to macroeconomic conditions common to all subjects.

In the literature, often strong assumptions are put on $(\tilde{w}'_{it}, v_{it})'$, such as independence of u_{it} from $\tilde{w}_{it}$ or iid of u_{it}'s, to estimate the parameters. But, other than the assumption of some finite moments, we will assume only *iid of* $(\tilde{w}'_{it}, v_{it})'$ *across i while allowing for arbitrary dependence and heterogeneity across t within a given i*. The iid assumption across i may not hold for some panels where the subjects are geographically close to one another (for example, many individuals from the same village). The model (3.1) also allows endogenous regressors and lagged dependent variables as regressors. The model will be generalized later to accommodate time-varying parameters; in the current form, only the intercept τ_t is allowed to vary across t.

Turning back to (3.1), stack the equations for unit i across t:

$$\begin{bmatrix} y_{i1} \\ \vdots \\ y_{iT} \end{bmatrix} = I_T \begin{bmatrix} \tau_1 \\ \vdots \\ \tau_T \end{bmatrix} + \begin{bmatrix} \tilde{c}'_i \\ \vdots \\ \tilde{c}'_i \end{bmatrix} \cdot \tilde{\alpha} + \begin{bmatrix} x'_{i1} \\ \vdots \\ x'_{iT} \end{bmatrix} \cdot \beta + \begin{bmatrix} \delta_i \\ \vdots \\ \delta_i \end{bmatrix} + \begin{bmatrix} u_{i1} \\ \vdots \\ u_{iT} \end{bmatrix}$$

$$(3.4)$$

where I_T is the regressor to estimate τ_t's, in the same way as 1 is attached to the intercept in the usual cross-section model. Define

$$y_i \equiv \begin{bmatrix} y_{i1} \\ \vdots \\ y_{iT} \end{bmatrix}, \quad x'_i \equiv \begin{bmatrix} x'_{i1} \\ \vdots \\ x'_{iT} \end{bmatrix}, \quad \text{and} \quad u_i \equiv \begin{bmatrix} u_{i1} \\ \vdots \\ u_{iT} \end{bmatrix}.$$

A typical panel data is made up of y_i, $\tilde{c}_i$ and x'_i (along with time dummies): for the wage example (3.3), the first six lines of a three-wave panel data for individual 1 and 2 look like Table 2.1.

TABLE 2.1 An Example of Three-Wave Panel Data

i	Wage ($/hr)	Race	Education (yr)	Work-hr/yr	ur (%)	Self
1	8.8	1	14	1924	5.4	1
1	8.2	1	14	2717	4.6	0
1	3.2	1	14	2844	4.5	1
2	17.4	0	13	1480	7.8	0
2	15.7	0	13	2005	7.2	0
2	17.7	0	13	2120	6.7	0

where "ur" is local unemployment rate and "self" is a dummy variable for self-employment; the wage column is for y_i, the race and education columns are for $\tilde{c}_i$, and the last three columns are for x'_i.

Define

$$\tau \equiv (\tau_1, ..., \tau_T)', \quad \Delta\tau \equiv (\tau_2 - \tau_1, ..., \tau_T - \tau_1)', \quad \tau^* \equiv (\Delta\tau', \tau_1)',$$

$$1_T \equiv T \times 1 \text{ vector of ones,}$$

$$m_T \equiv I_T \text{ with the first-column removed.}$$

Observe the following equivalent parameterization for τ when $T = 3$:

$$\begin{bmatrix} 1 & 0 & 0 \\ 0 & 1 & 0 \\ 0 & 0 & 1 \end{bmatrix} \begin{bmatrix} \tau_1 \\ \tau_2 \\ \tau_3 \end{bmatrix} = I_3\tau$$

$$= \begin{bmatrix} 0 & 0 & 1 \\ 1 & 0 & 1 \\ 0 & 1 & 1 \end{bmatrix} \begin{bmatrix} \tau_2 - \tau_1 \\ \tau_3 - \tau_1 \\ \tau_1 \end{bmatrix} \equiv (m_3, 1_3)\tau^*; \tag{3.5}$$

for a generic T, $I_T\tau = (m_T, 1_T)\tau^*$. In (3.4), I_T and $\tilde{c}_i$ were used for τ and $\tilde{\alpha}$. Equivalently, we can use m_T and c_i where

$$c_i \equiv (1, \tilde{c}'_i)';$$

the coefficients for m_T are $\Delta\tau$, the intercept coefficient for c_i is τ_1, and the slopes for c_i are $\tilde{\alpha}$. Using m_T and c_i is more convenient for programming to implement panel IVE and GMM, and thus they will be used mainly in the remainder; for this, more notations are needed.

Define

$$w_{it} \equiv (1, \tilde{w}'_{it})' = (1, \tilde{c}'_i, x'_{it})' = (c'_i, x'_{it})', \quad \text{and} \quad k \equiv k_c + k_x,$$

where k_c is the row dimension of c_i. With the $k_c \times T$ matrix

$$1'_T \otimes c_i = [c_i, ..., c_i],$$

(3.4) can be written as (note that c_i, not $\tilde{c}_i$, is used now):

$$\underset{T \times 1}{y_i} = \underset{T \times (T-1)}{m_T \cdot \Delta\tau} + \underset{T \times k_c}{(1'_T \otimes c_i)'\alpha} + \underset{T \times k_x}{x'_i \, \beta} + \underset{T \times 1}{1_T \delta_i} + u_i, \qquad (3.6)$$

$$= m_T \cdot \Delta\tau + \underset{T \times k}{w'_i \, \gamma} + v_i = \underset{T \times (k+T-1)}{q'_i} \, \eta + v_i,$$

where

$$\alpha \equiv (\tau_1, \tilde{\alpha}')', \quad w'_i \equiv ((1'_T \otimes c_i)', x'_i), \quad \gamma \equiv (\alpha', \beta')',$$

$$q'_i \equiv (m_T, w'_i), \quad \eta \equiv (\Delta\tau', \gamma')', \quad v_i \equiv 1_T \delta_i + u_i.$$

Hence, in the final form, we have

$$y_i = q'_i \eta + v_i. \qquad (3.7)$$

If $T = 1$, then $\Delta\tau = 0$ and $(1'_1 \otimes c_i)' = c'_i$: we get the usual cross-section model $y_i = w'_i \gamma + v_i$.

One may ask what happens if we use c_i but no time dummies, perhaps because all τ_t's are believed to be the same. Not using the time dummies, however, results in $(1/N) \sum_i v_{it} \neq 0$ for some t (that is, not imposing the moment condition $E(v_{it}) = 0$ for some t); using the time dummies assures $E(v_{it}) = 0$ for all t, as 1 in a cross-section regression imposes the mean-zero condition for the error term.

2.4 MOMENT CONDITIONS AND PANEL IVE AND GMM

The preceding section presented our main panel linear model. In this section, we present four types of temporal moment conditions in Subsection 2.4.1, introduce panel IVE and GMM in Subsection 2.4.2 which look the same as the cross section IVE and GMM in Section 2.2, and show how to set up instrument matrices in Subsection 2.4.3 to implement the panel IVE and GMM for the four moment conditions.

2.4.1 Four Moment Conditions

To estimate the parameter η in (3.7) $y_i = q'_i \eta + v_i$, we can use moment conditions in the form of orthogonality between regressors and error terms. Ignoring the related-effect problem for a while, for both unrelated and related-effect models, we take the following four temporal moment conditions as a basis for IVE: for all s and t indexing time periods,

(SUM)	(a) $E(\sum_t x_{it} v_{it}) = 0$	(b) $E(c_i \sum_t v_{it}) = 0$,	
(CON)	(a) $E(x_{it} v_{it}) = 0 \quad \forall t$	(b) $E(c_i v_{it}) = 0 \quad \forall t$,	
(PRE)	(a) $E(x_{is} v_{it}) = 0 \quad \forall s \leq t$	(b) $E(c_i v_{it}) = 0 \quad \forall t$,	
(EXO)	(a) $E(x_{is} v_{it}) = 0 \quad \forall s, t$	(b) $E(c_i v_{it}) = 0 \quad \forall t$,	

where SUM, CON, PRE, and EXO, respectively, stand for *summing, contemporaneous, predetermined*, and *strictly exogenous*; (b) follows from (a) replacing x_{it} with c_i.

The following implication arrows hold:

$$\text{SUM} \Leftarrow \text{CON} \Leftarrow \text{PRE} \Leftarrow \text{EXO}.$$

In SUM, x_{it} and v_{it} are allowed to be correlated as long as SUM holds. SUM is the moment condition for the LSE treating the panel data as $N \cdot T$ cross-section observations, because the moment condition for the LSE is

$$(1/N) \sum_i \sum_t x_{it} v_{it} \overset{p}{=} 0 \quad \Leftrightarrow \quad E(\sum_t x_{it} v_{it}) = 0.$$

In CON, only contemporaneous correlations are zero. In PRE, x_{is} is allowed to be correlated with v_{it} if $s > t$; for example, rational expectation models with $E(v_{it}|x_{i1}, ..., x_{it}) = 0$, but not necessarily with $E(v_{it}|x_{i1}, ..., x_{iT}) = 0$. In EXO, x_{is} and v_{it} are uncorrelated at all leads and lags. The four moment conditions will reappear in later chapters for limited dependent variable models.

Omitting some time periods in PRE and EXO, we can easily allow for endogenous regressors; for example, we may use

$$E(x_{is} v_{it}) = 0 \quad \forall s < t \quad (\text{not } s \leq t \text{ as in PRE } (a))$$

allowing a contemporaneous relation between x_{it} and v_{it}. How the above moment conditions ought to be specifically adjusted for various endogenous regressors will be shown in the next section through an example.

Recall the related-effect problem: δ_i is related to some components, say w_{it}^1, of w_{it}. One solution to this problem is as follows: with $w_{it} = (w_{it}^{o\prime}, w_{it}^{1\prime})\prime$, use w_{it}^o of some periods, for example $w_{i1}^o, ..., w_{it}^o$, as instruments for w_{it}^1. Other than this plain idea, there are at least three ways in IVE to deal with the problem (and all will be explored later in detail):

(a)   Remove the part of w_{it}^1 related to δ_i, and use the remaining part unrelated to δ_i as an instrument for w_{it}^1. For instance, if $w_{it}^1 = \delta_i + \omega_{it}$ with ω_{it} unrelated to δ_i, then use $w_{it}^1 - w_{i,t-1}^1$.

(b)   Remove δ_i from v_{it}, for example, by $v_{it} - v_{i,t-1}$, to use w_{it} as an instrument for the transformed error term.

(c)   Absorb the part of δ_i related to w_{it}^1 into $w_i'\gamma$, leaving in the error term only the part of δ_i unrelated to w_i. For example, if $\delta_i = \sum_{t=1}^{T} w_{it}^{1\prime}\zeta_t + v_i$ for some ζ_t's and v_i, with v_i unrelated to w_{it}^1, then absorb $\sum_{t=1}^{T} w_{it}^{1\prime}\zeta_t$ into the regression function and redefine $v_{it} \equiv v_i + u_{it}$.

$$(4.1)$$

In (a), the error term v_{it} stays intact, whereas it does not in (b) and (c). Because v_{it} is unobserved, transforming it in (b) requires transforming the model equation.

Call (a) "regressor-differencing," (b) "error-differencing," and (c) "δ-splitting" or "δ-projecting"; (a) and (b) will appear in this chapter; (c) will appear in the next chapter.

2.4.2 Panel LSE, IVE and GMM

Turning to panel IVE and GMM, in a SUM type moment condition

$$E(\underset{(k+T-1)\times T}{q_i} \cdot \underset{T\times 1}{v_i}) = E(\sum_t \underset{(k+T-1)\times 1}{q_{it}} \cdot \underset{1\times 1}{v_{it}}) = 0,$$

the number of moments is the same as the number of parameters. In this case, the following LSE is the most efficient under SUM:

$$h_{lse} \equiv (\sum_i q_i q_i')^{-1} \cdot \sum_i q_i y_i.$$

It is easy to show that, with $\hat{v}_i \equiv y_i - q_i' h_{lse}$,

$$\sqrt{N}(h_{lse} - \eta) \overset{d}{=} N(0, \ (\sum_i q_i q_i'/N)^{-1} \cdot (\sum_i q_i \hat{v}_i \hat{v}_i' q_i'/N) \cdot (\sum_i q_i q_i'/N)^{-1}).$$

With $T = 3$, the moment conditions due to 1 in c_i and two time dummies are

$$E(v_{i2}) = 0, \quad E(v_{i3}) = 0, \quad E(v_{i1} + v_{i2} + v_{i3}) = 0, \tag{4.2}$$

which is equivalent to $E(v_{it}) = 0$ for all t. If we do not include time dummies in q_i, we will be using only the third condition of (4.2). The formula for h_{lse} and its asymptotic distribution are analogous to those for the cross-section LSE.

If homoskedasticity holds in the sense that

$$E(v_i v_i' | w_{i1}, ..., w_{iT}) = \Omega, \quad \text{a constant matrix,} \tag{4.3}$$

we can do GLS (generalized LSE) estimating Ω by

$$\Omega_N \equiv (1/N) \sum_i \hat{v}_i \hat{v}_i'.$$

The GLS is

$$h_{gls} = \{\sum_i q_i \Omega_N^{-1} q_i'\}^{-1} \cdot \sum_i q_i \Omega_N^{-1} y_i;$$

$$\sqrt{N}(h_{gls} - \eta) \overset{d}{=} N(0, \ \{\sum_i q_i \Omega_N^{-1} q_i'/N\}^{-1}).$$

Although LSE and GLS are straightforward, SUM is too weak to be useful in general, and summing errors across time does not make a good sense although one exception will be noted later for errors-in-variable problem.

As for (more sensible) CON, PRE and EXO, there are more moments than parameters under these conditions, and we need IVE. Suppose we have an instrument matrix z_i such that $E(z_i v_i) = 0$, where z_i is a $K \times T$ matrix and $K \geq k + T - 1$; the specific form of z_i depends on the moment condition in use and will be shown in the next subsection. For a given z_i, the IVE is

$$h_{ive} = \{\sum_i q_i z_i' (\sum_i z_i z_i')^{-1} \sum_i z_i q_i'\}^{-1} \cdot \sum_i q_i z_i' (\sum_i z_i z_i')^{-1} \sum_i z_i y_i, \quad (4.4)$$

and

$$\sqrt{N}(h_{ive} - \eta) \Rightarrow N(0, \ A_N \cdot (\sum_i z_i \hat{v}_i \hat{v}_i' z_i' / N) \cdot A_N') \quad (4.5)$$

where $\hat{v}_i \equiv y_i - q_i' h_{ive}$, and

$$A_N \{\sum_i q_i z_i' / N (\sum_i z_i z_i' / N)^{-1} \sum_i z_i q_i' / N\}^{-1}$$

$$(\sum_i q_i z_i' / N)(\sum_i z_i z_i' / N)^{-1}.$$

The GMM estimator more efficient than the IVE is

$$h_{gmm} = (\sum_i q_i z_i' \cdot C_N^{-1} \cdot \sum_i z_i q_i')^{-1} \cdot \sum_i q_i z_i' \cdot C_N^{-1} \cdot \sum_i z_i y_i \quad (4.6)$$

where $C_N \equiv (1/N) \sum_i z_i \hat{v}_i \hat{v}_i' z_i'$ and

$$\sqrt{N}(h_{gmm} - \eta) \Rightarrow N(0, \ \{(\sum_i q_i z_i' / N) \cdot C_N^{-1} \cdot (\sum_i q_i z_i' / N)\}^{-1}). \quad (4.7)$$

Also, with $\tilde{v}_i \equiv y_i - q_i' h_{gmm}$, when $K > k + T - 1$,

$$\{(1/\sqrt{N}) \sum_i z_i \tilde{v}_i\}' \{(1/N) \sum_i z_i \tilde{v}_i \tilde{v}_i' z_i'\}^{-1} (1/\sqrt{N}) \sum_i z_i \tilde{v}_i \Rightarrow \chi^2_{K-(k+T-1)}$$
$$(4.8)$$

which can be used as a test statistic for $H_o : E(z_i v_i) = 0$. This is a GMM overidentification test. As in cross-section GMM, a small sample performance of h_{gmm} could be worse than that of h_{ive}.

Using $\hat{v}_i \hat{v}_i'$ in estimating asymptotic variances, we allow arbitrary serial correlations in $v_{i1}, ..., v_{iT}$. In the time-series literature, sometimes $u_{i1}, ..., u_{iT}$ are assumed to be autocorrelated of order one:

$$u_{it} = \rho \cdot u_{i,t-1} + \varepsilon_{it}, \quad |\rho| < 1, \quad \varepsilon_{i1}, ..., \varepsilon_{iT} \text{ are iid.}$$

An advantage of panel data is $(1/N) \sum_i \hat{v}_i \hat{v}_i'$ showing the autocorrelation pattern of u_{it}'s without specifying an equation like this.

In a cross-section model with a group structure, usually $u_{i1}, ..., u_{iT}$ are assumed to be uncorrelated. Then, $v_{i1}, ..., v_{iT}$ are correlated only through δ_i, and consequently $COR(v_{is}, v_{it})$ is the same for all $s \neq t$ ("equi-correlation"). If this sort of information on the error term serial correlation is imposed, then the asymptotic variance may be estimated more efficiently. Also such additional information can generate second-order (nonlinear) moment conditions that may be used to estimate η more efficiently; see, for example, Ahn and Schmidt (1995, 1997).

The preceding panel estimators LSE, IVE and GMM are almost the same as those for the cross-section model; the only difference is that there is the extra time dimension T in the variables defining the preceding estimators for panel data. Formulas (4.4) to (4.7) are all we need to implement IVE and GMM for linear panel data models. The only task left is forming z_i, which is more difficult than it looks due to redundancy in the moment conditions caused by time invariants. The following subsection shows the forms of z_i for CON, PRE, and EXO.

2.4.3 Setting Up Instrument Matrices

To show the specific form of z_i depending on the moment condition in use, suppose $T \cdot k$ CON moment conditions are used. Then we need

$$z_i \equiv \mathrm{diag}(w_{i1}, ..., w_{iT}),$$

for, with $T = 3$,

$$z_i v_i = \begin{bmatrix} w_{i1} & 0 & 0 \\ 0 & w_{i2} & 0 \\ 0 & 0 & w_{i3} \end{bmatrix}_{(3 \cdot k) \times 3} \cdot \begin{bmatrix} v_{i1} \\ v_{i2} \\ v_{i3} \end{bmatrix}_{3 \times 1} = \begin{bmatrix} w_{i1} v_{i1} \\ w_{i2} v_{i2} \\ w_{i3} v_{i3} \end{bmatrix}_{(3 \cdot k) \times 1}. \qquad (4.9)$$

The reason that we use w_i, not q_i, is due to the redundancy of the moment conditions: 1 in c_i renders $E(v_{it}) = 0 \; \forall t$, and thus the time dummies do not give any new moment conditions. We need at least as many instruments as the parameters:

$$T \cdot k \geq k + (T - 1), \qquad (4.10)$$

which holds always.

PRE gives a different number of moments for each t. For $T = 3$,

$$\begin{aligned} E(v_{i1} w_{i1}) &= 0 \quad (t = 1), \\ E(v_{i2} w_{i1}) &= E(v_{i2} w_{i2}) = 0 \quad (t = 2), \\ E(v_{i3} w_{i1}) &= E(v_{i3} w_{i2}) = E(v_{i3} w_{i3}) = 0 \quad (t = 3). \end{aligned}$$

Because c_i appears in all w_{it}'s, there are redundant moment conditions; for example, for $t = 2$, $E(v_{i2} w_{i1}) = E(v_{i2} w_{i2}) = 0$ includes redundant moment conditions as can be seen replacing w_{it} with c_i. Let

$$z_i = \mathrm{diag}\{w_{i1}, (x_{i1}', w_{i2}')', (x_{i1}', x_{i2}', w_{i3}')'\} \qquad (4.11)$$

to avoid the redundancy. This renders

$$
z_i v_i = \begin{bmatrix} w_{i1} & 0 & 0 \\ 0 & x_{i1} & 0 \\ 0 & w_{i2} & 0 \\ 0 & 0 & x_{i1} \\ 0 & 0 & x_{i2} \\ 0 & 0 & w_{i3} \end{bmatrix}_{[\{k_x \cdot (1+2+3)\}+k_c \cdot 3] \times 3} \cdot \begin{bmatrix} v_{i1} \\ v_{i2} \\ v_{i3} \end{bmatrix} = \begin{bmatrix} w_{i1} v_{i1} \\ x_{i1} v_{i2} \\ w_{i2} v_{i2} \\ x_{i1} v_{i3} \\ x_{i2} v_{i3} \\ w_{i3} v_{i3} \end{bmatrix}. \qquad (4.12)
$$

With T large, setting up z_i can be cumbersome. The condition analogous to (4.10) is

$$
k_x \cdot T(T+1)/2 + k_c \cdot T \geq k + (T-1), \qquad (4.13)
$$

which holds.

EXO gives even more moments than PRE, but its analytic expression is simpler using the Kronecker product: with $T = 3$,

$$
\begin{aligned}
z_i &= \operatorname{diag}\{(x'_{i1}, x'_{i2}, x'_{i3}, c'_i)', (x'_{i1}, x'_{i2}, x'_{i3}, c'_i)', (x'_{i1}, x'_{i2}, x'_{i3}, c'_i)'\} \\
&= I_3 \otimes (x'_{i1}, x'_{i2}, x'_{i3}, c'_i)'. \\
&\quad {}_{\{3 \cdot (k_x \cdot 3 + k_c)\} \times 3}
\end{aligned} \qquad (4.14)
$$

This kind of instrument can be seen in GMM for cross-section simultaneous equations where all equations share the same instruments. The condition analogous to (4.10) and (4.13) is

$$
k_x \cdot T^2 + k_c \cdot T \geq k + (T-1), \qquad (4.15)
$$

which also holds.

IVE for PRE and EXO can be computationally burdensome because the dimension of z_i can be huge. More problematic is the near singularity due to some time variants having little actual variation over time; for example, if the time span for the panel is short, $marriage_{it}$ may vary very little. In this case, using $marriage_{i1}$, $marriage_{i2}$, $marriage_{i3}$ as three separate instruments in (4.11) or (4.14) can result in $\sum_i z_i z'_i$ near singular. If this problem occurs, then treat $marriage_{it}$ as time invariant when it is used as instruments; that is, use only $marriage_{i1}$ as an instrument in c_i, not $marriage_{it}$, $t = 1, 2, 3$, in x_{it}.

Although we have assumed balanced panels so far, it is not difficult to allow for unbalanced panels: make q_i, y_i and z_i such that its time dimension is T_i varying across i, instead of T. In the panel IVE and GMM, the time dimension does not appear explicitly, for we only need products such as $q_i z'_i$, $z_i z'_i$ and $z_i y_i$ for each i that are free of the dimension T_i and to be summed up across i to yield those estimators.

2.5   IVE WITH DIFFERENCED REGRESSORS

The preceding section showed different forms for the instrument matrix z_i depending on the moment condition (CON, PRE, EXO) at hand. In reality, available moment conditions may not fit exactly any of these; for example, they can be weaker than PRE but stronger than CON. To appreciate this practical issue, in this section we will see how to set up z_i through an example where z_i consists of elements of w_{it} and their transformations. This will show how to adjust z_i to deal with endogenous regressors and related effect in Subsection 2.5.1. For related effect, we may have to "purify" certain regressors related to δ_i before they are used; for this task, linear projection is introduced in Subsection 2.5.2. Subsection 2.5.3 provides a brief illustrative empirical example on wage.

2.5.1   Classifying Regressors and Instrument Matrix

Recall (3.3): δ_i is ability, IQ, or productivity, and y_{it} is hourly wage to be explained by time invariants c_i and time variants x_{it} where

c_i: 1, RC (race), ED (education in years),

x_{it}: WH (working hours), UR (local unemployment rate),

SF (1 if self-employed and 0 otherwise),

u_{it}: Residential location.

Although not included in this example, usually gender, age, and age^2 are used as regressors to explain wage. Age varies across i and t, but only in a deterministic way for t; treating age as time variant can cause a trouble as will be shown later. In fact, what should be treated as time variant is not always clear. If SF varies over time for only a few people, then it is better to treat SF as time invariant, for otherwise the resulting estimates will be too sensitive to those few observations.

In the preceding example, δ_i may be observable to the employer of individual i but unobservable to econometricians. Comparing $v_{it} = \delta_i + u_{it}$ with c_i and x_{it}, assume the following:

(a)   RC$_i$ is not correlated with v_{it}.

(b)   ED$_i$ is correlated with v_{it} only through δ_i.

(c)   UR$_{it}$ is not correlated with v_{it}.   (5.1)

(d)   SF$_{it}$ is correlated with v_{it} only through δ_i.

(e)   WH$_{it}$ is correlated with v_{it} only through u_{it}.

The best way to understand these is to point out when (5.1) will not hold. In (a), $COR(\text{RC}_i, \delta_i) = 0$ will not hold if certain race is less (or more) productive, and $COR(\text{RC}_i, u_{it}) = 0$ will not hold if residential location is informative for race. In (c), $COR(\text{UR}_{it}, v_{it}) = 0$ will not hold if residential location is correlated with UR$_{it}$. In (d), $COR(\text{SF}_{it}, \delta_i) \neq 0$ is allowed (self-employed people may be more able because they can survive on their own, or they may be less able if nobody wants to hire them), but (d) would not hold if residential location is informative for SF$_{it}$. In (e), $COR(\text{WH}_{it}, \delta_i) = 0$, but this may not hold if able or productive people tend to work more (or less).

After the regressors are classified as in (5.1), to construct z_i, we should list all the moment conditions for each v_{it}, $t = 1, ..., T$. Suppose we take a simple-minded approach of not using any variable correlated with v_{it} in any fashion. Then only 1, RC_i and UR_{it} can be used as instruments. Because UR_{it} is time variant, we can impose various moment conditions on UR_{it}. Set $T = 3$ for a while.

Omitting SUM, which does not give enough moment conditions, suppose we use CON type conditions:

$$E(v_{it}) = 0 \quad \forall t, \quad E(RC_i v_{it}) = 0 \quad \forall t, \quad E(UR_{it} v_{it}) = 0 \quad \forall t. \tag{5.2}$$

Then, recalling (4.9) for the second matrix in the following,

$$z_i' = \begin{bmatrix} 1 & 0 & 0 & RC_i & 0 & 0 & UR_{i1} & 0 & 0 \\ 0 & 1 & 0 & 0 & RC_i & 0 & 0 & UR_{i2} & 0 \\ 0 & 0 & 1 & 0 & 0 & RC_i & 0 & 0 & UR_{i3} \end{bmatrix} \tag{5.3}$$

$$\Leftrightarrow \begin{bmatrix} 1 & RC_i & UR_{i1} & 0 & 0 & 0 & 0 & 0 & 0 \\ 0 & 0 & 0 & 1 & RC_i & UR_{i2} & 0 & 0 & 0 \\ 0 & 0 & 0 & 0 & 0 & 0 & 1 & RC_i & UR_{i3} \end{bmatrix}$$

where each of RC_i and UR_{it} gives three instruments. Either matrix can be used; the first corresponds to (5.2) better, whereas the second is written block-diagonally for v_{it}, $t = 1, 2, 3$.

Suppose we use PRE type conditions:

$$E(v_{it}) = 0 \quad \forall t, \quad E(RC_i v_{it}) = 0 \quad \forall t, \quad E(UR_{is} v_{it}) = 0 \quad \forall s \le t. \tag{5.4}$$

Then, recalling (4.12) for the second matrix in the following,

$$z_i' = \begin{bmatrix} 1 & 0 & 0 & RC_i & 0 & 0 & UR_{i1} & 0 & 0 & 0 & 0 & 0 \\ 0 & 1 & 0 & 0 & RC_i & 0 & 0 & UR_{i1} & 0 & UR_{i2} & 0 & 0 \\ 0 & 0 & 1 & 0 & 0 & RC_i & 0 & 0 & UR_{i1} & 0 & UR_{i2} & UR_{i3} \end{bmatrix}$$

$$\Leftrightarrow \begin{bmatrix} 1 & RC_i & UR_{i1} & 0 & 0 & 0 & 0 & 0 & 0 & 0 & 0 & 0 \\ 0 & 0 & 0 & 1 & RC_i & UR_{i1} & UR_{i2} & 0 & 0 & 0 & 0 & 0 \\ 0 & 0 & 0 & 0 & 0 & 0 & 0 & 1 & RC_i & UR_{i1} & UR_{i2} & UR_{i3} \end{bmatrix}$$

$$\tag{5.5}$$

which has more instruments than (5.3); compare the columns with UR_{it}'s in (5.3) and (5.5).

Suppose we use EXO type conditions

$$E(v_{it}) = 0 \quad \forall t, \quad E(RC_i v_{it}) = 0 \quad \forall t, \quad E(UR_{is} v_{it}) = 0 \quad \forall s, t. \tag{5.6}$$

Then, recalling (4.14),

$$z_i' = I_3 \otimes (\quad 1 \quad RC_i \quad UR_{i1} \quad UR_{i2} \quad UR_{i3} \quad) = I_3 \otimes (\quad 1 \quad RC_i \quad UR_i' \quad), \tag{5.7}$$

where $UR_i \equiv (UR_{i1}, UR_{i2}, UR_{i3})'$.

So far, we might have been too conservative using only 1, RC_i, and UR_{it} as instruments that are not related with v_{it} at all. Under some assumptions, however, we may use WH_{it} (work hours) and SF_{it} (self-employment) as well, for they are correlated only with a part of v_{it}. For WH_{it}, assume

$$E(WH_{is} \cdot v_{it}) = 0 \quad \forall s < t, \tag{5.8}$$

which is PRE without the contemporaneous orthogonality. As for SF_{it}, we introduce "linear projection" to extract the part of SF_{it} uncorrelated with δ_i and use the part as an instrument; this is the approach used in (4.1)(a). The specific form of z_i using WH_{it} and SF_{it} will be presented after linear projection is studied in the following subsection.

2.5.2 Linear Projection and Purifying Regressors

The linear projection of a random vector λ on a random vector ζ with $E|\lambda|^2 < \infty$ and $E|\zeta|^2 < \infty$ is defined as

$$\Pi(\lambda|\zeta) \equiv E(\lambda\zeta') \cdot E^{-1}(\zeta\zeta') \cdot \zeta = \vartheta' \cdot \zeta,$$

where $|\cdot|$ is the Euclidean norm,

$$\vartheta \equiv E^{-1}(\zeta\zeta') \cdot E(\zeta\lambda') \tag{5.9}$$

is the linear projection coefficient, and either $E(\zeta) = 0$ or ζ has 1 as its component. Then, with $\varepsilon \equiv \lambda - \vartheta'\zeta$,

$$E(\varepsilon\zeta') = E\{(\lambda - \vartheta'\zeta) \cdot \zeta'\} = E(\lambda\zeta') - E(\lambda\zeta') = 0. \tag{5.10}$$

Observe

$$COV(\varepsilon, \zeta) = E(\varepsilon\zeta') - E(\varepsilon) \cdot E(\zeta') = E(\varepsilon\zeta') = 0; \tag{5.11}$$

the second equality holds because either $E(\zeta) = 0$ or $E(\varepsilon) = 0$ from (5.10) corresponding to 1 in ζ. Thus, so long as the second moments exist, we can always decompose λ into two components $\vartheta'\zeta$ and ε, one correlated with ζ and the other uncorrelated with ζ:

$$\lambda = \vartheta'\zeta + \varepsilon; \tag{5.12}$$

no other assumptions are required for this decomposition. Some properties of $\Pi(\lambda|\zeta)$ are analogous to those of $E(\lambda|\zeta)$:

(a) $\Pi\{\Pi(\lambda|\zeta)|\zeta\} = \Pi(\lambda|\zeta),$
(b) $\Pi(a_1\lambda_1 + a_2\lambda_2|\zeta) = a_1\Pi(\lambda_1|\zeta) + a_2\Pi(\lambda_2|\zeta)$ $\qquad$ (5.13)

for constants a_j and random vectors λ_j with $E|\lambda_j|^2 < \infty$, $j = 1, 2$.

Turning back to SF_{it}, suppose

$$E(SF_{it}) \text{ and } E(\delta_i \cdot SF_{it}) \text{ are not functions of } t. \qquad (5.14)$$

Linearly project SF_{it} on 1 and δ_i to get

$$SF_{it} = \phi_i + (SF_{it} - \phi_i) \equiv \phi_i + \lambda_{it}, \qquad (5.15)$$

where ϕ_i is the linear projection, and $\lambda_{it} \equiv SF_{it} - \phi_i$; λ_{it} *is uncorrelated with* δ_i *by construction.* Hence, transformations of SF_{it} that remove δ_i can be used as instruments: for example,

$$SF_{it} - SF_{i,t-1} = \lambda_{it} - \lambda_{i,t-1}, \qquad (5.16)$$

$$SF_{it} - (1/T) \sum_t SF_{it} = \lambda_{it} - (1/T) \sum_t \lambda_{it}. \qquad (5.17)$$

We prefer (5.16) to (5.17), for (5.17) can complicate the asymptotic variance of the resulting estimator by involving all time periods.
Define

$$\Delta SF_{it} \equiv SF_{it} - SF_{i,t-1} \quad and \quad \Delta SF_i \equiv (\Delta SF_{i2}, \Delta SF_{i3})'.$$

Omitting now the CON case, which is easy, suppose that we use the following PRE type conditions; recall (5.1) and (5.8):

$$\begin{aligned}
&v_{i1} \text{ is orthogonal to } z_{i1} = (1, RC_i, UR_{i1})'; \\
&v_{i2} \text{ is orthogonal to } z_{i2} = (1, RC_i, UR_{i1}, UR_{i2}, WH_{i1}, \Delta SF_{i2})'; \\
&v_{i3} \text{ is orthogonal to } z_{i3} = \\
&\qquad (1, RC_i, UR_{i1}, UR_{i2}, UR_{i3}, WH_{i1}, WH_{i2}, \Delta SF_{i2}, \Delta SF_{i3})'.
\end{aligned} \qquad (5.18)$$

Then z_i' is block-diagonal for the three error terms:

$$z_i' = \begin{bmatrix} z_{i1}' & 0 & 0 \\ 0 & z_{i2}' & 0 \\ 0 & 0 & z_{i3}' \end{bmatrix}. \qquad (5.19)$$

If we use EXO type conditions for UR_{it}, then z_i' becomes

$$\begin{bmatrix} & 0 & 0 & 0 & 0 & 0 \\ (1, RC_i, UR_i') \otimes I_3 & WH_{i1} & \Delta SF_{i2} & 0 & 0 & 0 \\ & 0 & 0 & WH_{i1} & WH_{i2} & \Delta SF_i' \end{bmatrix}, \qquad (5.20)$$

which can be easily rewritten block-diagonally as in (5.19) if desired. In the panel IVE literature, Arellano and Bover (1995) use regressors in levels or in differences and list instruments block-diagonally for each period as we do here.

2.5.3 An Empirical Example on Wage

The data appendix has a small ($N = 334$) teaching-purpose panel drawn from Panel Study of Income Dynamics with three waves (1984–1986) and 10 columns:

c1:	edu (education in years)	c2:	hr (work-hours per year)
c3:	wage ($ wage per hour)	c4:	family earnings in $ per year
c5:	self (dummy for self-employed)	c6:	sal (dummy for salaried)
c7:	mar (dummy for married)	c8:	kid (number of children)
c9:	age	c10:	ur (local unemployment %)

with the summary statistics for the first wave being (c4 not used)

	edu	hr	wage	self	sal	mar	kid	age	ur
MEAN	13.55	2162	16.44	0.198	0.434	0.925	1.13	41.25	7.46
SD	2.94	799	12.57	0.399	0.496	0.264	1.12	10.01	1.81

For GMM, we allow edu, hr, mar, and kid to be endogenous for wage, to use $(1, age, age^2/100)$' as time-invariant instruments and $(sal, self, ur)$' as time-variant instruments.

Usually in practice, ln(wage) is used as y and ln(hr) is used as a regressor. A small fraction of the data show wage = 0 and hr = 0; for them we used ln(wage) = 0 and ln(hr) = 0. This is certainly not the best way to deal with the problem ln(0) (a better way is to use a sample selection model), but it is simpler and at least assures no wage for no hours worked. The results for the ln(wage) equation are shown in Table 2.2, with t-values in ($\cdot$).

TABLE 2.2 Results for ln(wage) Equation

	LSE	BET	WIT	GMM-PRE	GMM-EXO
$\tau_2 - \tau_1$	.008(.29)			−.004(.15)	.00(.47)
$\tau_3 - \tau_1$	.006(.21)		.002(.04)	.001(.04)	.004(.17)
τ_1	.637(.94)	.413(.58)		1.377(1.2)	.412(.45)
age	.040(1.3)	.043(1.3)	.079(1.4)	.062(1.1)	.076(1.5)
age^2/100	−.031(−.9)	−.033(−.9)	−.081(−1.3)	−.053(−.7)	−.076(−1.1)
edu	.066(5.4)	.064(5.2)		.010(.24)	.064(2.0)
kid	.008(.29)	.003(.11)	.044(.76)	.027(.16)	−.064(−.41)
ln(hr)	−.009(−.53)	.013(.57)	−.105(−3.2)	.030(.36)	−.009(−.15)
mar	.101(.96)	.114(.88)	.008(.06)	−.634(−.91)	−.069(−.15)
sal	.241(4.2)	.259(3.7)	.091(2.0)	.271(2.9)	.125(2.1)
self	−.413(−4.4)	−.454(−4.2)	−.200(−1.8)	−.291(−2.6)	−.278(−3.0)
ur	−.016(−.9)	−.012(−.6)	−.030(−1.5)	−.039(−2.1)	−.031(−2.4)
PV (p-value for GMM overidentification test):				.288	.035

Two estimators, "BET" and "WIT," will be explained in the next section; here we compare only LSE, GMM-PRE, and GMM-EXO.

First, the intercept does not seem to change over time; the 3-year period was "calm" economically. Second, age and $age^2/100$ show that wage increases at decreasing rate as age goes up. Third, edu has its return of about 6.5% per year in LSE and GMM-EXO (significant), and about 10% in GMM-PRE (insignificant); the coefficient of education attracted considerable attention under the name "returns to schooling." Fourth, sal has a significant positive effect, whereas self and ur have significant negative effects. Fifth, estimating $E(vv')$ using the LSE residuals, we find

$$COR(v_1, v_2) = 0.730, \quad COR(v_1, v_3) = 0.665, \quad \text{and} \quad COR(v_2, v_3) = 0.665,$$

which shows rather slowly decreasing serial correlation; recall that if u_{it}'s are independent over time, then equicorrelation should hold because serial correlation is driven only by δ_i.

Despite that LSE may be inconsistent because it does not allow endogeneity for the regressors, that the sample size is small, and that GMM-EXO requires very strong assumptions on instruments, overall, the results are not too different across the three estimators (in sal and self, however, some estimates are twice as big as some other estimates). The GMM overidentification test with level 5% rejects EXO while failing to reject PRE.

2.6 IVE WITH DIFFERENCED ERRORS

In the preceding section, we illustrated how to set up the instrument matrix z_i through an example, and then we showed that a transformation of regressors or "regressor differencing" can deal with endogenous regressors and related effect. One shortcoming of this approach was that the validity of instruments depends too much on assumptions. Panel data can provide noncontroversial instruments as well that amount to differencing the model equation, which, however, comes at some cost which we will illustrate shortly: the coefficients of the time invariant regressors are not identified, and the variation of the regressors may get reduced substantially.

We explore "error differencing" (recall (4.1b)) in Subsection 2.6.1, with an empirical example on crime and punishment given in Subsetion 2.6.2. In Subsection 2.6.3, the "between-group estimator" is examined, which is the opposite of error differencing in the sense that the error terms are added up rathen than differenced; an empirical example for a production function is also provided in Subsection 2.6.3.

2.6.1 Within-Group Estimator

Define idempotent and symmetric mean-differencing matrix

$$Q_T \equiv I_T - 1_T 1_T'/T \tag{6.1}$$

to transform (3.6) into

$$Q_T y_i = Q_T m_T \cdot \Delta \tau + Q_T (1_T' \otimes c_i)' \alpha + Q_T x_i' \beta + Q_T (1_T \delta_i) + Q_T u_i \tag{6.2}$$

where

$$Q_T y_i = (y_{i1} - \bar{y}_{i.}, ..., y_{iT} - \bar{y}_{i.})', \quad \bar{y}_{i.} \equiv (1/T) \sum_t y_{it}; \quad (6.3)$$

$Q_T y_i$ is said to be "demeaning" y_i. The mean differencing eliminates the second and fourth terms on the right-hand side (that is, all time invariants, observed or not) to leave

$$Q_T y_i = Q_T m_T \cdot \Delta \tau + Q_T x_i' \beta + Q_T u_i = Q_T w_i^{*\prime} \gamma^* + Q_T u_i, \quad (6.4)$$

where

$$\underset{T \times (T-1+k_x)}{w_i^{*\prime}} \equiv (m_T, x_i'), \quad \gamma^* \equiv (\Delta \tau', \beta')'.$$

LSE to (6.4) under $E(w_i^* Q_T u_i) = 0$ is called the "within-group estimator (WIT)":

$$g_{wit} = (\sum_i w_i^* Q_T w_i^{*\prime})^{-1} \cdot \sum_i w_i^* Q_T y_i,$$

$$\sqrt{N}(g_{wit} - \gamma^*) \overset{d}{=} N(0, \ \Psi_N^{-1} \cdot (1/N) \sum_i (w_i^* Q_T \hat{u}_i \hat{u}_i' Q_T w_i^{*\prime}) \cdot \Psi_N^{-1}), \quad (6.5)$$

where $\Psi_N \equiv (1/N) \sum_i w_i^* Q_T w_i^{*\prime}$ and $Q_T \hat{u}_i = Q_T y_i - Q_T w_i^{*\prime} g_{wit}$; here the group refers to the individual i. WIT is also called the "fixed-effect estimator." In WIT, the coefficients of time invariants are not identified, which is the main weakness of WIT.

In WIT, the regressors and the error become, respectively, $x_{it} - \bar{x}_{i.}$ and $u_{it} - \bar{u}_{i.}$, where $\bar{x}_{i.} \equiv (1/T) \sum_t x_{it}$ and $\bar{u}_{i.} \equiv \sum_t u_{it}$. For these to be orthogonal, we need EXO. First-differencing, however, avoids this strong requirement: for

$$\Delta y_{it} = \Delta x_{it}' \beta + \Delta u_{it}, \quad (6.6)$$

PRE $E(x_{is} u_{it}) = 0 \ \forall s \leq t$ implies $E(\Delta x_{is} \Delta u_{it}) = 0 \ \forall s \leq t - 1$. Anderson and Hsiao (1981, 1982) removed δ_i not by demeaning but by first-differencing a model with $y_{i,t-1}$ as a regressor; they proposed to use $y_{i,t-2} - y_{i,t-3}$ or $y_{i,t-2}$ as an instrument for $y_{i,t-1} - y_{i,t-2}$. Because the error term in the differenced model is $u_{it} - u_{i,t-1}$, the instruments are valid if u_{it}'s are serially uncorrelated; if u_{it} is of "moving average of order one" ($u_{it} = \varepsilon_{it} + \rho \varepsilon_{i,t-1}$, where $\varepsilon_{i1}, ..., \varepsilon_{iT}$ are iid), then $y_{i,t-3} - y_{i,t-4}$ or $y_{i,t-3}$ can be used as an instrument for $y_{i,t-1} - y_{i,t-2}$. If we indeed impose the zero serial correlation assumption of u_{it}''s, then we can use more lagged y_{it}'s as instruments (Arellano and Bond, 1991). Zero serial correlation can occur in rational expectation models, which, in fact, contain conditional orthogonality, stronger than unconditional orthogonality.

Removing δ_i requires care in practice, because some time variants such as age$_{it}$ vary over time in a deterministic way: when demeaning or first-differencing is applied to such variables, demeaned or first-differenced versions become linearly dependent on demeaned or first-differenced m_T, respectively. To see this, let $T = 3$ and compare m_3 and age$_{it}$ before and after mean differencing:

$$
\begin{bmatrix} 0 & 0 & \text{age}_{i1} \\ 1 & 0 & \text{age}_{i2} \\ 0 & 1 & \text{age}_{i3} \end{bmatrix} \Rightarrow \begin{bmatrix} -1/3 & -1/3 & -1 \\ 2/3 & -1/3 & 0 \\ -1/3 & 2/3 & 1 \end{bmatrix} \Rightarrow \begin{bmatrix} 2/3 & -1/3 & 0 \\ -1/3 & 2/3 & 1 \end{bmatrix}
$$

$$(6.7)$$

where the second arrow follows from losing one row in mean differencing (this is essentially the same as losing one wave in first-differencing); we dropped the first row. In the last 2×3 matrix, one column is linearly dependent on the other two; we should remove any one column to prevent singularity of the inverted matrix in g_{wit}. This also holds more generally for $T > 3$: remove either one column in m_T or age$_{it}$ from x_{it}. For job experience, the same problem can occur if it increases by one every period as age does.

Depending on what is removed to prevent singularity, the parameter identification changes. Suppose we remove the time dummy for period 2. To see the effect of this action, observe that the first column of the 2×3 matrix in (6.7) is linearly dependent on the other two columns:

$$
\begin{bmatrix} 2/3 \\ -1/3 \end{bmatrix} = -2 \cdot \begin{bmatrix} -1/3 \\ 2/3 \end{bmatrix} + \begin{bmatrix} 0 \\ 1 \end{bmatrix}.
$$

$$(6.8)$$

In (6.4), suppose $w_i^{*\prime} = (m_3, \text{age}_{it})$. Then $Q_T w_i^{*\prime} \gamma^*$ is, other than its first redundant row,

$$
(\tau_2 - \tau_1) \cdot \begin{bmatrix} 2/3 \\ -1/3 \end{bmatrix} + (\tau_3 - \tau_1) \cdot \begin{bmatrix} -1/3 \\ 2/3 \end{bmatrix} + \beta_{\text{age}} \cdot \begin{bmatrix} 0 \\ 1 \end{bmatrix}
$$
$$
= \{-2(\tau_2 - \tau_1) + (\tau_3 - \tau_1)\} \cdot \begin{bmatrix} -1/3 \\ 2/3 \end{bmatrix} + \{(\tau_2 - \tau_1) + \beta_{\text{age}}\} \cdot \begin{bmatrix} 0 \\ 1 \end{bmatrix}.
$$

$$(6.9)$$

Hence, with period 2 dummy removed from m_3, WIT estimates

$$
-2(\tau_2 - \tau_1) + (\tau_3 - \tau_1) \quad \text{and} \quad (\tau_2 - \tau_1) + \beta_{\text{age}} \qquad (6.10)
$$

as the coefficients for the period 3 dummy and age_{it}; in Table 2.2, the numbers in the rows for $\tau_3 - \tau_1$ and β_{age} in the WIT column are for these new parameters. If age_{it} is removed instead of the time dummy for period 2, then, doing analogously to (6.8) to (6.10), we can show that

$$(t - 1)\beta_{age} + (\tau_t - \tau_1), \quad t = 2, ..., T$$

are identified; for Table 2.2, we get 0.078 (1.31) and 0.158 (1.42) for these two parameters with $T = 3$. If one is not aware of this identification isssue, then these numbers may be mistaken for $\tau_2 - \tau_1$ and $\tau_3 - \tau_1$, respectively.

As mentioned already, the major shortcoming of WIT is losing $\tilde{c}_i$ along with δ_i. Sometimes the following scheme is employed to recover the coefficients of $\tilde{c}_i$ (for example, Kerkhofs *et al.*, 1999). First, time-average equation (3.1) and replace β with its WIT $\hat{\beta}$ to get

$$(1/T) \sum_t y_{it} - (1/T) \sum_t x'_{it} \hat{\beta} \cong (1/T) \sum_t \tau_t + \tilde{c}'_i \tilde{\alpha} + \delta_i + (1/T) \sum_t u_{it}.$$
(6.11)

Second, $(1/T) \sum_t \tau_t$ and $\tilde{\alpha}$ are estimated by the LSE of the left-hand side on 1 and $\tilde{c}_i$. But the validity of the scheme is problem specific. For the scheme to work, it is necessary to have

$$E[\tilde{c}_i \cdot \{\delta_i + (1/T) \sum_t u_{it}\}] = 0.$$
(6.12)

If T is not too small to have $(1/T) \sum_t u_{it} \cong 0$, then $COR(\tilde{c}_i, u_{it}) \neq 0$ can be allowed as well as $COR(x_{it}, \delta_i) \neq 0$ that was allowed by $\hat{\beta}$. For the returns to schooling example, however, this scheme will not work because $COR(\tilde{c}_i, \delta_i) \neq 0$, which violates the moment condition (6.12).

2.6.2 An Empirical Example on Crime and Punishment

Although WIT allows endogeneity of regressors due to δ_i, it does not allow endogeneity due to u_{it}. In Table 2.2, hr (and kid and mar) may be related to u_{it}; the significant negative estimate for ln(hr) might be due to this problem, as we would expect a higher wage as ln(hr) goes up. For the table, a Wald test (explained in the next chapter) for LSE = WIT and PRE = WIT returned p-values, respectively, 0.017 and 0.002, rejecting the equalities. The following example on crime and punishment illustrates the endogeneity problems further; with or without the endogeneity problems, crime and punishment is an interesting issue on its own.

Cornwell and Trumbull (1994) have analyzed ln(crime rate) using a data on North Carolina counties ($N = 90$ and $T = 7$); see Table 2.3. BET is the "between-group estimator," which is the simple cross-section LSE for time-averaged variables (explained in detail in the next subsection), WIT-IVE is explained in the following paragraph.

TABLE 2.3 Explaining ln(Crime Rate)

	BET (SD)	WIT (SD)	WIT-IVE (SD)
P(arrest)	−0.648 (0.088)	−0.355 (0.032)	−0.455 (0.618)
P(convict)	−0.528 (0.067)	−0.282 (0.021)	−0.336 (0.371)
P(imprison)	0.297 (0.231)	−0.173 (0.032)	−0.196 (0.200)
Punishment severity	−0.236 (0.174)	−0.002 (0.026)	−0.030 (0.030)
Number of police officers per capita	0.364 (0.060)	0.413 (0.027)	0.504 (0.617)

Crime rate = Ratio of crimes to county population

P(arrest) = Ratio of arrests to offenses

P(convict) = Ratio of convictions to arrests

P(imprison) = Proportion of convictions resulting in prison sentence

Punishment severity = Average prison sentence length in days

	Crime	P(arrest)	P(convict)	P(imprison)	Severity	Police Officers
Mean	0.032	0.309	0.689	0.426	8.955	0.00192
SD	0.018	0.171	1.690	0.087	2.658	0.00273

Cornwell and Trumbull (1994) are concerned about two endogeneity problems. One is $COR(x_{it}, \delta_i)$; for example, police practice varies across counties and some county police tend to underreport crimes, which then exaggerates P(arrest). The other is the simultaneity between y_{it} and $police_{it}$: not only police can influence crime rate, but also crime rate can influence the number of police, that is, $COR(police_{it}, u_{it})$ may not be zero. BET can be used if both sources of endogeneity are not present; WIT can be used if only the first is present; for both endogeneities, WIT-IVE is an IVE to the mean-differenced model.

Looking at BET and WIT, P(arrest) and P(convict) are significant in BET and WIT, whereas P(imprison) is so only in WIT; *police* is significant for both BET and WIT but has the wrong sign. In WIT-IVE, *police* is insignificant; but all the other variables are so as well, which is likely to be due to "weak" instruments or reduced variation in the regressors. The magnitude of crime-deterring effects of P(arrest), P(convict), and P(imprison) is decreasing along the legal process steps. It is disappointing to see the insignificant effect of punishment severity, but with the average punishment being as low as 9 days, this is understandable. From the summary statistics table, the probability of the eventual imprisonment given committing a crime is less than 0.1: $0.309*0.689*0.426 = 0.091$. Coupling this number with the 9-day average punishment, the expected eventual punishment is less than one day; here we are glossing over factors such as type of crime.

2.6.3 Between-Group Estimator

If we take temporal average of all variables for each individual, then the time dimension is gone. The LSE to this cross-section data is called the "between group (BET)" estimator. Formally, with $\bar{y}_{i.} \equiv (1/T) \sum_t y_{it}, \bar{q}_{i.} \equiv (1/T) \sum_t q_{it}$, and $\bar{v}_{i.} \equiv (1/T) \sum_t v_{it}$, BET is the LSE applied to

$$\bar{y}_{i.} = \bar{q}'_{i.}\eta + \bar{v}_{i.}, \quad i = 1, ..., N. \tag{6.13}$$

That is,

$$h_{bet} = \{\sum_i \bar{q}_{i.}\bar{q}'_{i.}\}^{-1} \cdot \sum_i \bar{q}_{i.}\bar{y}_{i.}, \tag{6.14}$$

$$\sqrt{N}(h_{bet} - \eta) \overset{d}{=} N(0, \ (\sum_i \bar{q}_{i.}\bar{q}'_{i.}/N)^{-1} \cdot (\sum_i \bar{q}_{i.}\bar{q}'_{i.}\bar{v}^2_{i.}/N) \cdot (\sum_i \bar{q}_{i.}\bar{q}'_{i.}/N)^{-1}).$$

For unbalanced panels, BET may be the easiest estimator to use. For the sake of comparison, BET was given in Table 2.2: BET is little different from LSE (but the BET intercept is $(\tau_1 + \tau_2 + \tau_3)/3$).

BET does not remove related effect, but it removes much of measurement errors. To see this, consider an errors-in-variable model:

$$y_{it} = x^{*\prime}_{it}\beta + \delta_i + u_{it} \quad \text{and} \quad x_{it} = x^*_{it} + \varepsilon_{it} \tag{6.15}$$

$$\Rightarrow \quad y_{it} = x'_{it}\beta + \delta_i - \varepsilon'_{it}\beta + u_{it}, \tag{6.16}$$

where $\{\varepsilon_{it}\}$ are measurement error vectors iid across i and t and independent of $\{u_{it}\}$ and $\{x^*_{it}\}$, and x_{it} is an error-ridden regressor vector that is observed instead of x^*_{it}. First-difference (6.16) to get

$$y_{it} - y_{i,t-1} = (x_{it} - x_{i,t-1})'\beta - (\varepsilon_{it} - \varepsilon_{i,t-1})'\beta + u_{it} - u_{i,t-1}. \tag{6.17}$$

The LSE of Δy_{it} on Δx_{it} is inconsistent for β due to the relation between $x_{it} - x_{i,t-1}$ and $\varepsilon_{it} - \varepsilon_{i,t-1}$. The variation of Δx_{it} in (6.17) is likely to be smaller than that of x_{it} in (6.16), whereas the variation of the error term gets bigger due to $V(\varepsilon_{it} - \varepsilon_{i,t-1}) = V(\varepsilon_{it}) + V(\varepsilon_{i,t-1})$. This means that the IVE for (6.17) is likely to have larger standard errors than the IVE for (6.16). But BET can remove much of ε_{it} by averaging: $(1/T) \sum_t \varepsilon_{it} \cong 0$ if T is not too small. In this regard, LSE and GLS with SUM type moments may work as well, for the summation over t in SUM does the same job; recall that BET was almost the same as LSE in Table 2.2. In practice, one may want to weigh the biases due to related-effect and measurement error. If the latter is the greater, then LSE or BET may be preferred to IVE.

To see how to detect the errors-in-variable problem, consider $y_{it} - y_{i,t-s}$ for any $s \neq t$: analogously to (6.17), we get

$$y_{it} - y_{i,t-s} = (x_{it} - x_{i,t-s})'\beta - (\varepsilon_{it} - \varepsilon_{i,t-s})'\beta + u_{it} - u_{i,t-s}. \quad (6.18)$$

The LSE for this has a bias that is a function of s. Griliches and Hausman (1986) have suggestd LSE for (6.18) with different s: if the LSE varies much as s varies, then this is an indication of an errors-in-variable problem. To be specific, the LSE bias converges in probability to (recall $x_{it} = x_{it}^* + \varepsilon_{it}$ and independence betwee x_{it}^*'s and ε_{it}'s)

$$-E^{-1}\{ \sum_{t=s+1}^{T} (x_{it} - x_{i,t-s})(x_{it} - x_{i,t-s})' \}$$

$$\sum_{t=s+1}^{T} E\{(x_{it} - x_{i,t-s})(\varepsilon_{it} - \varepsilon_{i,t-s})'\}\beta$$

$$= -E^{-1}\{ \sum_{t=s+1}^{T} (x_{it} - x_{i,t-s})(x_{it} - x_{i,t-s})' \} \cdot$$

$$\sum_{t=s+1}^{T} E\{(\varepsilon_{it} - \varepsilon_{i,t-s})(\varepsilon_{it} - \varepsilon_{i,t-s})'\} \cdot \beta$$

$$= -E^{-1}\{ \sum_{t=s+1}^{T} (x_{it} - x_{i,t-s})(x_{it} - x_{i,t-s})' \} \cdot$$

$$\{2(T-s) \cdot E(\varepsilon_{it}\varepsilon_{it}') \cdot \beta\}, \quad (6.19)$$

where 2 comes from $E\{(\varepsilon_{it} - \varepsilon_{i,t-s})(\varepsilon_{it} - \varepsilon_{i,t-s})'\} = 2 \cdot E(\varepsilon_{it}\varepsilon_{it}')$, and $T - s$ comes from $\sum_{t=s+1}^{T}$. The two matrices in (6.19) are functions of s. Heuristically, $|x_{it} - x_{i,t-s}|$ decreases as s goes down; because $E(\varepsilon_{it}\varepsilon_{it}')$ is a constant and $T - s$ increases as s goes down, (6.19) becomes more negative if $\beta > 0$ as s decreases.

Griliches and Mairesse (1998) considered various ways of combining first-differencing, mean differencing, and averaging. Then they estimated the Cobb-Douglas production function for a French firm-level panel data with $N = 441$ and $T = 13$ (over 1967–1979). Table 2.4 shows part of their Table 6.1.

TABLE 2.4 Estimates and Measurement Errors

	Estimate (t-value)	V(capital)	Measurement error
Level, y_{it}:	0.304 (34.8)	0.3023	$\varepsilon_{it} \Rightarrow 1$
BET, $\bar{y}_{i.}$:	0.315 (10.1)	0.2851	$(1/T)\sum_t \varepsilon_{it} \Rightarrow 0$
WIT, $y_{it} - \bar{y}_i$:	0.146 (12.0)	0.0245	$\varepsilon_{it} - (1/T)\sum_t \varepsilon_{it} \Rightarrow 1$
LD, $y_{iT} - y_{i1}$:	0.147 (3.7)	0.1282	$\varepsilon_{iT} - \varepsilon_{i1} \Rightarrow 2$
FD, Δy_{it}:	0.061 (3.4)	0.0085	$\varepsilon_{it} - \varepsilon_{i,t-1} \Rightarrow 2$

The response variable of the final estimated model is given in the first column (LD (FD) stands for the "last (first) difference"), the estimates for ln(capital) and their t-values are given in the second column, V(capital) in the third column stands for the net variance of ln(capital)-based regressor net of its relationship to the other regressors, and finally in the last column, if T is large (so that $(1/T)\sum_t \varepsilon_{it} \cong 0$), the *effective* number of the measurement errors in each model is $1, 0, 1, 2, 2$, respectively, as shown by "$\Rightarrow$."

The big difference between FD and LD suggests an errors-in-variable problem as mentioned just before (6.19); FD indeed seems to be suffering from a bigger negative bias than LD. Given the usual inaccurate measurement of capital, this is not surprising. In general, as we go from level data to differenced data, the variation in the regressors declines whereas the errors-in-variable problem gets aggravated. These two factors, errors in variables and small regressor variation in the differeced model, tend to reduce t-values and push estimate magnitudes toward zero; see Table 2.4 and also the crime example. The second factor was a motivating force for IVE in the preceding sections, which was used instead of differencing the model. The IVE that uses differenced regressors as instruments while keeping the model equation intact, however, does not quite solve the problem, for the differenced regressors as instruments have a smaller variation.

Given the regressor variations and the errors in variables, the table seems to favor WIT and LD over FD in removing δ_i. But WIT and LD have some shortcomings. A problem with WIT is that the error term in WIT involves all of $u_{i1}, ..., u_{iT}$. Thus, for a given period, it is difficult to use the other periods' regressors as instruments; for example, if only u_{it} and $u_{i,t-1}$ appeared for the equation at t, regressors in periods other than t and $t - 1$ might be used as instruments. A problem with LD is that, when two waves are far apart, there is a higher chance for time-varying parameters. Thus, what is a good estimator to use for a given data depends on sevaral factors: sources of endogeneity, availability of instruments, parameter constancy, measurement errors, and so on.

2.7 AN EMPIRICAL EXAMPLE ON PRODUCTION FUNCTION

This section presents an empirical example on Cobb–Douglas production function for panel IVE and GMM. The data set was originally collected by Mexico's

Commerce Department and subsequently used in a number of world bank projects. We drew one industry (plastic) that has 140 firms over 5 years (1986–1990). Our goal is to illustrate some of the estimators that appeared up to now and see whether statistical inference is stable as orthogonality conditions and the assumption of related/unrelated-effect change. See Griliches and Mairesse (1998) and the references therein for more on production function estimation with (panel data) IVE and errors-in-variable problems; they also present detailed discussions on sources of error terms in production functions.

The following variables are available:

Y^* (output): Value added divided by producer price index

K (capital): Machine, equipment, construction, transport (in real terms)

L (labor): Total number of workers employed

Day: Days of operation

Export: Export amount (in real terms)

Interest: Interest payment on debt (in real terms)

Invest: Acquisition of new capital (in real terms)

Share: Employees profit-sharing scheme index

Sharedum: 1 if there is any profit sharing scheme in place

Wage: Total remuneration of the year divided by L

White: The proportion of white-collar workers in L

We use the log of capacity-adjusted output, $Y = Y^*$ (365/day), as the response variable. Other than these variables, the constant 1 and time dummies (td) are used. The summary statistics of the variables are shown in Table 2.5.

TABLE 2.5 Summary Statistics

	MIN	LQ	MED	UQ	MAX	SD
Y	0.001	0.080	0.207	0.504	4.328	0.558
K	0.002	0.049	0.137	0.520	7.805	1.068
L	3	57	110	215	1135	150.39
day	173	283	298	305	365	32.24
export	0.000	0.016	0.049	0.128	2.255	0.193
interest	0.000	0.000	0.008	0.047	2.345	0.170
invest	0.000	0.000	0.006	0.028	0.929	0.080
share	0.000	0.000	0.070	0.390	113.23	4.738
sharedum	0	0	1	1	1	0.458
wage	0.650	3.020	6.280	9.980	39.640	5.614
white	0.000	0.180	0.260	0.350	0.740	0.128

The median of L is 110, which means that the firms are not too small on average. Some firms report that they operate 365 days, which is not totally implausible in a country like Mexico. The measurement unit for share is not clear from the data source. Sharedum shows that more than 50% of the firms have a profit-sharing scheme of some kind. The variable *white* indicates that the proportion of the white-collar workers is small: the upper quartile is 0.35.

We classify the instruments into two. The first group, say z_1, are assumed not to be simultaneously related to $\ln(Y)$:

$$z_1 : \ln(\text{interest}), \ln(\text{share}), \text{sharedum}, \ln(\text{wage}), \text{white}.$$

The second group, say z_2, are allowed to be simultaneously related to $\ln(Y)$:

$$z_2 : \ln(K), \ln(L), \ln(\text{export}), \ln(\text{invest}), \ln(Y).$$

We use three sets of orthogonality assumptions to get three sets of estimates.

For the first estimator (RELATED-PRE), we allow related effect and assume that both z_{1t} and z_{2t} are predetermined. This makes

$$z_{1\tau} - z_{1,\tau-1} \quad \text{for } \tau = 2, ..., t, \quad \text{and} \quad z_{2\tau} - z_{2,\tau-1}, \quad \text{for } \tau = 2, ..., t - 1$$

valid instruments; first-differencing is to remove the parts of z_{1t} and z_{2t} that are correlated with the unit-specific effect. The predeterminedness is to allow the possibility that firms may adjust their future z_{1t} and z_{2t} in response to the past error terms.

For the second estimator (RELATED-EXO), we assume that z_{2t} is still predetermined, whereas z_{1t} is strictly exogenous, and allow related effect. This rules out adjusting z_{1t} in response to the past error terms. The valid instruments are now

$$z_{1\tau} - z_{1,\tau-1} \quad \text{for } \tau = 2, ..., T, \quad \text{and} \quad z_{2\tau} - z_{2,\tau-1} \quad \text{for } \tau = 2, ..., t - 1.$$

For the third estimator (UNRELATED-PRE), we assume that both z_{1t} and z_{2t} are predetermined but disallow related effect. This makes

$$z_{1\tau} \quad \text{for } \tau = 1, ..., t, \quad \text{and} \quad z_{2\tau} \quad \text{for } \tau = 1, ..., t - 1$$

valid instruments, for first-differencing is unnecessary.

The estimated model is

$$\ln(Y_{it}) = \tau_t + A_{it} + \beta_K \cdot \ln(K_{it}) + \beta_L \cdot \ln(L_{it}) + \delta_i + u_{it}, \tag{7.1}$$

where A_{it} is specified as a linear functions of the variables in the model other than $\ln(Y_{it})$, $\ln(K_{it})$, and $\ln(L_{it})$. A_{it} may be viewed as an ad-hoc efficiency measure of the firm i at time t. For the three sets of estimates, we also report the p-value of the GMM specification test.

TABLE 2.6 Production Function Estimates

Variable	Related−PRE	Related−EXO	Unrelated−PRE
td2	−0.4449 (−5.92)	−0.3582 (−12.0)	−0.5490 (−11.6)
td3	−0.9450 (−7.12)	−0.7836 (−16.1)	−1.1537 (−13.7)
td4	−1.0715 (−7.12)	−0.9156 (−16.0)	−1.3907 (−14.9)
td5	−1.0870 (−6.25)	−0.8991 (−13.6)	−1.4492 (−13.4)
one	−6.1025 (−12.6)	−5.3832 (−15.0)	−5.1411 (−21.2)
lnK	0.2092 (3.98)	0.2528 (7.39)	0.0597 (2.90)
lnL	0.9907 (12.11)	0.9413 (17.5)	0.8370 (21.9)
lnexpo	−0.0311 (−0.79)	0.0449 (1.97)	0.1104 (6.60)
lninter	−0.0003 (−0.06)	−0.0025 (−1.07)	0.0035 (1.09)
lninvest	0.0185 (1.56)	0.0133 (2.48)	0.0499 (6.27)
lnshare	0.0340 (1.91)	0.0328 (8.01)	0.0776 (10.8)
sharedum	0.1709 (2.03)	0.2024 (8.99)	0.4542 (12.0)
lnwage	0.4761 (5.69)	0.4010 (13.1)	0.6316 (11.8)
white	0.9883 (2.65)	0.1829 (2.21)	0.6127 (4.85)
GMM test p−value	0.405	0.108	0.077

Turning to the estimates (and t-values in parentheses) in Table 2.6, focus on the first estimator that is based on the weakest assumptions and so the most reliable among the three. The negative coefficients of the time dummies indicate that this is a period of economic downturn (at least for this industry). The returns-to-scale measurement determined by the sum of the coefficients of $\ln K$ and $\ln L$ is 1.2. Among the remaining variables with fairly high t-values, $\beta_{\ln \text{invest}}$ is positive (as one would expect, for new machines mean new technique) and marginally significant. $\beta_{\ln \text{share}}$ and β_{sharedum} are positive and significant. $\beta_{\ln \text{wage}}$, which is positive, may be a proxy for the morale of the workers. What is surprising to an extent is the positive and significant coefficient of *white*: as *white* goes up by 1%, the output also goes up by 1%. The GMM specification test renders a p-value of 0.405; the model specification is not rejected.

As for the second estimator, because there are many more instruments, the t-values are much higher. The magnitude and sign of the estimates stay more or less the same, with two exceptions: $\beta_{\ln \text{expo}}$ becomes significant and positive, and β_{white} drops five times in its magnitude while still being significant. The p-value of the GMM specification test drops to 0.1 from 0.4.

As for the third estimator for unrelated effect, many estimates are more or less doubled in their magnitude compared with the two related-effect estimators, with the exceptions being (β_{one}), $\beta_{\ln K}$, and $\beta_{\ln L}$; both $\beta_{\ln K}$ and $\beta_{\ln L}$ became smaller reducing the scale economy down to 0.9 from 1.2. The p-value of the GMM specification test is 0.077, smaller than the other two p-values.

In summary, despite the substantial difference between the moment conditions, the two related-effect estimators returned close estimates, and the difference between the two seems almost negligible compared with the difference between the unrelated-effect and related-effect estimators.

3

TOPICS FOR PANEL LINEAR MODELS

3.1 INTRODUCTION

In Chapter 2, we set up our main panel linear model and examined panel instrumental variable estimator (IVE) and generalized method of moment (GMM), which looked analogous to cross-section IVE and GMM. With the basics of panel linear model built up, this section discusses various topics on panel linear models; nonlinear panel models will be dealt with in Chapters 4 through 6. For the reader who may have skipped Chapter 1, part of Chapter 1 will be repeated in this chapter. In the following paragraphs, we preview the topics discussed in this chapter one by one. Sections 3.4 through 3.6 are optional.

As it will become clear soon, minimum distance estimation (MDE) is quite handy in panel data, which is explained in Section 3.2. In panel IVE, often matrices become excessively large as T goes up; although theoretically straightforward, using large matrices is compuatationally burdensome. One way to avoid this problem is to estimate each wave separately and then combine the estimates for different waves; MDE is useful for this task. If the parameters vary as t varies, then there will be no reason to combine the estimates for different waves. The MDE provides a test statistic for constancy of parameters across time. In cases when time-constant parameters are rejected, time-varying parameters are allowed for also in Section 3.2.

Chapter 2 focused on "related effect": the unit-specific error δ_i is allowed to be related to regressors. For related effect, we mentioned *three* approaches, two of which were explained in Chapter 2. The first was "regressor differencing" or "regressor transforming": transformed regressors free of the part related to δ_i were used as instruments. The second was "error- or first-differencing": the panel model was first-differenced to rid of δ_i. Section 3.3 introduces the third "δ-splitting" or "δ-projecting" approach for related effect. Here again, MDE will be used.

One variable used frequently in practice for x_{it} is the lagged dependent variable $y_{i,t-1}$; with $y_{i,t-1}$ included in x_{it}, the model is called a "dynamic model." Once $y_{i,t-1}$ is allowed for, there is no reason why lagged regressors should not be included in x_{it}; both $y_{i,t-1}$ and $x_{i,t-1}$ capture inertia or momentum in the data over time. In fact, we already know one important source of inertia: the time-invariant variables, observed (c_i) and unobserved (δ_i). Furthermore, because our behavior depends not just on the past but also on the expectation of future variables, $E(y_{i,t+1})$ or $E(x_{i,t+1})$ may appear in the equation at time t where $E(\cdot)$ is taken at time t. These issues for dynamic models will be discussed in Section 3.4.

Our behavior is influenced not just by our past and the expected future variables, but also by our neighbors' behavior. In Section 3.5, complementing Section 3.4 on temporal dependence, "spatial dependence" is introduced. We will discuss spatial dependence in a cross-section framework first, and then we will move on to panel data spatial dependence tests.

The final section to this chapter, Section 3.6, examines independent leftover topics, which do not fit well into other sections. Subsection 3.6.1 addresses the issue of efficiency gain for endogenous regressor parameters as more instruments become available; this subsection shows the historical development of the panel IVE literature. Subsection 3.6.2 discusses Wald-type specification tests; as the reader can see by now, our emphasis has been on estimation, not so much on tests; here we make up for this imbalance somewhat. Subsection 3.6.3 presents quasi-differencing and panel vector autoregression; the former is for time-varying effects of δ_i, and the latter can be useful to the reader keen on Granger causality. Subsection 3.6.4 briefly addresses the question of whether to pool multiple time series or not to get a panel data when T is large, and then the issue of "long-run versus short-run effects" is examined, which is helpful for interpreting panel results vis-à-vis cross-section results.

3.2   WAVE-BY-WAVE ESTIMATION AND TIME-VARYING PARAMETERS

When the number of instruments varies across time, putting together different moment conditions for different periods as done in Chapter 2 for predetermined-ness (PRE) moment conditions can be cumbersome. In this section, we will explore a two-stage alternative that is easier in computation: one need only to estimate each wave separately (in Subsection 3.2.1) and then combine the estimates later using an MDE (in Subsection 3.2.2). This includes the inefficient but intuitive way of combining the estimates for different periods by simply averaging them. Another benefit of the two-stage scheme is that unbalanced panels can be taken care of more easily as to be shown also in this section. The two-stage idea leads to a simple test for constancy of parameters across t; in case of rejection, time-varying parameters are allowed for in Subsection 3.2.3.

3.2.1 Wave-by-Wave Estimation

Consider wave t matrix equation with k_t-many instruments and parameters γ_t:

$$Y_t = W_t \gamma_t + V_t \tag{2.1}$$

where

$$\underset{N \times 1}{Y_t} \text{ (response)}, \quad \underset{N \times k}{W_t} \text{ (regressors)}, \quad \underset{N \times 1}{V_t} \text{ (error)}, \quad \underset{N \times k_t}{Z_t} \text{ (instruments)}; \tag{2.2}$$

they are stacked (over individuals) versions for y_{it}, w_{it}, v_{it}, and z_{it}, respectively. The IVE $g_{t,ive}$ for the parameter γ_t is

$$g_{t,ive} \equiv \{W_t' Z_t (Z_t' Z_t)^{-1} Z_t' W_t\}^{-1} W_t' Z_t (Z_t' Z_t)^{-1} Z_t' Y_t. \tag{2.3}$$

The GMM g_t is

$$g_t \equiv \{W_t' Z_t (Z_t' D_t Z_t)^{-1} Z_t' W_t\}^{-1} W_t' Z_t (Z_t' D_t Z_t)^{-1} Z_t' Y_t, \tag{2.4}$$

where D_t is $\mathrm{diag}(\hat{v}_{it}^2, i = 1, ..., N)$ and $(\hat{v}_{1t}, ..., \hat{v}_{Nt})' \equiv \hat{V}_t \equiv Y_t - W_t g_{t,ive}$.
Using the vector notations, instead of the matrices,

$$g_{t,ive} - \gamma_t = \{\sum_i w_{it} z_{it}'/N \cdot (\sum_i z_{it} z_{it}'/N)^{-1} \cdot \sum_i z_{it} w_{it}'/N\}^{-1} \tag{2.5}$$
$$\cdot \sum_i w_{it} z_{it}'/N \cdot (\sum_i z_{it} z_{it}'/N)^{-1} \sum_i z_{it} v_{it}/N,$$

$$g_t - \gamma_t = \{\sum_i w_{it} z_{it}'/N \cdot (\sum_i z_{it} z_{it}' \hat{v}_{it}^2/N)^{-1} \cdot \sum_i z_{it} w_{it}'/N\}^{-1} \tag{2.6}$$
$$\cdot \sum_i w_{it} z_{it}'/N \cdot (\sum_i z_{it} z_{it}' \hat{v}_{it}^2/N)^{-1} \sum_i z_{it} v_{it}/N.$$

It is possible that there may not be enough instruments when t is close to one; those periods cannot be used then, which will entail efficiency loss. If T is small and this problem does occur, wave-by-wave estimation may not be a good idea.

When we use all waves together, an unbalanced panel can be cumbersome, for each person may require a different number of instruments, which is one reason why we have been limiting our discussion to balanced panels. But if we estimate each wave separately, unbalanced panels are easy to handle using a "membership" function:

$$1_{it} = 1 \text{ if } i \text{ is observed at } t, \text{ and } 0 \text{ otherwise.}$$

For unbalanced panel, attach this to all sums in (2.5) and (2.6):

$$g_{t,ive} - \gamma_t = \{\sum_i 1_{it} w_{it} z'_{it}/N \cdot (\sum_i 1_{it} z_{it} z'_{it}/N)^{-1} \cdot \sum_i 1_{it} z_{it} w'_{it}/N\}^{-1} \quad (2.7)$$

$$\cdot \sum_i 1_{it} w_{it} z'_{it}/N \cdot (\sum_i 1_{it} z_{it} z'_{it}/N)^{-1} \sum_i 1_{it} z_{it} v_{it}/N,$$

$$g_t - \gamma_t = \{\sum_i 1_{it} w_{it} z'_{it}/N \cdot (\sum_i 1_{it} z_{it} z'_{it} \hat{v}_{it}^2/N)^{-1} \cdot \sum_i 1_{it} z_{it} w'_{it}/N\}^{-1} (2.8)$$

$$\cdot \sum_i 1_{it} w_{it} z'_{it}/N \cdot (\sum_i 1_{it} z_{it} z'_{it} \hat{v}_{it}^2/N)^{-1} \sum_i 1_{it} z_{it} v_{it}/N.$$

For GMM, let $\hat{\psi}_{it} \equiv A_t z_{it} v_{it}$, with A_t being the $k \times k_t$ matrix in front of $\sum_i z_{it} v_{it}/N$ in (2.6); $\hat{\psi}_{it} = \psi_{it} + o_p(1)$ where

$$\psi_{it} \equiv \{E(w_{it} z'_{it}) E^{-1}(z_{it} z'_{it} v_{it}^2) E(z_{it} w'_{it})\}^{-1} E(w_{it} z'_{it}) E^{-1}(z_{it} z'_{it} v_{it}^2) z_{it} v_{it};$$

ψ_{it} is an "influence function" for g_t, whereas $\hat{\psi}_{it}$ is an estimate for ψ_{it}. Then we have

$$g_t - \gamma_t = (1/N) \sum_i \psi_{it} + o_p(1/\sqrt{N}). \quad (2.9)$$

The estimation error $g_t - \gamma_t$ is written as the average of ψ_{it}'s; that is, ψ_{it} shows the contribution of each i to $g_t - \gamma_t$. Influence functions will be used in the next subsection for MDE. For unbalanced panels, $\hat{\psi}_{it}$ should be defined analogously as $\tilde{A}_t 1_{it} z_{it} v_{it}$, with $\tilde{A}_t$ being the $k \times k_t$ matrix in front of $\sum_i 1_{it} z_{it} v_{it}/N$ in (2.8); ψ_{it} is then the probability limit of $\hat{\psi}_{it}$.

3.2.2 Minimum Distance Estimation (MDE)

Suppose $T = 2$ and we want to combine two k-dimensional estimates g_1 (for γ_1) and g_2 (for γ_2), because it is believed that $\gamma_1 = \gamma_2 (\equiv \gamma)$, which can be written as

$$\begin{bmatrix} \gamma_1 \\ \gamma_2 \end{bmatrix} = \begin{bmatrix} I_k \\ I_k \end{bmatrix} \cdot \gamma \Rightarrow \begin{bmatrix} g_1 \\ g_2 \end{bmatrix} \cong \begin{bmatrix} I_k \\ I_k \end{bmatrix} \cdot \gamma. \quad (2.10)$$

This suggests an easy way of estimating γ: regard $g \equiv (g_1', g_2')'$ as a response variable and $R \equiv [I_k, I_k]'$ as a regressor to get the least squares estimator (LSE) of g on R. Because $R'R = I_k + I_k = 2I_k$, and $R'g = g_1 + g_2$, the LSE is

$$(R'R)^{-1}R'g = (g_1 + g_2)/2, \tag{2.11}$$

the simple average of g_1 and g_2. But, as mentioned already, an weighted average will be better as in the following.

For a $K > k$, consider a $K \times 1$ estimator θ_N for θ with

$$\sqrt{N}(\theta_N - \theta) \Rightarrow N(0, W_N); \tag{2.12}$$

recall that we use "$\Rightarrow N(0, W_N)$" for "$\Rightarrow N(0, W)$ and $W_N =^p W$." We want to estimate a $k \times 1$ parameter β with θ_N and the restriction

$$\theta = R \cdot \beta \tag{2.13}$$

for a known $K \times k$ matrix R of rank k; this general framework includes the preceding paragraph as a special case when $\theta_N = g$ and $\beta = \gamma$. Again regard θ as a response variable and R as a regressor. If we do the LSE, we would multiply $\theta = R\beta$ by R' and solve the equation for $\beta = (R'R)^{-1}R'\theta$, which suggests an estimator $(R'R)^{-1}R'\theta_N$ for β as in (2.11).

In fact, we can multiply $\theta = R\beta$ by any $k \times K$ matrix so long as the resulting equation is solvable for β. Analogously to LSE versus generalized LSE (GLS), the best choice of the $k \times K$ matrix turns out to be $R'W_N^{-1}$. To see this, rewrite $\theta = R\beta$ as

$$\theta_N = R\beta + \theta_N - \theta, \quad \text{where } \theta_N - \theta \text{ is the error term.} \tag{2.14}$$

Because the components of $\theta_N - \theta$ have different variances, GLS is better than LSE, and the GLS is the MDE

$$b_{mde} = (R'W_N^{-1}R)^{-1}R'W_N^{-1}\theta_N, \tag{2.15}$$

with its asymptotic variance

$$\sqrt{N}(b_{mde} - \beta) \Rightarrow N(0, (R'W_N^{-1}R)^{-1}).$$

This MDE includes the simple average (or "equally weighted") version as a special case with $W_N = I_K$ in (2.15); the asymptotic variance is, however, not $(R'R)^{-1}$.

Formula (2.15) can also be obtained by minimizing

$$(\theta_N - Rb)' \cdot W_N^{-1} \cdot (\theta_N - Rb) \tag{2.16}$$

with respect to (wrt) b. As in GMM, this minimand at $b = b_{mde}$ is useful:

$$N \cdot (\theta_N - Rb_{mde})' \cdot W_N^{-1} \cdot (\theta_N - Rb_{mde}) \Rightarrow \chi^2_{K-k}. \tag{2.17}$$

This is an "overidentification (over-id)" test statistic for $\theta = R\beta$ on whether the $k \times 1$ β satisfies K-many equations or not despite $K > k$; note that (2.16) can be minimized regardless of whether or not $\theta = R\beta$ actually holds. There are more general versions of MDE, say for nonlinear restrictions, but the preceding MDE is enough for our purpose; see Lee (1992), Newey and McFadden (1994), Lee (1996), Greenwood and Nikulin (1996) and the references therein for more on MDE, which is also called "minimum χ^2 estimator."

Formula (2.10) was a simple motivational example, whereas (2.13) was a general setup. Now we examine MDE for our main panel data model with $T = 3$. Suppose we have GMM $g_N \equiv (g_1', g_2', g_3')'$ for $\gamma \equiv (\gamma_1', \gamma_2', \gamma_3')'$; recall (2.4). Suppose we impose the restriction on the model that the slope coefficients μ_t in γ_t, $t = 1, 2, 3$, are the same, whereas the intercepts τ_t's may be different where $\gamma_t = (\tau_t, \mu_t')'$. Denoting the $(k-1) \times 1$ common slope parameter vector as μ, these restrictions are

$$\begin{bmatrix} \tau_1 \\ \mu_1 \\ \tau_2 \\ \mu_2 \\ \tau_3 \\ \mu_3 \end{bmatrix} = \begin{bmatrix} 1 & 0 & 0 & 0 \\ 0 & 0 & 0 & I_{k-1} \\ 0 & 1 & 0 & 0 \\ 0 & 0 & 0 & I_{k-1} \\ 0 & 0 & 1 & 0 \\ 0 & 0 & 0 & I_{k-1} \end{bmatrix} \cdot \begin{bmatrix} \tau_1 \\ \tau_2 \\ \tau_3 \\ \mu \end{bmatrix}. \tag{2.18}$$

Denote the middle matrix with zeros and I_{k-1} as R; some of the zeros in R are zero vectors defined conformably for the identity matrices. Also define

$$\gamma_o \equiv (\tau_1, \tau_2, \tau_3, \mu')'.$$

For MDE under (2.18), the main difficulty in practice is in getting W_N: because g_1, g_2 and g_3 are obtained separately in the first stage, their covariance matrices are not readily available in the first stage.

To get the asymptotic variance matrix estimate W_N for $\sqrt{N}(g_N - \gamma)$, define $\hat{\psi}_i \equiv (\hat{\psi}_{i1}', \hat{\psi}_{i2}', \hat{\psi}_{i3}')'$ to get (recall (2.9))

$$W_N = (1/N) \sum_i \hat{\psi}_i \hat{\psi}_i'. \tag{2.19}$$

Then

$$g_{mde} = (R'W_N^{-1}R)^{-1} \cdot R'W_N^{-1}g_N, \qquad (2.20)$$

$$\sqrt{N}(g_{mde} - \gamma_o) \Rightarrow N(0, (R'W_N^{-1}R)^{-1}),$$

$$N \cdot (g_N - R \cdot g_{mde})'W_N^{-1}(g_N - R \cdot g_{mde}) \Rightarrow \chi^2_{2(k-1)}$$

which is a test statistic for (2.18); the dimension of the leftmost vector in (2.18) is $3k$, whereas that of the rightmost vector is $(k - 1) + 3$, which yields $3k - ((k - 1) + 3) = 2(k - 1)$. When (2.18) is rejected, we may want to know during which periods the constancy of the slope parameter fails. For this, the following sequential test can be used.

Let m_t denote the t-th wave estimator for μ_t. Under $H_o : \mu_t = \mu_{t-1}$,

$$N \cdot (m_t - m_{t-1})' \cdot C_N^{-1} \cdot (m_t - m_{t-1}) \Rightarrow \chi^2_{k-1}, \qquad (2.21)$$

where C_N is a consistent estimator for the asymptotic variance C of $\sqrt{N}(m_t - m_{t-1})$; singular C cases are dealt with later in (6.8). To get C_N, define a scalar $\hat{\psi}_{1it}$ and a $(k - 1) \times 1$ vector $\hat{\psi}_{sit}$ such that $\hat{\psi}_{it} \equiv (\hat{\psi}_{1it}, \hat{\psi}'_{sit})'$, $t = 1, 2, 3$ (in the subscripts, "s" is for the slope). Define an "effective influence function" estimator $\hat{\psi}^*_{sit}$ for the slopes as

$$\hat{\psi}^*_{sit} = \hat{\psi}_{sit} - \{\sum_i \hat{\psi}_{sit}\hat{\psi}_{1it} / \sum_i \hat{\psi}^2_{1it}\} \cdot \hat{\psi}_{1it}, \qquad (2.22)$$

which is based on the linear projection idea. This yields

$$\sqrt{N}(m_t - \mu_t) = (1/\sqrt{N}) \sum_i \psi^*_{sit} + o_p(1), \quad t = 1, ..., T, \qquad (2.23)$$

where ψ^*_{sit} is the "true" effective influence function. Then,

$$C_N = (1/N) \sum_i (\hat{\psi}^*_{sit} - \hat{\psi}^*_{si,t-1})(\hat{\psi}^*_{sit} - \hat{\psi}^*_{si,t-1})' \overset{p}{=} C.$$

Using the test statistic (2.21) for some two periods will shed light on slope changes over the periods.

3.2.3 Wage Example and Time-Varying Parameters

Recall the pedagogical three-wave wage panel in Chapter 2. Now we estimate each wave separately. To avoid an insufficient number of instruments, assume strict exogeneity (EXO) on sal, self, and ur; the time-invariant instruments are the same as before: 1, age, age^2. There are 10 parameters and 12 instruments for each wave:

$$1, \text{age}_1, \text{age}_1^2, \text{sal}_1, \text{sal}_2, \text{sal}_3, \text{self}_1, \text{self}_2, \text{self}_3, \text{ur}_1, \text{ur}_2, \text{ur}_3.$$

We estimate each wave separately, and then impose (2.18) with MDE. We obtain the results shown in Table 3.1 (t-values in ($\cdot$)).

Table 3.1 GMM and MDE for ln(Wage)

	Wave-1 GMM	Wave-2 GMM	Wave-3 GMM	MDE
τ_1	7.64 (0.54)			−0.15 (−0.10)
τ_2		−0.72 (−0.22)		−0.09 (−0.06)
τ_3			0.32 (0.12)	−0.12 (−0.08)
age	−0.07 (−0.23)	0.17 (0.34)	0.08 (0.82)	0.11 (1.65)
age^2/100	0.11 (0.30)	−0.20 (−0.34)	−0.09 (−0.68)	−0.12 (−1.36)
edu	0.07 (0.51)	−0.07 (−0.15)	0.04 (0.75)	0.03 (0.70)
kid	0.39 (0.51)	−0.55 (−0.45)	−0.12 (−0.27)	−0.17 (−0.68)
ln(hr)	−0.30 (−0.33)	0.21 (0.32)	−0.12 (−0.55)	0.02 (0.13)
mar	−3.85 (−0.79)	0.11 (0.01)	0.93 (0.52)	0.06 (0.07)
sal	0.43 (0.56)	0.32 (0.60)	0.44 (2.22)	0.29 (2.58)
self	−0.18 (−0.25)	−0.24 (−0.37)	−0.39 (−1.41)	−0.37 (−2.71)
ur	0.00 (0.02)	−0.03 (−0.26)	−0.01 (−0.26)	−0.02 (−0.91)
p−value (over−id)	0.943	0.023	0.607	
p−value for slope constancy (over−id)				0.000

Due to weak instruments, all but one (sal for wave 3) estimates are insignificant for waves 1 through 3. When they are combined with MDE, sal and self become significant, and age and age^2 gain much in significance. MDE is mostly an average of the three corresponding estimates in waves 1 through 3. Compared with the GMM-EXO in the preceding chapter for the same wage example, edu and ur for the MDE lose their significance.

Surprisingly, the GMM over-id test for wave 2 is rejecting, whereas those for wave 1 and 3 are not. Given the small sample size and relatively large number of parameters and instrument matrix dimension, this could very well be an artifact of numerical instability. Probably because of this peculiar behavior of wave 2 estimation, the MDE over-id test rejects the MDE restriction (constancy of the slope parameters) with ease.

If we reject the slope constancy, then we need to allow the slope coefficients to time-vary by generalizing the main linear model into

$$
\begin{aligned}
y_{it} &= \underset{1 \times k_c}{c_i'\, \alpha_t} + \underset{1 \times k_x}{x_{it}'\, \beta_t} + \delta_i + u_{it} &\qquad (2.24)\\
&\equiv \underset{1 \times k}{w_{it}'\gamma_t} + v_{it}, \quad \gamma_t \equiv (\alpha_t', \beta_t')'.
\end{aligned}
$$

Because the first component of α_t is the intercept, which varies across t, now we do not need any time dummy variable.

Stacking the model (2.24) for unit i across t, we get

$$
\begin{aligned}
\underset{T\times 1}{y_i} &= \underset{T\times(T\cdot k_c)}{(I_T \otimes c_i)'}\alpha + \underset{T\times(T\cdot k_x)}{x_i'}\beta + \underset{T\times 1}{1_T}\delta_i + u_i \qquad (2.25)\\
&\equiv \underset{T\times(T\cdot k)}{w_i'}\gamma + v_i, \quad i = 1, ..., N,
\end{aligned}
$$

where $\alpha \equiv (\alpha_1', ..., \alpha_T')'$ is a $(T\cdot k_c)\times 1$ vector, $\beta \equiv (\beta_1', ..., \beta_T')'$ is a $(T\cdot k_x)\times 1$ vector, $x_i' \equiv \mathrm{diag}(x_{i1}', ..., x_{iT}')$ is a $T\times(T\cdot k_x)$ block-diagonal matrix, and

$$
w_i' \equiv [\ (I_T \otimes c_i)' \quad x_i'\ ], \quad \gamma \equiv (\alpha', \beta')'.
$$

Applying IVE to (2.25) is straightforward. The only change needed is that there be at least $T\cdot k$ many instruments. For this, we should impose at least contemporary (CON) type moment conditions. Because this is just enough, PRE and strict-exogeneity (EXO) seem to be better suited for the time-varying coefficient model.

It is possible to generalize (2.24) further by allowing the effect of δ_i on y_{it} to vary across t as done in Holtz-Eakin *et al.* (1988). Let $\Phi = (\Phi_1, ..., \Phi_T)'$, and suppose we have

$$
\underset{T\times 1}{y_i} = \underset{T\times(T\cdot k_c)}{(I_T \otimes c_i)'}\alpha + \underset{T\times(T\cdot k_x)}{x_i'}\beta + \underset{T\times 1}{\Phi}\cdot\delta_i + u_i. \qquad (2.26)
$$

This, however, does not alter the regressor-differencing approach for (2.25), because it is based on orthogonality between $\Phi_t\delta_i + u_{it}$ and instruments; Φ_t becomes troublesome only if one tries to remove $\Phi_t\delta_i$ as in error differencing. This shows an advantage of regressor differencing over error differencing. The model (2.26) will appear again in Section 3.6 for panel vector autoregression.

3.3 MINIMUM DISTANCE ESTIMATION FOR RELATED-EFFECT

In (4.1) of the preceding chapter, we examined a couple of ideas to deal with related effect. In this section, the δ-splitting (or δ-projecting) idea for related effect in Chamberlain (1982) is studied using MDE: the unit-specific effect δ_i is linearly projected on regressors to explicitly account for the part of δ_i related to the regressors, rather than purging out δ_i one way or another.

Chamberlain (1982) rewrote δ_i as (recall $c_i = (1, \tilde{c}_i')'$)

$$
\delta_i = 1\cdot\zeta_o + \tilde{c}_i'\zeta_{\tilde{c}} + \sum_{\tau=1}^{T} x_{i\tau}'\zeta_\tau + v_i, \quad \text{where } v_i \equiv \delta_i - \zeta_o - \tilde{c}_i'\zeta_{\tilde{c}} - \sum_{\tau=1}^{T} x_{i\tau}'\zeta_\tau;
$$

$$(3.1)$$

δ_i is linearly projected on $(c_i', x_{i1}', ..., x_{iT}')'$, and $(\zeta_c', \zeta_1', ..., \zeta_T')'$ are the linear projection coefficients where $\zeta_c \equiv (\zeta_o, \zeta_{\tilde{c}}')'$. Recall the panel linear model

$$
y_{it} = \tau_t + \tilde{c}_i'\tilde{\alpha} + x_{it}'\beta + \delta_i + u_{it}.
$$

Substitute (3.1) into this to get

$$
y_{it} = \tau_t + \zeta_o + \tilde{c}_i'(\tilde{\alpha} + \zeta_{\tilde{c}}) + x_{it}'(\beta + \zeta_t) + \sum_{\tau \neq t} x_{i\tau}' \zeta_\tau + v_{it}, \quad v_{it} \equiv v_i + u_{it}; \quad (3.2)
$$

v_{it} is now defined as $v_i + u_{it}$ (it has been $\delta_i + u_{it}$ so far). With δ_i gone, each wave can be estimated by LSE, or by an IVE if u_{it} is correlated with some components of $c_i, x_{i1}, ..., x_{iT}$. Chamberlain (1982)'s formulation does not involve $\tilde{c}_i$ in (3.1), but we included $\tilde{c}_i$ for a reason given later.

To understand the Chamberlain's (1982) MDE which is a two-stage method, set $T = 2$ and $\tau_1 = \tau_2 = \zeta_o = \tilde{c}_i = 0$ for a while to get, instead of (3.2),

$$
y_{i1} = x_{i1}'(\beta + \zeta_1) + x_{i2}'\zeta_2 + v_{i1}, \quad y_{i2} = x_{i1}'\zeta_1 + x_{i2}'(\beta + \zeta_2) + v_{i2}. \quad (3.3)
$$

The first stage is estimating each wave "reduced form" (RF) parameter vectors separately:

$$
\pi_{11} \equiv \beta + \zeta_1, \quad \pi_{12} \equiv \zeta_2, \quad \text{and} \quad \pi_{21} \equiv \zeta_1, \quad \pi_{22} \equiv \beta + \zeta_2. \quad (3.4)
$$

Although there are only three "structural form" (SF) parameter vectors β, ζ_1, and ζ_2, there are (more than enough) four RF parameter vectors. The second stage is estimating the SF parameters using the RF estimates and the relation (3.4) between the SF and RF. With this key point understood, in the following we will show the MDE in detail.

Maintain $T = 2$ for a while and return to (3.2). Denote the RF parameters for $1, \tilde{c}_i, x_{i1}, x_{i2}$ in the t-th wave as $\chi_{t1}, \chi_{t\tilde{c}}, \pi_{t1}, \pi_{t2}$, respectively:

$$
\begin{aligned}
\chi_{11} &= \tau_1 + \zeta_o, \quad \chi_{1\tilde{c}} = \tilde{\alpha} + \zeta_{\tilde{c}}, \quad \pi_{11} = \beta + \zeta_1, \quad \pi_{12} = \zeta_2, \quad (3.5) \\
\chi_{21} &= \tau_2 + \zeta_o, \quad \chi_{2\tilde{c}} = \tilde{\alpha} + \zeta_{\tilde{c}}, \quad \pi_{21} = \zeta_1, \quad \pi_{22} = \beta + \zeta_2.
\end{aligned}
$$

In the SF parameters in (3.2) for $t = 1, 2$, we can identify a $(2 + k_{\tilde{c}} + 3k_x) \times 1$ vector

$$
\vartheta \equiv (\tau_1 + \zeta_o, \tau_2 + \zeta_o, \ (\tilde{\alpha} + \zeta_{\tilde{c}})', \ \beta', \zeta_1', \zeta_2')';
$$

$\tilde{\alpha}$ is not separable from $\zeta_{\tilde{c}}$. Stack (3.5) to get

$$
\theta \equiv
\begin{bmatrix}
\chi_{11} \\
\chi_{1\tilde{c}} \\
\pi_{11} \\
\pi_{12} \\
\chi_{21} \\
\chi_{2\tilde{c}} \\
\pi_{21} \\
\pi_{22}
\end{bmatrix}
=
\begin{bmatrix}
1 & 0 & 0 & 0 & 0 & 0 \\
0 & 0 & I_{k_{\tilde{c}}} & 0 & 0 & 0 \\
0 & 0 & 0 & I_{k_x} & I_{k_x} & 0 \\
0 & 0 & 0 & 0 & 0 & I_{k_x} \\
0 & 1 & 0 & 0 & 0 & 0 \\
0 & 0 & I_{k_{\tilde{c}}} & 0 & 0 & 0 \\
0 & 0 & 0 & 0 & I_{k_x} & 0 \\
0 & 0 & 0 & I_{k_x} & 0 & I_{k_x}
\end{bmatrix}
\begin{bmatrix}
\tau_1 + \zeta_o \\
\tau_2 + \zeta_o \\
\tilde{\alpha} + \zeta_{\tilde{c}} \\
\beta \\
\zeta_1 \\
\zeta_2
\end{bmatrix}
\equiv \Psi \cdot \vartheta,
$$

$$
(3.6)
$$

where Ψ is the big matrix in the middle.

Denote the estimator for θ as θ_N, a stacked version of the RF estimators for the two waves: with $\xi_t \equiv (\chi_{t1}, \chi'_{t\tilde{c}}, \pi'_{t1}, \pi'_{t2})'$, $t = 1, 2,$

$$\underset{2(1+k_{\tilde{c}}+2k_x)\times 1}{\theta} = (\xi'_1, \xi'_2)' \quad \text{and} \quad \theta_N = (\xi'_{N1}, \xi'_{N2})', \tag{3.7}$$

where ξ_{Nj} is the RF estimator for ξ_j, $j = 1, 2$. Let Ω_N denote an estimator for the asymptotic variance of $\sqrt{N}(\theta_N - \theta)$; Ω_N can be estimated using the influence function estimates for θ_N as shown in the preceding section around (2.9) and (2.19). The MDE is

$$\vartheta_N = (\Psi'\Omega_N^{-1}\Psi)^{-1} \cdot \Psi'\Omega_N^{-1}\theta_N; \tag{3.8}$$

$$\sqrt{N}(\vartheta_N - \vartheta) \Rightarrow N(0, (\Psi'\Omega_N^{-1}\Psi)^{-1}),$$

$$N \cdot \{\theta_N - \Psi \cdot \vartheta_N\}'\Omega_N^{-1}\{\theta_N - \Psi \cdot \vartheta_N\} \Rightarrow \chi^2_{k_{\tilde{c}}+k_x}.$$

Because the lagged or future regressors appear in (3.2) only because of δ_i, one reason for (3.6) to be rejected is that y_{it} depends on lagged regressors or the expected values of future regressors other than through δ_i.

When $T = 3$, the analog for (3.5) in a matrix form is

$$\begin{bmatrix} \chi_{11} & \chi'_{1\tilde{c}} & \pi'_{11} & \pi'_{12} & \pi'_{13} \\ \chi_{21} & \chi'_{2\tilde{c}} & \pi'_{21} & \pi'_{22} & \pi'_{23} \\ \chi_{31} & \chi'_{3\tilde{c}} & \pi'_{31} & \pi'_{32} & \pi'_{33} \end{bmatrix}$$

$$= \begin{bmatrix} \tau_1 + \zeta_o & (\tilde{\alpha} + \zeta_{\tilde{c}})' & (\beta + \zeta_1)' & \zeta'_2 & \zeta'_3 \\ \tau_2 + \zeta_o & (\tilde{\alpha} + \zeta_{\tilde{c}})' & \zeta'_1 & (\beta + \zeta_2)' & \zeta'_3 \\ \tau_3 + \zeta_o & (\tilde{\alpha} + \zeta_{\tilde{c}})' & \zeta'_1 & \zeta'_2 & (\beta + \zeta_3)' \end{bmatrix}. \tag{3.9}$$

The last three columns of the right-hand side matrix can be written as

$$I_3 \otimes \beta' + 1_3 \otimes (\zeta'_1, \zeta'_2, \zeta'_3). \tag{3.10}$$

The identified SF parameters is a $(3 + k_{\tilde{c}} + 4k_x) \times 1$ vector

$$\vartheta \equiv (\tau_1 + \zeta_o, \tau_2 + \zeta_o, \tau_3 + \zeta_o, \ (\tilde{\alpha} + \zeta_{\tilde{c}})', \ \beta', \zeta'_1, \zeta'_2, \zeta'_3)', \tag{3.11}$$

and we need

$$\underset{3(1+k_{\tilde{c}}+3k_x)\times 1}{\theta} = (\xi'_1, \xi'_2, \xi'_3)' \quad \text{and} \quad \theta_N = (\xi'_{N1}, \xi'_{N2}, \xi'_{N3})'. \tag{3.12}$$

Make a matrix Ψ such that $\theta = \Psi\vartheta$ holds analogously to (3.6). Then (3.8) holds with the degree of freedom in (3.8) replaced by (with $T = 3$)

$$T(1 + k_{\tilde{c}} + Tk_x) - \{T + k_{\tilde{c}} + (T + 1)k_x\};$$

if $T = 2$, this becomes $k_{\tilde{c}} + k_x$.

Chamberlain (1984) showed an application of the MDE to three-wave (1969–1971) panel data ($N = 1454$) drawn from the National Longitudinal Survey. The response variable is the logarithm of hourly earnings of young men, and the regressors are union membership (U_1, U_2, U_3) and two other time variants, as well as time invariants such as schooling, sex and race. Focusing on U_1, U_2 and U_3, the unrestricted reduced form estimates are as follows (standard errors in parentheses):

	U_1	U_2	U_3
1969	0.171 (0.025)	*0.042* (0.026)	*−0.009* (0.025)
1970	*0.048* (0.023)	0.150 (0.028)	*0.010* (0.026)
1971	*0.046* (0.023)	*0.041* (0.030)	0.132 (0.030)

Recalling the last three columns of (3.9), a pair of italic entries in a given column should be close, and this is borne out by this table. Thus, although past and future union memberships are significant, this dynamic aspect seems to be solely due to the relation between (U_1, U_2, U_3) and δ. Imposing the restrictions, the MDE is

β: 0.107 (0.016),

ζ_1: -0.023 (0.030), ζ_2: -0.067 (0.040), ζ_3: -0.082 (0.037).

If we ignore the unit-specific effect, then $\beta \cong 0.15$ from the diagonal of the preceding table, which is much larger than 0.107 for β here.

As an application of the Chamberlain's idea, Behrman and Wolfe (1989) estimated the effect of schooling on nutrition equations for Nicaraguan women. They used a group-structure cross-section data with $N = 500$ and $T = 2$ (two sisters from each household), where δ_i is the common unobserved family background between the two sisters. By taking the inter-sister difference, which amounts to the within group estimator (WIT), they estimated the effect of schooling. They also estimated one sister equation using the other sister's schooling as a regressor; that is, (3.3) is used with x_{i1} and x_{i2} being the sisters' schooling. Denoting the coefficient for own and the sister's schooling as π_{11} and π_{12}, respectively, they estimated the net effect $\pi_{11} - \pi_{12}$ of schooling. In (3.4), $\pi_{11} - \pi_{12} = \beta$ if $\zeta_1 = \zeta_2$ that is plausible in their study; this idea is in Chamberlain (1980, p. 235). See also Ashenfelter and Krueger (1994) who used a sample of twins.

The main advantage of the Chamberlain's approach is that the linear projection does not require any restriction (other than the existence of the second moments), differently from assuming that $E(\delta|c_i, x_{i1}, ..., x_{iT})$ is a linear function of c_i and $x_{i1}, ..., x_{iT}$. The problem of nonidentified $\tilde{\alpha}$ can be avoided simply by omitting $\tilde{c}_i$ from the variables on which δ_i is projected. In this case, however, the resulting error term in the RF's may be correlated with $\tilde{c}_i$, which then requires an instrument vector for $\tilde{c}_i$. That is, regarding identifying $\tilde{\alpha}$, the following two cases hold. First, if $COR(\tilde{c}_i, \varepsilon_{it}) = 0$, where ε_{it} is the model error term as in (3.2) without $\tilde{c}_i$ used for projection, or if $COR(\tilde{c}_i, \varepsilon_{it}) \neq 0$ but there is an instrument for $\tilde{c}_i$, then drop $\tilde{c}_i$ from the projection set and identify $\tilde{\alpha}$. Second, if $COR(\tilde{c}_i, \varepsilon_{it}) \neq 0$ and there is no instrument for $\tilde{c}_i$, then $\tilde{c}_i$ should be included in the projection set and $\tilde{\alpha}$ cannot be identified.

Among the three approaches for related effect in (4.1) of Chapter 2, in terms of the weakness of assumptions and the ability to identify $\tilde{\alpha}$, roughly the following can be said. The error differencing uses the weakest assumptions but cannot identify $\tilde{\alpha}$. The regressor-differencing uses the strongest assumptions and can identify $\tilde{\alpha}$. The strength of the assumptions for the δ-splitting approach falls in between these two, and it may or may not identify $\tilde{\alpha}$. In practice, often we apply these methods together and try to infer what assumptions went wrong if the estimates differ by much.

If the strength of the assumptions is similar across estimators, then the choice of an estimator will depend largely on computational ease and small sample performance. Error differencing, compared with regressor differencing, may make computation easier by removing redundant moment conditions. But efficiency-wise, there is nothing to gain by error differencing relative to regressor differencing (Schmidt *et al.*, 1992) if all moment conditions are used and GMM is employed in regressor-differencing. Ziliak (1997) compared various MME's based on PRE conditions for small sample performance, and one of his findings is that the inefficient GMM with the identity matrix as the weighting matrix is less biased than the efficient GMM. In fact, this seems to hold also for MDE: the inefficient MDE using the identity weighting matrix is often less biased; see Hansen *et al.* (1996) and Ziliak (1997) for the literature on small sample problems in IVE, GMM and MDE. The main culprit for the poor performance of the efficient GMM and MDE appears to be the relation between the estimated sample moment and the estimated weighting matrix; see, however, Koenker *et al.* (1994) for a twist. More discussion and references on this and a related issue, "weak instrument," will be provided when nonlinear GMM is reviewed in Chapter 5.

3.4 DYNAMIC MODELS

Our behavior may be affected not just by current variables, but also by the past or expected future variables. Usually models with lagged variables or expected future variables are called "dynamic models"; in the more narrower sense, models with lagged response variables as regressors are called "dynamic models." Anybody using panel (or time-series) data runs into the question of whether or not to use dynamic models, and if so, on what basis and to what extent. As far as estimation goes, dynamic models are not special, for our IVE framework easily allows lagged or expected future variables as regressors.

There are many sources for dynamics, which are not necessarily mutually exclusive. We saw two sources already: time invariants $\tilde{c}_i$ and δ_i appearing at all periods and temporal moment conditions allowing relations between u_{is} and x_{it} over time. Besides these, there are other sources as well. First, y_{it} may depend on $y_{i,t-1}$ and other lagged responses, for example, due to "habit persistence." Second, analogously to the first, u_{it} may depend on $u_{i,t-1}$ and other lagged errors. Third, $x_{i,t-1}$ and other lagged time-variant regressors may affect y_{it}. Fourth, expected future responses or regressors may also influence y_{it}. These aspects will be examined in this section.

Recall the linear model:

$$y_{it} = \tau_t + \tilde{c}_i'\tilde{\alpha} + x_{it}'\beta + v_{it} \quad \text{and} \quad v_{it} = \delta_i + u_{it}. \tag{4.1}$$

Removing δ_i in (4.1), we get

$$y_{it} - y_{i,t-1} = \tau_t - \tau_{t-1} + (x_{it} - x_{i,t-1})'\beta + u_{it} - u_{i,t-1}$$
$$\Leftrightarrow \quad y_{it} = y_{i,t-1} + \tau_t - \tau_{t-1} + (x_{it} - x_{i,t-1})'\beta + u_{it} - u_{i,t-1}; \tag{4.2}$$

the first-difference model yields a dynamic model with $y_{i,t-1}$, 1, and $x_{it} - x_{i,t-1}$ as regressors, and with the restriction that $y_{i,t-1}$ has unit root. Now subtract the $y_{i,t-2}$-equation from the y_{it}-equation to get

$$y_{it} = y_{i,t-2} + \tau_t - \tau_{t-2} + (x_{it} - x_{i,t-2})'\beta + u_{it} - u_{i,t-2}; \tag{4.3}$$

here, dependence on the past seems to be through $t - 2$. The hidden dynamics operating only through δ_i is made explicit by lagged variables.

Equations (4.2) and (4.3) show that *the same underlying model may lead to seemingly different dynamic models.* If one uses all of

$$y_{i,t-1}, \; y_{i,t-2}, \; 1, \; x_{it}, \; x_{i,t-1}, \; \text{and} \; x_{i,t-2}$$

as regressors, the two dynamic models differ in parameter restrictions (for example, (4.2) has the restriction that $y_{i,t-2}$ and $x_{i,t-2}$ have zero coefficients) and error term serial correlation structure. The question of which one between (4.2) and (4.3) is to be estimated depends on the estimator; for example, if LSE is used, then it will depend on which one of $u_{it} - u_{i,t-1}$ and $u_{it} - u_{i,t-2}$ has the smaller variance. If IVE is used, then it will depend on the moment conditions used, which differ across (4.2) and (4.3) because the regressors and error terms differ.

More generally than (4.1), suppose (4.1) holds with δ_i replaced by $\Phi_t\delta_i$ (Φ_t is the time-varying effect of δ_i) where $\Phi_t/\Phi_{t-1} = \phi$ $\forall t$ and ϕ is an unknown constant. Multiply the $y_{i,t-1}$-equation by ϕ and subtract it from the y_{it}-equation to get

$$y_{it} = \phi y_{i,t-1} + \tau_t - \phi\tau_{t-1} + c_i'(1-\phi)\tilde{\alpha} + x_{it}'\beta - x_{i,t-1}'\phi\beta + u_{it} - \phi u_{i,t-1}. \tag{4.4}$$

There is no restriction of unit root for $y_{i,t-1}$, but the coefficient of $x_{i,t-1}$ is restricted to be that of $y_{i,t-1}$ times that of x_{it} times -1. In (4.2) to (4.4), the source of dynamics has been δ_i.

Now consider a model without δ_i but with a serial relation on u_{it}:

$$y_{it} = \tau_t + \tilde{c}_i'\tilde{\alpha} + x_{it}'\beta + u_{it}, \tag{4.5}$$
$$u_{it} = \rho \cdot u_{i,t-1} + e_{it}, \quad u_{i0} = 0, \quad e_{i1}, ..., e_{iT} \text{ are iid}$$

where ρ is an unknown constant with $|\rho| < 1$. The quasi-differencing $y_{it} - \rho y_{i,t-1}$ renders

$$y_{it} = \rho y_{i,t-1} + \tau_t - \rho \tau_{t-1} + \tilde{c}_i'(1-\rho)\tilde{\alpha} + x_{it}'\beta - x_{i,t-1}'\rho\beta + e_{it}; \tag{4.6}$$

the source of dynamics is the serial dependence in u_{it}, and lagged y_{it} and lagged x_{it} are used to account for $u_{i,t-1}$. The regression parameters in (4.6) are restricted in the same way as in (4.4).

Equations (4.4) to (4.6) show that *different underlying models can lead to seemingly the same dynamic model*, whereas (4.1) to (4.3) showed that the same underlying model can lead to seemingly different dynamic models. With the same y_{it} as the response variable, the regression parameter restrictions are the same for (4.4) and (4.6), and the only difference between (4.4) and (4.6) is the error term serial correlation: the error term in (4.4) is serially correlated even if u_{it}'s are iid, whereas the error term in (4.6) is not under iid e_{it}'s. Differently from (4.2) and (4.3), the same regression parameters are estimated in (4.4) and (4.6) regardless of the estimator in use (so long as it is consistent), and estimating the error term serial correlation will tell which one of the two underlying models holds.

So far, our discussion might have given the impression that $y_{i,t-1}$ appears only to account for unobservables δ_i or $u_{i,t-1}$. But this is not necessarily the case. If y_{it} is salary, and if y_{it} is determined such that the new salary y_{it} is the old salary $y_{i,t-1}$ plus an adjustment, then $y_{i,t-1}$ should appear in the model without regard to unobservable variables. If $y_{i,t-1}$ appears for its own sake, this is called a "true state dependence," whereas the opposite case of $y_{i,t-1}$ appearing only for other variables is called a "spurious state dependence." An interesting example for state dependence is the effect of advertizing: if there is state dependence, then advertising will have a long-run effect, for once a consumer buys a brand, he or she will be "hooked" onto the brand (that is, state dependence is present). If there is no state dependence, then advertising will have only a temporary effect, for buying a brand currently due to the current advertising will not affect the future purchase. The marketing literature seems to show no state dependence, but there are also some evidences for weak state dependence (depending on the product); see Keane (1997), Chintagunta *et al.* (2001), Erdem and Sun (2001) and the references therein for more on this. Erdem and Sun (2001) also explored the possibility of testing for true state dependence: if $x_{i,t-1}$ turns out to be relevant (that is, significant) in an equation without $y_{i,t-1}$ despite that a prior knowledge rules out the direct effect of $x_{i,t-1}$ on y_{it}, then this may be an evidence for omiited $y_{i,t-1}$ (that is, true state dependence).

If

$$P(y_{it} \le a | y_{i,t-1}) \ne P(y_{it} \le a) \quad \text{for some } a, \tag{4.7}$$

then there is a "prima facie" (or apparent) state dependence. But if there is a random variable, say λ, such that

$$P(y_{it} \le a | y_{i,t-1}, \lambda) = P(y_{it} \le a | \lambda) \quad \forall a, \tag{4.8}$$

then the state dependence is spurious. But because we can hardly ever search completely for all such λ, it will be rather difficult in reality to rule out spurious dependence and conclude a true state dependence. Regardless of whether the state dependence is true or spurious, the magnitude of the coefficient of $y_{i,t-1}$ will depend on the time span between t and $t - 1$: if it is small, the coefficient should be large in general, for y_{it} has little chance to differ from $y_{i,t-1}$; if the time span is large, the coefficient is likely to be small.

Often in practice, regardless of true or spurious state dependence, $y_{i,t-1}$ is used as a regressor, because this increases the model fitness (say R^2) and tends to result in error terms with little serial correlation, whereas the error terms exhibit substantial serial correlations without $y_{i,t-1}$ in the model as a regressor; (4.1) to (4.6) explain this phenomenon to an extent. Typically, for the model $y_{it} = \rho y_{i,t-1} +, ...$, most of R^2 is contributed by $y_{i,t-1}$ whereas the other regressors contribute little. When $y_{i,t-1}$ is used as a regressor, we can rewrite the model, say $y_{it} = \rho y_{i,t-1} +, ...$, as $y_{it} - y_{i,t-1} = (\rho - 1)y_{i,t-1} +, ...$ Despite this equivalence, however, the latter usually yields a substantially lower R^2 than the former because $y_{it} - y_{i,t-1}$ is used as the response variable. The $y_{it} - y_{i,t-1}$ equation shows that *if $y_{i,t-1}$ appears on the right-hand side, essentially the change in y_{it}, not y_{it} itself, is explained by $y_{i,t-1}$ and the other regressors.*

Using $y_{i,t-1}$ as a regressor begs the question of what explains y_{it}: if y_{it} is explained by $y_{i,t-1}$, what then explains $y_{i,t-1}$? If we substitute the $y_{i,t-1}$-equation to remove $y_{i,t-1}$ on the righ-hand side, then $y_{i,t-2}, x_{it}, x_{i,t-1}, ...$ appear on the right-hand side. Continuing to do this will result in a model with $x_{it}, ..., x_{i1}$ and y_{i1} on the right-hand side; what explains y_{i1} at the end? The answer to this question depends on the data and what we want to know. Suppose y_{it} is salary. Then we can go all the way back to the time when the person received his or her first salary which can be explained by his or her characteristics and the labor market conditions at that time. But the panel data in hand may have started long after this period, in which case we just have to keep y_1 as a regressor and use the panel data from $t = 2$ and on. Here y_1 saves us from having to include all x_{it} with $t \le 0$ in the model. But this is a mixed blessing, for y_1 or any lagged response in the regressors may make most time-invariant regressors useless; recall (4.2) where all time invariants would have been removed along with δ_i. If we want to know the effects of time-invariant regressors, it may be better not to use any lagged response variable as a regressor.

As the past explains the present, we can also think of expected future variables affecting the present; for example, if a baby is expected next period, then the parents may choose to work more this period. Let I_t be the information available at t, and consider an extension of (4.1):

$$y_{it} = \tau_t + \tilde{c}'_i \tilde{\alpha} + x'_{it} \beta + E_t(x_{i,t+1})' \gamma + \delta_i + u_{it} \qquad (4.9)$$

where

$$E_t(x_{i,t+1}) \equiv E(x_{i,t+1} | I_t) \text{ and } I_t \text{ includes } c_i, y_{is}, x_{is} \; \forall i \text{ and } s \leq t;$$

all individuals are assumed to be equally informed. Note $I_{t-1} \subseteq I_t \; \forall t$.

Take the first-difference to get

$$
\begin{aligned}
y_{it} - y_{i,t-1} \;=\; & \tau_t - \tau_{t-1} + (x_{it} - x_{i,t-1})' \beta \qquad (4.10) \\
& + \{E_t(x_{i,t+1}) - E_{t-1}(x_{it})\}' \gamma + u_{it} - u_{i,t-1}.
\end{aligned}
$$

Rewrite this as

$$
\begin{aligned}
y_{it} - y_{i,t-1} \;=\; & \tau_t - \tau_{t-1} + (x_{it} - x_{i,t-1})' \beta + (x_{i,t+1} - x_{it})' \gamma \qquad (4.11) \\
& + \{E_t(x_{i,t+1}) - x_{i,t+1} - E_{t-1}(x_{it}) + x_{it}\}' \gamma + u_{it} - u_{i,t-1}.
\end{aligned}
$$

Define the composite error term

$$\varepsilon_{it} \equiv \{E_t(x_{i,t+1}) - x_{i,t+1} - E_{t-1}(x_{it}) + x_{it}\}' \gamma + u_{it} - u_{i,t-1}.$$

Observe

$$E\{E_t(x_{i,t+1}) - x_{i,t+1} | I_{t-1}\} = E[E\{E_t(x_{i,t+1}) - x_{i,t+1} | I_t\} | I_{t-1}] = 0. \quad (4.12)$$

If $E(u_{it} c_i) = 0 \; \forall t$ and $E(u_{it} x_{is}) = 0$ for $s \leq t$, then we get the following moment conditions:

$$E(\varepsilon_{it} c_i) = 0, \quad t = 2, ..., T-1 \quad \text{and} \quad E(\varepsilon_{it} x_{is}) = 0 \quad \forall s \leq t-1. \quad (4.13)$$

The parameters in (4.11) can be estimated by IVE.

(4.9) can be generalized further into

$$
\begin{aligned}
y_{it} \;=\; & \tau_t + \tilde{c}'_i \tilde{\alpha} + x'_{it} \beta_o + x'_{i,t-1} \beta_1 + E_t(x_{i,t+1})' \gamma + \delta_i + u_{it} \quad (4.14) \\
=\; & \tau_t + \tilde{c}'_i \tilde{\alpha} + x'_{it} \beta_o + x'_{i,t-1} \beta_1 + x'_{i,t+1} \gamma + \\
& \{E_t(x_{i,t+1}) - x_{i,t+1}\}' \gamma + \delta_i + u_{it}
\end{aligned}
$$

to get a dynamic model with the past and expected future regressors. Recall that the δ-splitting approach in (3.2) also resulted in $x_{i,t-1}$ and $x_{i,t+1}$ on the right-hand side, which was, however, only to account for δ_i.

3.5 SPATIAL DEPENDENCE AND ITS TESTS USING PANEL DATA

So far, we assumed that the panel data are iid across individuals. But this may not hold at least in two cases. One is "block-sampling" where a block of households in the same town or village are sampled and observed over T periods along with other blocks. Cross-section data with a group structure (N groups with T_i observations for group i) can be treated as an iid (across i) panel data, but block-sampled panels cannot. The other is aggregation; aggregate county or city data may exhibit dependence, whereas individuals do not. In the two cases, geographical proximity matters, and the relation across i is called "spatial dependence." Cross-country panels often used in the economic development/growth literature have this problem. Spatial dependence can have a group structure (dependence only within a block or a group), or all subjects may be related to all the other subjects in the data.

Failure to account for spatial dependence is often many-fold underestimation of the standard error of the estimator in use, leading to a false sense of statistical significance. For the economic development literature, Deaton (1995, p. 1818), for instance, stated that "many studies will have to be redone ... there will have to be a good deal of revision of conclusions." To see the main problem, for a cross-section linear model $y_i = x_i'\beta + u_i$, the asymptotic variance of the LSE depends positively on

$$V[(1/\sqrt{N})\sum_i x_i u_i] = E\{(1/N)\sum_i \sum_j x_i x_j u_i u_j\}.$$

A small positive spatial dependence among u_i and u_j, $i \neq j$, will quickly add up to a sizable number. Under some assumptions on T_i and N, one can devise "spatial-correlation-robust asymptotic variance" for cross-section data with a group structure: reorder the data as an unbalanced panel and use

$$(1/N)\sum_i (\sum_{t=1}^{T_i} \sum_{\tau=1}^{T_i} x_{it} x_{i\tau}' \cdot \hat{u}_{it}\hat{u}_{i\tau}),$$

instead of the usual $(1/N)\sum_i x_i x_i' \hat{u}_i^2$ where $\hat{u}_i$ is the residual for u_i.

Whereas spatial dependence can be tested with cross-section data, panel data are particularly advantageous because we can see whether the temporal pattern of variables are similar across i. In the following, we introduce cross-section spatial dependence drawing upon Anselin (1988) and Anselin and Bera (1998), and then distribution-free tests for panel spatial dependence. See, for example, Bell and Bockstael (2000) for a more recent literature and an application of GMM to spatial correlation.

Consider a cross-section "spatial error dependence" model: for $i = 1, ..., N$, a scalar y_i and u_i, and a vector x_i,

$$y_i = x_i'\beta + u_i, \quad u_i = \rho \cdot w_i'U + v_i, \quad U = (u_1, ..., u_N)', \quad (5.1)$$

$\{v_i\}$ are iid, $E(v_i|x_1, ..., x_N) = 0$, ρ is an unknown scalar, $|\rho| < 1$, (5.2)

where $w_i \equiv (w_{i1}, w_{i2}, ..., w_{iN})'$ is a known $N \times 1$ weighting vector such that

$$w_{ij} = w_{ji} \geq 0, \quad w_{ii} = 0 \quad \text{and} \quad \sum_{j=1}^{N} w_{ij} = 1 \quad \forall i. \quad (5.3)$$

Define

$$Y \equiv (y_1, ..., y_N)', \quad X \equiv (x_1, ..., x_N)', \quad V \equiv (v_1, ..., v_N)',$$
$$W \equiv (w_1, ..., w_N)' \quad (N \times N \text{ weighting matrix})$$

to get

$$Y = X\beta + U, \quad \text{and} \quad U = \rho \cdot WU + V \Rightarrow U = (I_N - \rho W) \cdot V;$$

$\rho \neq 0$ means spatial error dependence.

In the spatial dependence literature, w_{ij} is specified as a known function of the distance between i and j. If i has four adjacent regions (each, west, south, and north), then the four regions may be given the equal weight $1/4$, whereas the other regions may be given the weight zero. Alternatively, the percentage of the j-th border in the i-th total border length may be used for w_{ij}; if $w_{ij} \neq w_{ji}$, we can symmetrize W by redefining w_{ij} and w_{ji} as $(w_{ij} + w_{ji})/2$. Whether $\rho = 0$ or not, the LSE for (5.1) is consistent due to (5.2). But if $\rho \neq 0$, then the asymptotic variance of the LSE should be adjusted for the spatial error dependence. These features are analogous to those for heteroskedasticity in that, although heteroskedasticity does not make LSE inconsistent, it affects the asymptotic variance.

In (5.1), one may think of x_i as being subject to the same transformation as u_i is subject to. This is natural: if the unobservable are influenced spatially, then the observable are likely to be influenced in the same way. The models (5.1) and (5.2) allow this, but they do not allow a direct influence of a neighbor's regressor or error term, say x_{i+1} or u_{i+1}, entering into the y_i-equation.

One generalization for (5.1) in this regard is to add "spatially lagged dependent variables": with λ being an unknown constant, $|\lambda| < 1$,

$$y_i = \lambda \cdot w_i'Y + x_i'\beta + u_i \quad \text{and} \quad u_i = \rho \cdot w_i'U + v_i. \quad (5.4)$$

Differently from (5.1), (5.4) has a simultaneity problem among the elements of Y, and the LSE is inconsistent; IVE, however, will do. As in dynamic panel data models, there occurs the question of interpreting the spatially lagged dependent variables Y. One may take (5.4) as such: y_i is influenced by y_j's, $j \neq i$ ("true spatial dependence"). Alternatively, obtain from (5.4)

$$(I_N - \lambda W) \cdot Y = X \cdot \beta + U \Rightarrow Y = (I_N - \lambda W)^{-1}X \cdot \beta + (I_N - \lambda W)^{-1}U.$$

Use $(I_N - \lambda W)^{-1} = I_N + \lambda W + \lambda^2 W^2 + \cdots$ to see that x_j's and u_j's, $j \neq i$, affect y_i directly in (5.4).

Turning to a test for spatial dependence using panel data, the "Spearman's rank correlation" between two random vectors $e_i \equiv (e_{i1}, ..., e_{iT})'$ and $e_j \equiv (e_{j1}, ..., e_{jT})'$ is

$$r_{ij} \equiv s_{ij}/(s_{ii} \cdot s_{jj})^{1/2}.$$

where

$$s_{ij} \equiv (T - 1)^{-1} \sum_t \{R_{it} - (T + 1)/2\} \cdot \{R_{jt} - (T + 1)/2\},$$

and $(R_{i1}, ..., R_{iT})$ is the ranks of the components of e_i; $(T + 1)/2$ is the average rank.

Define a test statistic

$$T_2 \equiv \binom{N}{2}^{-1} \sum_{i<j} r_{ij}^2. \tag{5.5}$$

If

$$\{e_{it}\} \text{ are iid across } i \text{ and } t \text{ with a density function,} \tag{5.6}$$

then Frees (1995) showed that

$$N\{T_2 - (T-1)^{-1}\} \Rightarrow a(T)\{\chi_{1,T-1}^2 - (T-1)\} + b(T) \cdot \{\chi_{2,T(T-3)/2}^2 - T(T-3)/2\} \tag{5.7}$$

where

$$a(T) \equiv 4(T + 2)/\{5(T - 1)^2(T + 1)\} \quad \text{and}$$
$$b(T) \equiv 2(5T + 6)/\{5T(T - 1)(T + 1)\},$$

and $\chi_{1,T-1}^2$ and $\chi_{2,T(T-3)/2}^2$ are independent of each other and follow χ_{T-1}^2 and $\chi_{T(T-3)/2}^2$, respectively. If e_i is an error vector, because error terms are not observed, we have to use residuals. Frees (1995, Corollary 3) shows that (5.7) is still valid for the residuals, if (5.6) holds and

$$\text{the density is symmetric about zero.} \tag{5.8}$$

Usually spatial correlation is positive, but there are instances where it is negative (for example, migration among regions). The purpose of squaring r_{ij} in T_2 is to prevent negative entries from canceling positive entries. If spatial dependence is non-negative, or if the negative entries do not cancel too much of the positive entries, then we can use a much simpler version than T_2:

$$T_1 \equiv \binom{N}{2}^{-1} \sum_{i<j} r_{ij}; \quad (N - 1)(T - 1) \cdot T_1 + (T - 1) \Rightarrow \chi_{T-1}^2; \tag{5.9}$$

this can be found in Hettmansperger (1984, pp. 197 and 210): K^* in page 197 follows χ_{T-1}^2, and K^* is then written as $(N - 1)(T - 1) \cdot T_1 + (T - 1)$ in page 210. The null model allows "exchangeability" (thus some form of dependence) within i: the joint distribution of $e_{i1}, ..., e_{iT}$ is permutation-free, which is weaker than (5.6). It is not clear what happens to T_1 if residuals are used.

Applying T_1 to the three-wave wage data, first we obtain the residuals for the GMM under the PRE condition; of course, other estimators may be used as well. Second, for each individual, the ranks for the three residuals are calculated (for example, 1, 3, 2 or 3, 1, 2, ...). Third, for each two individuals i and j, the rank correlation r_{ij} is obtained. Fourth, the test statistic and the p-value are

$$(N - 1)(T - 1) \cdot T_1 + (T - 1) = 2.152 \quad \text{and} \quad p\text{-value} = 0.341. \quad (5.10)$$

Hence no spatial correlation is not rejected; here we ignore the problem of using residuals.

Denoting the 3×1 residual vector for individual i as $\hat{v}_i$, the autocorrelation matrix for $\hat{v}_i$ is

$$\begin{bmatrix} 1 & 0.73 & 0.67 \\ 0.73 & 1 & 0.70 \\ 0.67 & 0.70 & 1 \end{bmatrix}. \quad (5.11)$$

Judging from the off-diagonal terms, which are not much different, the serial correlation seems to come from δ_i; if u_{i1}, u_{i2}, and u_{i3} are iid, then this equicorrelation case satisfies the exchangeability requirement. Due to δ_i, it is important to allow at least exchangeability; independence would be too restrictive for panel data error terms.

3.6 EFFICIENCY GAIN, WALD-TYPE TESTS, PANEL VAR, AND LONG-RUN AND SHORT-RUN EFFECTS

This section examines five topics. The first is an efficiency gain issue on estimating parameters of endogenous regressors with increasingly more instruments; examining this gives us a chance to look at the part of the panel IVE literature not discussed in the preceding sections. The second is Wald type specification tests for panel data, which can be used in addition to the over-id tests in GMM and MDE that have appeared already. The third is quasi-differencing and panel vector autoregression (VAR), useful for Granger-causality analysis. The fourth is the issue of whether to pool time-series or not if T is large as well as N. Finally, the fifth is "long-run versus short-run effects." The last two topics are related and thus put together in the same section.

3.6.1 Efficiency Gain for Endogenous Regressors

In the wage example that has appeared already, one of the main interests is on the effect of education (ED); see Card (1999) for a survey on this long-standing issue. Although ED can vary over time, in most data on adults, ED hardly changes over time. Because ED is likely to be correlated with the time-invariant error δ_i standing for IQ or ability, a related-effect estimator is called for. But differencing the model equation will not do, for ED_i is removed along with δ_i; it is necessary to estimate the model without purging out all time invariants. This can be done by IVE with regressor differencing, the early literature of which, however, has been limited more or less to summation (SUM) type moment conditions with a non-block-diagonal instrument matrix, under either homoskedasticity or heteroskedasticity of a known form. In the following discussion, we will set $T = 3$ and review this literature, and then discuss the efficiency gain issue as more instruments become available.

Recall that in (5.2) to (5.7) of Chapter 2 on the wage example, only the time dummies, RC_i (race) and UR_{it} (local unemployment rate) were used as the source for instruments for ED_i. Under SUM, the instrument matrix z_i' is

$$
\begin{bmatrix}
0 & 0 & 1 & RC_i & UR_{i1} \\
1 & 0 & 1 & RC_i & UR_{i2} \\
0 & 1 & 1 & RC_i & UR_{i3}
\end{bmatrix},
\tag{6.1}
$$

which is, however, insufficient for the number of parameters is greater than the column number of z_i'. Hausman and Taylor (1981) noted that the time-invariant part of the time-variant variables may be used as instruments as well for endogenous time-invariant variables; that is, $UR_{i.} \equiv (1/T)\sum_t UR_{it}$ can be used as an instrument for ED_i. Thus Hausman and Taylor (1981) augmented z_i' into

$$
\begin{bmatrix}
0 & 0 & 1 & RC_i & UR_{i1} & UR_{i.} \\
1 & 0 & 1 & RC_i & UR_{i2} & UR_{i.} \\
0 & 1 & 1 & RC_i & UR_{i3} & UR_{i.}
\end{bmatrix},
\tag{6.2}
$$

where $UR_{i.}$ may be correlated with ED_i; highly educated people may live in low unemployment area.

Going one step further from Hausman and Taylor (1981), Amemiya and MaCurdy (1986) have suggested including the time-invariant variables generated from the exogenous time-variant variables. In the wage example, z_i' gets three new columns in place of $UR_{i.}$:

$$
\begin{bmatrix}
0 & 0 & 1 & RC_i & UR_{i1} & UR_{i1} & UR_{i2} & UR_{i3} \\
1 & 0 & 1 & RC_i & UR_{i2} & UR_{i1} & UR_{i2} & UR_{i3} \\
0 & 1 & 1 & RC_i & UR_{i3} & UR_{i1} & UR_{i2} & UR_{i3}
\end{bmatrix}.
\tag{6.3}
$$

Breusch *et al.* (1989) further extend the instrument matrix by including the time-invariant variables generated from the time-variant variables correlated with δ_i under the assumption that the correlated part is time invariant; recall (5.14) through (5.16) from Chapter 2. This allows using a transformation of self-employment dummy SF_{it}, and the instrument matrix z_i' becomes ($\Delta SF_{it} \equiv SF_{it} - SF_{i,t-1}$)

$$
\begin{bmatrix}
0 & 0 & 1 & RC_i & UR_{i1} & UR_{i1} & UR_{i2} & UR_{i3} & \Delta SF_{i2} & \Delta SF_{i3} \\
1 & 0 & 1 & RC_i & UR_{i2} & UR_{i1} & UR_{i2} & UR_{i3} & \Delta SF_{i2} & \Delta SF_{i3} \\
0 & 1 & 1 & RC_i & UR_{i3} & UR_{i1} & UR_{i2} & UR_{i3} & \Delta SF_{i2} & \Delta SF_{i3}
\end{bmatrix}.
$$

$$
\tag{6.4}
$$

In (6.1) to (6.4), we have increasingly more time-invariant instruments generated by time-variant variables. But comparing (5.3), (5.5), and (5.7) of Chapter 2 with (6.2) to (6.4) above, the latter use only SUM type conditions, whereas the former use far more. This has implication for efficiency gain as shown in the following.

After the above three papers on IVE with increasingly more instruments, there came up a question on the efficiency gain. Cornwell and Ruppert (1988) applied the IVE's with (6.2), (6.3) and (6.4) to the returns-to-schooling problem and noted that the efficiency gain was limited to the coefficient of the endogenous time invariant regressor ED_i. This was plausible, for the new instruments are all time-invariant. They drew data from the Panel Study of Income Dynamics (PSID), 1976–1982 with $N = 595$. Define

EXP = Work experience   WKS = Weeks worked

MS = Dummy for married   UNION = Dummy for union member

ED = Education in years   FEM = Dummy for female.

Using WKS and MS (and some other variables) as time-variant instruments, and FEM (and some other variable) as a time-invariant instrument, Table 3.2 represents part of their Table 1 (standard errors in parenthesis) explaining ln(wage); HT, AM, and BMS stand for, respectively, Hausman and Taylor, Amemiya and MaCurdy, and Breusch, Mizon and Schmidt.

TABLE 3.2 ln(Wage)-Equation Estimation with Increasing Number of Instruments

	GLS	HT	AM	BMS
EXP	.0565 (.0028)	.0605 (.0029)	.0602 (.0029)	.0601 (.0029)
EXP^2	−.00045(.00005)	−.00042(.00005)	−.00042(.00005)	−.00042(.00005)
WKS	.00088(.00058)	.00089(.00059)	.00089(.00059)	.00088(.00058)
MS	−.0436 (.0182)	−.0487 (.0183)	−.0487 (.0183)	−.0488 (.0182)
UNION	.0197 (.0143)	.0134 (.0145)	.0140 (.0144)	.0156 (.0143)
ED	.0941 (.0170)	.2004 (.0783)	.1585 (.0586)	.1067 (.0314)
FEM	−.3482 (.1515)	−.3559 (.1531)	−.3484 (.1523)	−.3385 (.1518)

Except for ED, there is little difference across the estimators. The estimate for MS has a negative sign, which is rather strange (maybe due to the ignored endogeneity of MS). The key variable ED shows a puzzling pattern: as more instruments are used, the estimate magnitude drops to the GLS estimate, and the standard errors drop signaling efficiency gain here. The latter is natural, whereas the former does not hold anymore when different specifications are used by Baltagi and Khanti-Akom (1990); what does seem to hold, however, is that the estimate for ED is smaller in GLS than in IVE in most cases.

Baltagi and Khanti-Akom (1990) used (almost) the same data set as Cornwell and Ruppert (1988) used, but with different classifications of the instruments. They observed that efficiency gain was not limited to the endogenous time-invariant regressor and that the efficiency gain was much smaller than that in Cornwell and Ruppert (1988). We will show that there should be *no efficiency gain for the endogenous time-variant variables so long as SUM is used*; for such a gain, we need at least CON or better (that is, PRE or EXO).

Let $T = 2$ and consider a time-variant 2×1 random vector $m_i \equiv (m_{i1}, m_{i2})'$. Also consider two time-invariant random variables d_i and e_i. Consider approximating m_i by d_i and e_i. There are a couple of different ways. One way is to choose λ_d and λ_e in

$$\left[\begin{array}{c} m_{i1} \\ m_{i2} \end{array} \right] - \lambda_d \cdot \left[\begin{array}{c} d_i \\ d_i \end{array} \right] - \lambda_e \cdot \left[\begin{array}{c} e_i \\ e_i \end{array} \right], \tag{6.5}$$

such that this deviation is small in a sense. In this case, both m_{i1} and m_{i2} are fitted by $\lambda_d d_i + \lambda_e e_i$ which is time invariant. Another way is to choose $\lambda_{d1}, \lambda_{d2}, \lambda_{e1}$ and λ_{e2} in

$$\left[\begin{array}{c} m_{i1} \\ m_{i2} \end{array} \right] - \lambda_{d1} \cdot \left[\begin{array}{c} d_i \\ 0 \end{array} \right] - \lambda_{d2} \cdot \left[\begin{array}{c} 0 \\ d_i \end{array} \right] - \lambda_{e1} \cdot \left[\begin{array}{c} e_i \\ 0 \end{array} \right] - \lambda_{e2} \cdot \left[\begin{array}{c} 0 \\ e_i \end{array} \right], \tag{6.6}$$

such that this is small in a sense. Here m_{i1} is fitted by $\lambda_{d1} d_i + \lambda_{e1} e_i$ and m_{i2} is fitted by $\lambda_{d2} d_i + \lambda_{e2} e_i$: that is, d_i and e_i can generate a time-variant feature, so long as d_i and e_i are not independent of m_{i1} and m_{i2}. Approximation (6.5) imposes $\lambda_{d1} = \lambda_{d2}$ and $\lambda_{e1} = \lambda_{e2}$ in comparison with (6.6).

Recall the wage example where WH$_{it}$ (working hours) is the endogenous time-variant variable. Let $d_i = $ UR$_{i1}$ and $e_i = $ UR$_{i2}$. Then it is possible that WH$_{i1}$ is explained by UR$_{i1}$, whereas WH$_{i2}$ is explained by UR$_{i1}$ (lagged unemployment rate) and UR$_{i2}$ (current unemployment rate). Using (6.3) or (6.4) leads to (6.5), whereas using (5.5) or (5.19) from Chapter 2 leads to (6.6). Hence, with the moment conditions as in CON, PRE, and EXO, there can be efficiency gain for the endogenous time-variant regressors as well as for the endogenous time-invariant regressors.

Baltagi and Khanti-Akom (1990) use a SUM type moment condition where there should be no efficiency gain for the endogenous time-variant regressors. Nevertheless, they noted an efficiency gain in one endogenous time-variant variable: job experience (JE$_{it}$). As noted in their paper, barring unemployment spells,

$$JE_{it} = JE_{i1} + t - 1. \tag{6.7}$$

With time dummies already in, the only part of JE$_{it}$ left to be explained by time-invariant instruments is the time-invariant JE$_{i1}$. So it is not surprising to see an efficiency gain in JE$_{it}$. JE$_{it}$ is better to be regarded as time invariant as age$_{it}$ is so.

3.6.2 Wald-Type Specification Tests

So far we have seen two specification tests: the GMM test and the MDE test. Both are over-id tests in the sense that there are more than enough restrictions in terms of moments for the GMM test and in terms of parameter restrictions for the MDE test. Another type of test, "Wald test," was given in (2.21): it compares two estimators that are consistent for the same parameter under H_o while expected to converge to different values under H_a. This type of test is in fact widely used; for example, one popular way to test for related-effect is comparing GLS (or LSE) to WIT by constructing analogously to (2.21). Because the identified parameters in GLS and WIT are different, we need effective influence functions to construct a test statistic analogous to (2.21); the steps for this task are essentially the same as (2.22) and (2.23).

In comparing two $k \times 1$ vector estimators a_N and b_N, suppose that a_N is $\sqrt{N}$-consistent for β and efficient under H_o while inconsistent under H_a, and that b_N is $\sqrt{N}$-consistent for β under both H_o and H_a while inefficient under H_o. Then

$$N \cdot (b_N - a_N)'(V_{Nb} - V_{Na})^{-1}(b_N - a_N) \Rightarrow \chi^2_\rho \qquad (6.8)$$

where V_{Nb} (V_{Na}) is a symmetric p.s.d. consistent estimator for the asymptotic variance V_b (V_a) of $\sqrt{N}(b_N - \beta)$ $(\sqrt{N}(a_N - \beta))$, and $\rho = rank(V_b - V_a)$; if $\rho < k$, then the middle matrix in (6.8) is the Moore-Penrose inverse, and the condition

$$P(rank(V_{Nb} - V_{Na}) = rank(V_b - V_a)) \to 1 \quad as \quad N \to \infty$$

is required (see Andrews, 1987). Formula (6.8) can be used to test for H_o, and such a test is called "Hausman test" in econometrics, because Hausman (1978) showed that $V_{Nb} - V_{Na}$ is a consistent estimator for the asymptotic variance of $\sqrt{N}(b_N - a_N)$ under H_o.

The advantage of Hausman tests is the simplicity in obtaining the middle variance matrix when $\rho = k$ without getting (effective) influence functions. But model assumptions other than those tested in H_o may not hold, rendering $V_{Nb} - V_{Na}$ non positive definite; this occurs quite frequently in practice. In this case, (6.8) does not work, and one needs to estimate the asymptotic variance for $\sqrt{N}(b_N - a_N)$ using the (effective) influence functions.

It has been known for a long time in statistics (see, for example, Bickel *et al.*, 1993) that an inefficient $\sqrt{N}$-consistent estimator's influence function, say ζ_i with $E(\zeta) = 0$, can be written as $\eta_i + \xi_i$ where η_i with $E(\eta) = 0$ is the efficient estimator's influence function and $E(\eta \xi') = 0$. Following this, we can write the asymptotic variance of $\sqrt{N}(b_N - \beta)$ as $E(\eta \eta') + E(\xi \xi')$ and that of $\sqrt{N}(a_N - \beta)$ as $E(\eta \eta')$. Hence,

$$(\text{asy.var. for } b_N) - (\text{asy.var. for } a_N) = E(\xi \xi') = \text{asy.var. for } (b_N - a_N)$$

for ξ_i is an influence function for $\sqrt{N}\{b_N - \beta - (a_N - \beta)\}$. Given the fact that the main idea of Hausman (1978) was known long before, the name "Hausman test" seems overused in econometrics.

For a linear hypothesis $H_o : R\beta = r$ where β is a $k \times 1$ parameter vector, R is a known $f \times k$ matrix of rank f, and r is a known $f \times 1$ vector, a Wald test statistic is

$$N(Rb_N - r)' \cdot (R\Omega_N R')^{-1} \cdot (Rb_N - r) \Rightarrow \chi_f^2 \qquad (6.9)$$

where $\sqrt{N}(b_N - \beta) \Rightarrow N(0, \Omega)$ and Ω_N is a consistent estimator for Ω. Here two estimators for the parameter $R\beta$ are compared: one is r, which is consistent under H_o while inconsistent under $H_a : R\beta \neq r$, and the other is Rb_N, which is consistent under both H_o and H_a. Hence both r and Rb_N are consistent for $R\beta$ under H_o, whereas r and Rb_N are consistent for r and $R\beta$, respectively, under $H_a : R\beta \neq r$. Because r is efficient under H_o (r has zero variance), (6.9) also has a flavor of the Hausman test.

Recall (2.17):

$$N \cdot (\theta_N - Rb_{mde})' \cdot W_N^{-1} \cdot (\theta_N - Rb_{mde}) \Rightarrow \chi_{K-k}^2. \qquad (6.10)$$

Again, θ_N and Rb_{mde} are two different estimators for the same parameter $\theta = R\beta$ under H_o. The tests in (6.8), (6.9), and (6.10) all take the same form: the difference between two estimators for the same parameter under H_o weighted by some matrix. But they differ in computing the weighting matrix and the appropriate degree of freedom. In the full rank cases of Wald type tests, if we have the influence function estimates, say $\hat{\psi}_{1i}$ and $\hat{\psi}_{2i}$, for the two estimators, the middle matrix can be estimated by

$$\{(1/N) \sum_i (\hat{\psi}_{1i} - \hat{\psi}_{2i})(\hat{\psi}_{1i} - \hat{\psi}_{2i})'\}^{-1}. \qquad (6.11)$$

In (6.8), (6.11) becomes $(V_{Nb} - V_{Na})^{-1}$ due to the special assumptions for Hausman tests; (6.11) can be used for all Hausman tests. In (6.9), one influence function disappears because r is a constant. Formula (6.10) is rather special: the fact that the MDE minimizes the left-hand side of (6.10) leads to the reduced degree of freedom $K - k$, not K that one might expect given the dimension of $\theta_N - Rb_{mde}$.

There are testing ideas other than over-id tests and Wald tests. The most appropriate for methods-of moment estimator (MME) would be methods-of-moment tests where moment conditions not used for estimation but implied by the model assumptions are tested for. For example, if moment conditions A and B are implied by the model assumptions but only A is used to estimate the model parameters, then we can check if the estimated parameters satisfy B or not. If not, part of the model assumptions is false.

We can delve into the moment test, but we will not do so because the moment test can be implemented by a Wald test: obtain two estimators b_N using A and

a_N using both A and B, and compare a_N and b_N. Note that in the moment test, we would be getting only b_N. With some regularity conditions, the moment test and the Wald test can be shown to be asymptotically equivalent under the null hypothesis. The moment test may be called a LM (Lagrangean multiplier) or a score test, for the moment test uses only part of available moment conditions for estimation, and then tests for the unused ones.

3.6.3 Quasi-Differencing and Panel Vector-Autoregression (VAR)

Holtz-Eakin *et al.* (1988) considered a "vector autoregressive (VAR)" model between two variables x_{it} and y_{it}, where the y_{it}-equation is

$$y_{it} = \alpha_{0t} + \sum_{j=1}^{J} \alpha_{jt} y_{i,t-j} + \sum_{j=1}^{J} \beta_{jt} x_{i,t-j} + \Phi_t \delta_i + u_{it};$$

δ_i now carries a time-varying effect Φ_t on y_{it}. The lagged y_{it}'s on the right-hand side give the word "autoregressive"; adding the lagged x_{it}'s then yields the expression "vector autoregressive." Taking the right-hand side as the linear projection of y_{it} on

$$1, \ y_{i,t-1}, \ ..., \ y_{i,t-J}, \ x_{i,t-1}, \ ..., \ x_{t-J}, \ \text{and} \ \delta_i$$

yields PRE type moment conditions:

$$E(u_{it}) = 0, \quad E(y_{is} u_{it}) = 0, \quad E(x_{is} u_{it}) = 0, \quad E(\delta_i u_{it}) = 0 \quad \forall s < t.$$

Define $\phi_t \equiv \Phi_t / \Phi_{t-1}$ and get the $\phi_t y_{i,t-1}$ equation:

$$
\phi_t y_{i,t-1} = \phi_t \alpha_{0,t-1} \quad + \quad \sum_{j=1}^{J} \phi_t \alpha_{j,t-1} y_{i,t-j-1}
$$
$$
+ \quad \sum_{j=1}^{J} \phi_t \beta_{j,t-1} x_{i,t-j-1} + \Phi_t \delta_i + \phi_t u_{i,t-1}.
$$

Now remove δ_i by the quasi-differencing $y_{it} - \phi_t y_{i,t-1}$:

$$
y_{it} = \alpha_{0t} - \phi_t \alpha_{0,t-1} \quad + \quad (\phi_t + \alpha_{1t}) \cdot y_{i,t-1}
$$
$$
+ \quad \sum_{j=2}^{J} (\alpha_{jt} - \phi_t \alpha_{j-1,t-1}) \cdot y_{i,t-j} \tag{6.12}
$$
$$
-\phi_t \alpha_{J,t-1} \cdot y_{i,t-J-1} \quad + \quad \beta_{1t} \cdot x_{i,t-1} + \sum_{j=2}^{J} (\beta_{jt} - \phi_t \beta_{j-1,t-1}) \cdot x_{i,t-j}
$$
$$
-\phi_t \beta_{J,t-1} \cdot x_{i,t-J-1} \quad + \quad u_{it} - \phi_t u_{i,t-1}.
$$

As a digression, more generally than demeaning and (quasi) differencing, $S \cdot y_i$ where S is a $T \times T$ matrix such that each row sum is zero eliminates all time-invariants in the y_{it}-equation. This includes "forward-differencing" as in Keane and Runkle (1992) and Arellano and Bover (1995); for example $y_{it} - y_{i,t+1}$. Although involving all periods is problematic in demeaning, demeaning at least avoids the question of choosing s in differencing $y_{it} - y_{i,s}$; in a group structure cross-section model, demeaning is the natural way to remove δ_i, for there is no order within each group.

Turning back to (6.12), with $\varepsilon_{it} \equiv u_{it} - \phi_t u_{i,t-1}$, the preceding PRE type moment conditions imply

$$E(\varepsilon_{it}) = 0, \quad E(y_{is}\varepsilon_{it}) = 0, \quad \text{and} \quad E(x_{is}\varepsilon_{it}) = 0 \quad \forall s < t - 1,$$

with which the coefficients of the lagged y_{it} and x_{it} variables in (6.12) can be estimated along with the intercept if $T \geq J + 3$. Note that identifying the original parameters α_{jt}'s and β_{jt}'s has been made difficult due to the quasi-differencing. But a certain task does not require identifying the original parameters. For example, a Granger noncausality test of x_t for y_t is

$$H_o : \beta_{jt} = 0 \quad \forall j \text{ and } t,$$

which implies

$$H_o : \text{the coefficients of lagged } x_{it}\text{'s are all zero in (6.12)};$$

this is a test for whether the past and current x_{it}'s help linearly predict the one-step ahead future y_{it}. Holtz-Eakin *et al.* (1988) applied this test to wage and work-hours equations to find that the work hour does not Granger-cause wage. Holtz-Eakin *et al.* (1989) applied the test to revenues and expenditures of local governments to find that expenditures do not Granger-cause revenues, although revenues Granger-cause expenditures.

Although the Granger noncausality of x_t for y_t is defined as (Granger, 1969, 1980)

$$P(y_t \leq a | I_{t-1}) - P(y_t \leq a | I_{t-1} \text{ without } x_{t-1}, x_{t-2}, ...) = 0 \quad \forall a, \quad (6.13)$$

where I_{t-1} is all the information available at $t - 1$, (6.13) with $I_{t-1} = \{y_{t-1}, y_{t-2}, ..., x_{t-1}, x_{t-2}, ...\}$ is often taken as an operational definition of Granger noncausality. The problem of the Granger noncausality is that it critically depends on I_t. If there is a variable driving both x_t and y_t but omitted from I_{t-1}, then one will reject the Granger noncausality. Because we will never get the complete information in practice, rejecting the Granger noncausality can be misleading; accepting it is also subject to the following problem.

Let I_{t-1} denote the information available at hand other than a random variable ξ. Suppose that

$$P(y_t \leq a | \xi, I_{t-1}) - P(y_t \leq a | \xi, I_{t-1} \text{ without } x_{t-1}, x_{t-2}, ...)$$

is positive for some values of ξ while negative for some other values, and that $P(y_t \leq a | I_{t-1}) = P(y_t \leq a | I_{t-1}$ without $x_{t-1}, x_{t-2}, ...) \; \forall a$. In this case, one may falsely conclude that Granger noncausality holds despite x_t Granger-causing y_t differently depending on the value of ξ.

3.6.4 Pool or Not and Long-Run versus Short-Run Effects

So long as N is large, our panel data estimators will work. If T is large as well, we may replace β in $y_{it} = x'_{it}\beta + \delta_i + u_{it}$ with β_i, and estimate β_i (and δ_i) using the time-series data for i; there seems to be no good reason to pool the data across i to get a panel. Pooling the data will be beneficial, however, if there is restriction $\beta_i = \beta \; \forall i$ (or if β_i's are close to one another), or if u_{it}'s autocorrelation pattern is similar across i. If β_i varies across i, then pooling can cause a bias while lowering the variance, leading to the classic trade-off between bias and variance. But the bias does not occur always; for example, with $\beta_i = \bar{\beta} + \varepsilon_i$ and $E(\varepsilon_i) = 0$,

$$y_{it} = x'_{it}\beta_i + \delta_i + u_{it} = x'_{it}\bar{\beta} + \delta_i + x'_{it}\varepsilon_i + u_{it}$$

where the error term is now $\delta_i + x'_{it}\varepsilon_i + u_{it}$, which is heteroskedastic, but $E(\beta_i) = \bar{\beta}$ can be estimated just the same.

Baltagi *et al.* (2000) estimated per capita cigarette consumption (y_{it}) equation for 46 ($= N$) states over 30 ($= T$) years:

$$\ln(y_{it}) = \rho \cdot \ln(y_{i,t-1}) + \beta_m \ln(m_{it}) + \beta_n \ln(n_{it}) + \beta_p \ln(p_{it}) + \cdots , \quad (6.14)$$

where m_{it} is the per capita income, n_{it} is the minimum price of cigarettes in the neighboring states, p_{it} is the price of cigarettes, and $y_{i,t-1}$ accounts for habit formation. Although not shown in (6.14), time-invariant regressors and time-dummies were used as well; time dummies are important because of law changes on health warning labels, tobacco advertising, and public-place smoking. In (6.14), β_m, β_n and β_p stand for short-run effect (elasticities), whereas the long-run effects are $\beta_m/(1 - \rho)$, $\beta_n/(1 - \rho)$ and $\beta_p/(1 - \rho)$. Because T is fairly large, there comes the question of whether or not to pool. Table 3.3 shows part of their Table 1 on the elasticities with t-values in ($\cdot$).

TABLE 3.3 Tobacco Consumption Elasticities

		Short−Run		Long−Run	
	ρ	β_m	β_p	β_m	β_p
LSE	0.90 (103)	0.04 (3.3)	−0.19 (11)	0.44 (3.5)	−1.95 (12)
WIT	0.83 (66)	0.10 (4.2)	−0.30 (13)	0.60 (4.3)	−1.79 (12)
WIT−IVE	0.60 (17)	0.19 (6.4)	−0.50 (13)	0.47 (7.1)	−1.25 (18)
FD−IVE	0.51 (9.5)	0.10 (2.9)	−0.35 (12)	0.21 (2.7)	−0.71 (7.5)

In Table 3.3, WIT-IVE is an IVE to the mean-difference model, and FD-IVE is an IVE to the first-differenced model; due to rounding errors, the long-run numbers do not match exactly the short-run numbers divided by $1 - \rho$. WIT controls for δ_i, but if u_{it} is autocorrelated, then $\ln(y_{i,t-1})$ is related to u_{it}, rendering WIT inconsistent; WIT-IVE and FD-IVE avoid both sources of bias by the extra IVE step to the transformed equations free of δ_i. The magnitude of LSE is the greatest for ρ but the smallest for β_m and β_p in the short run. WIT falls between LSE and WIT-IVE and FD-IVE in terms of the estimate magnitude. The short-run effects are fairly small, whereas the long-run effects are much bigger. Although spatial correlation is controlled for by n_{it}, the error terms across i may be correlated, which would lower the t-values in Table 3.3 by two- to three-folds if properly accounted for.

Baltagi *et al.* (2000) compared the previous panel estimators with the estimators applied to individual time series. The comparison is on out-of-sample prediction mean squared errors. They concluded that panel estimators are much better than those for individual time series; the main reason seems to be the instability of the latter over time. This makes a good case for pooling even when T is large. See Baltagi *et al.* (2000) and Hoogstrate *et al.* (2000) for more on whether or not to pool. Among the pooled data estimators, LSE and WIT performed better for the prediction criterion. But if prediction is the goal, one should not bother with endogeneity problems at all; LSE should be the best for mean-squared-error prediction. Thus it is not surprising at all to see LSE doing well.

Turning to short-run versus long-run effects consider a panel data model

$$y_{it} = \sum_{s=0}^{m} x'_{i,t-s}\beta_s + u_{it}, \quad \beta_s > 0 \;\; \forall s, \quad (6.15)$$

$x_{i1}, ..., x_{iT}$ are positively correlated.

For example, a research input (x_{it}) will take time to bear fruit, which means that x_{it} and its lagged variables appear in the output y_{it} equation. Also, if the lagged response is substituted out successively in (6.14), we will arrive a model like (6.15). Here, β_s's are short-run responses of y_{it} to x_{it}, whereas $\sum_s \beta_s$ is the long-run response when x_{it} is the same for all t. In time-series or panel data, we can estimate β_s's. In cross-section data, however, lagged x_{it}'s (that is, $\sum_{s=1}^{m} x'_{i,t-s}\beta_s$) are omitted and the LSE will be inconsistent for β_0 due to the omitted variable bias, and omitting lagged x_{it}'s will make the estimate for x_{it} upward biased due to the positive correlation and $\beta_s > 0$; that is, the LSE will typically give a number greater than β_0 (but smaller than $\sum_s \beta_s$). If $x_{i,t-s} = x_{it}$ for all s, then there will be no omitted variable bias, and the cross-section LSE gives the long-run effect.

This explains the tendency for estimates in cross-section data to have bigger magnitudes than estimates in time-series or panel data: an insufficient number of lagged x_{it}'s are included in the cross section; see Baltagi and Griffin (1984) and Pirotte (1999) and the references therein for more details. If the sum of omitted lagged x_{it}'s changes little over time, the sum can be represented as δ_i (the sum can be picked up also by $y_{i,t-1}$ if $y_{i,t-1}$ is included in the regressor; in this case, $y_{i,t-1}$ becomes relevant due to the misspecified dynamics in x_{it}'s). Thus, panel differencing estimators controlling for δ_i tend to estimate short-run responses, whereas (cross-section) estimators not controlling for δ_i tend to be biased toward the long-run effect.

In this short-run and long-run interpretation, x_{it} affects y_{it} directly in the short run, and indirectly in the long-run through δ_i which is the x_{it}'s effects accumulated over time; the cross-section estimator bias due to $COR(x_{it}, \delta_i)$ is not taken as a bias any more. Here, δ_i is affected by x_{it} in the sense that x_{it}'s are repeated over time and accumulated in δ_i; if, however, $COR(x_{it}, \delta_i)$ is due to δ_i affecting x_{it}, say δ_i being genes, then the long-run interpretation is not appropriate.

Recall the crime example in the preceding chapter. There, other than police, the between group estimator (BET) is greater than WIT in magnitude; this phenomenon of BET being greater than WIT is often seen in practice. One may interpret these as long-run versus short-run effects: WIT measures the short-run effect of increasing x_{it} in a given county, whereas BET using panel as a pooled-cross-section measures the long-run effect. When different counties are compared, it is likely that different police practices or procedures have been implemented for a long time in different counties to render long-run effects.

4

PANEL DATA ESTIMATORS FOR BINARY RESPONSES

4.1 INTRODUCTION

In the preceding chapters, we studied instrumental variable estimators (IVE) for linear panel data models. In this and the following chapter, we study panel data with limited responses: binary response, count response, censored response, and multinomial response. We do not examine ordered discrete response (ODR), but we will indicate where ODR can be accommodated easily within the binary response framework; the computer program appendix contains three programs for ODR as well. For length considerations, this chapter deals only with binary responses, but most comments in this introduction also apply to the following chapter.

As in the preceding chapters, we focus on "related-effect" panel models where the time-invariant error δ_i is allowed to be related to regressors. Reviews on (cross-section) limited response models can be found in, for example, Powell (1994) and Lee (1996). See Heckman (1981), Maddala (1987), and the references therein for mostly "unrelated-effect" panel data models for limited responses where δ_i is unrelated to the regressors.

Our panel binary response model is basically the same as the panel linear model except that the continuous response is latent and observed only as binary. Recall the linear model with the time-invariant regressor vector $\tilde{c}_i$, the time-variant regressor vector x_{it}, the time-varying error u_{it}, and the continuous response denoted now as y_{it}^*:

$$
\begin{aligned}
y_{it}^* &= \tau_t + \tilde{c}_i'\tilde{\alpha} + x_{it}'\beta + \delta_i + u_{it} \quad (\tau_t \text{ is time-varying intercept}) \qquad (1.1) \\
&= \tau_t + \tilde{w}_{it}'\tilde{\gamma} + v_{it}, \\
&\quad \text{where } \tilde{w}_{it} = (\tilde{c}_i', x_{it}')', \quad \tilde{\gamma} = (\tilde{\alpha}', \beta')', \quad v_{it} = \delta_i + u_{it}; \\
y_{it} &= 1[y_{it}^* > 0], \quad \{(y_{it}, \tilde{w}_{it}')'\}_{t=1}^T, \ i = 1, ..., N, \text{ are observed, iid across } i
\end{aligned}
$$

where $1[A] = 1$ if A holds and 0 otherwise. Also recall

$$
\begin{aligned}
c_i &\equiv (1, \tilde{c}_i')', \quad w_{it} \equiv (1, \tilde{c}_i', x_{it}')' = (c_i', x_{it}')', \\
\alpha &\equiv (\tau_1, \tilde{\alpha}')', \quad \text{and} \quad \gamma \equiv (\alpha', \beta')';
\end{aligned}
$$

the coefficient for c_i (w_{it}) is α (γ), and what is estimated is

$$
\tau_1, \tau_2 - \tau_1, ..., \tau_T - \tau_1, \gamma \iff \tau_1, ..., \tau_T, \gamma.
$$

Here, only the intercept is allowed to vary over time whereas the slopes are fixed; but as explained in the preceding chapters, allowing for time-varying slopes is not difficult. Unless otherwise noted, we will use these notations throughout.

Although IVE has been applied to linear models fruitfully, IVE is not applicable in general to models with limited responses, for the model equations are not solvable for the error term. To see this, suppose $E(v_{it}\tilde{w}_{it}) \neq 0$, but $E(v_{it}z_{it}) = 0$ for an instrument vector z_{it}. Because the y_{it}-equation is not solvable for v_{it}, we cannot write $E(v_{it}z_{it})$ in terms of the observed variables y_{it}, $\tilde{w}_{it}$, z_{it} and the parameters. Without IVE, the relation between $\{w_{i1}, ..., w_{iT}\}$ and $\{u_{i1}, ..., u_{iT}\}$ becomes difficult to deal with in limited response models. As for the relation between $\{w_{i1}, ..., w_{iT}\}$ and δ_i, among the three approaches for related-effect in the preceding chapters (error- or first-differencing, regressor differencing or transforming, and δ-splitting or δ-projecting), regressor differencing (and the ensuing IVE) is infeasible. Yet error differencing is still applicable: there exist first-difference type estimators for limited response models using only Δy_{it} and $\Delta \tilde{w}_{it}$; because first-differencing removes $\tilde{c}_i'\tilde{\alpha}$ and δ_i, $\tilde{\alpha}$ is not identified then. In this case, we will redefine δ_i as $\delta_i + \tilde{c}_i'\tilde{\alpha}$ and stop mentioning $\tilde{c}_i$ at all. The δ-splitting approach is not directly applicable, but its more restrictive version is so where δ_i is specified as a linear function of $\{w_{i1}, ..., w_{iT}\}$, say $\delta_i = \sum_{t=1}^T w_{it}'\zeta_t + e_i$, with e_i unrelated to $\{w_{i1}, ..., w_{iT}\}$. In this case, because ζ_t's get merged with γ, the parameter identification becomes harder; as in the first-differencing approach, the coefficients of time invariants are not identified.

Because of the infeasibility of regressor differencing and IVE, if we are interested in time invariants in panel limited response models, then we have no alternative but to assume that the regressors are unrelated to δ_i, unless we specify fully the relation between δ_i and $\{w_{i1}, ..., w_{iT}\}$. Suppose δ_i and u_{it}

are random variables distributed independently of $w_{i1}, ..., w_{iT}$. Then τ_t and γ can be estimated consistently simply using estimators for cross-section models. Unless γ changes across time, a more efficient estimator combining these cross-section estimators can be found with a minimum distance estimation (MDE). Furthermore, imposing a parametric assumption on δ_i and u_{it} and using the structure $\delta_i + u_{it}$ will lead to an even more efficient estimator (so long as the parametric assumptions are valid).

One interesting question an unrelated-effect panel data model can answer is the contribution of individual variance of δ_i and u_{it} to $V(\delta_i + u_{it})$: $V(\delta_i)$ is an "intersubject" or "between-group" variation, and $V(u_{it})$ may be called an "intrasubject" or "within-group" variation; here, one individual's over time data are taken as a group. Even if $V(\delta_i + u_{it})$ is not identified due to limited responses, still the ratio $V(\delta_i)/V(u_{it})$ or $V(\delta_i)/V(\delta_i + u_{it})$ may be identified. Unrelated effect is not of our interest and will not be discussed further; if interested, one can follow the sketch in this and the preceding paragraph, as well as consult other books on panel data.

Section 4.2 introduces conditional logit of Anderson (1970) and Chamberlain (1980) for $T = 2$; Section 4.2 also includes a subsection on kernel nonparametric estimation, which appears in the remaining sections. Section 4.3 explores methods for extending the $T = 2$ conditional logit for $T \geq 3$, which are also useful for other panel data estimators developed for the $T = 2$ cases only; also discussed in this section is Honoré and Kyriazidou's (2000b) conditional logit allowing a lagged response in regressors. Section 4.4 introduces various panel probit estimators; one particular estimator in Chamberlain (1980, 1984) is studied in detail, whereas others in Avery *et al.* (1983) and Arellano and Carrasco (1999) are given a brief look. Section 4.5 introduces Manski's (1987) semiparametric estimator, consistent but slowly converging, along with its smoothed version. Section 4.6 reviews Lee's (1999) $\sqrt{N}$-consistent semiparametric estimator. Section 4.7 provides an empirical example for conditional logit and panel probit. Time-constrained readers may want to read only Subsections 4.2.1, 4.2.2, 4.3.1, 4.3.2, and 4.4.1 to move on to the next chapter.

4.2 CONDITIONAL LOGIT FOR $T = 2$

Although our interest is on estimators based on weak distributional assumptions, those estimators for panel binary response are somewhat restrictive in some aspects as to be shown later in this chapter. For this reason and for their importance in the literature, we study two nearly parametric estimators for panel binary response: conditional logit in Sections 4.2 and 4.3 and panel probit in Section 4.4.

In this section, we examine conditional logit for $T = 2$ only, the computational ease of which may give it a name "LSE for panel binary responses." In the following section, we extend it to $T \geq 3$. This division into two sections is partly due to the length considerations; more important, however, many related-effect estimators are devised only for two periods, and how to extend a two-period estimator to more than two periods is a nontrivial practical issue per se.

Subsection 4.2.1 quickly reviews cross-section logit and then introduces conditional logit. Subsection 4.2.2 provides a few remarks along with a brief empirical example on health care demand. Although it looks somewhat out of place, Subsection 4.2.3 reviews kernel nonparametric estimation, for it appears in all remaining sections of this chapter; see, for example, Härdle (1990) for more on nonparametric estimation.

4.2.1 Cross-section Logit and Panel Conditional Logit

Consider a typical cross-section binary response model with the error term following a logistic distribution:

$$y_i = 1[x_i'\beta + u_i > 0], \quad x_i \text{ is a } k \times 1 \text{ regressor vector,}$$

$$\beta \text{ is a parameter vector,} \quad u_i \text{ is an error term independent of } x_i,$$

$$P(u_i/\sigma \leq \lambda) = e^\lambda/(1 + e^\lambda) \quad \forall \lambda, \quad \text{for an unknown positive constant } \sigma,$$

$$(x_i', y_i)', \quad i = 1, ..., N, \quad \text{are observed and iid.}$$

Because logistic distribution is symmetric about 0,

$$
\begin{aligned}
P(y_i &= 1|x_i) = P(u_i > -x_i'\beta|x_i) = P(u_i/\sigma > -x_i'\beta/\sigma|x_i) \\
&= P(u_i/\sigma < x_i'\beta/\sigma|x_i) = \exp(x_i'\beta/\sigma)/\{1 + \exp(x_i'\beta/\sigma)\} \\
\Rightarrow \quad &P(y_i = 0|x_i) = 1/\{1 + \exp(x_i'\beta/\sigma)\}.
\end{aligned}
$$

For this model, the cross-section logit is the maximum likelihood estimator (MLE) for $(\beta_1/\sigma, ..., \beta_k/\sigma)'$ obtained by maximizing the log-likelihood function

$$\sum_i [(1 - y_i) \cdot \ln\{1/(1 + \exp(x_i'a))\} + y_i \cdot \ln\{\exp(x_i'a)/(1 + \exp(x_i'a))\}]$$

with respect to (wrt) a. Because β is identified only up to the unknown σ, often we set $\sigma = 1$ to simplify the notations; this however should not be construed as $\sigma = 1$ being true.

Turning to panel binary response with $T = 2$, recall (1.1) and assume

$$u_{it}/\sigma \text{ is logistic independently of } (\delta_i, \tilde{c}_i, x_{i1}, x_{i2}), \textit{ iid across } t \text{ and } i \quad (2.1)$$

$$\Rightarrow P(y_{it} = 1|\delta_i, \tilde{c}_i, x_{i1}, x_{i2}) = P(u_{it} > -\tau_t - \tilde{c}_i'\tilde{\alpha} - x_{it}'\beta - \delta_i|\delta_i, \tilde{c}_i, x_{i1}, x_{i2})$$

$$= \exp(\tau_t/\sigma + \tilde{c}_i'\tilde{\alpha}/\sigma + x_{it}'\beta/\sigma + \delta_i/\sigma)/$$

$$\{1 + \exp(\tau_t/\sigma + \tilde{c}_i'\tilde{\alpha}/\sigma + x_{it}'\beta/\sigma + \delta_i/\sigma)\},$$

$$\Rightarrow P(y_{it} = 0|\delta_i, \tilde{c}_i, x_{i1}, x_{i2}) = 1/\{1 + \exp(\tau_t/\sigma + \tilde{c}_i'\tilde{\alpha}/\sigma + x_{it}'\beta/\sigma + \delta_i/\sigma)\},$$

for some unknown positive constant σ that is not a function of t. With this understood, set $\sigma = 1$ from now on to simplify notations.

Observe, omitting i and "$|\delta_i, \tilde{c}_i, x_{i1}, x_{i2}$,"

$$P(y_1 = 0, y_2 = 1|y_1 + y_2 = 1)$$
$$= P\{y_1 = 0, y_2 = 1|(y_1 = 0, y_2 = 1) \text{ or } (y_1 = 1, y_2 = 0)\}$$
$$= P(y_1 = 0)P(y_2 = 1)/$$
$$\{P(y_1 = 0)P(y_2 = 1) + P(y_1 = 1)P(y_2 = 0)\}$$
$$= \exp(\tau_2 + \tilde{c}'\tilde{\alpha} + x_2'\beta + \delta)/$$
$$\{\exp(\tau_2 + \tilde{c}'\tilde{\alpha} + x_2'\beta + \delta) + \exp(\tau_1 + \tilde{c}'\tilde{\alpha} + x_1'\beta + \delta)\}$$
$$= \exp(\Delta\tau + \Delta x'\beta)/\{1 + \exp(\Delta\tau + \Delta x'\beta)\}, \qquad (2.2)$$

dividing through by $\exp(\tau_1 + \tilde{c}'\tilde{\alpha} + x_1'\beta + \delta)$, where

$$\Delta\tau \equiv \tau_2 - \tau_1 \quad \text{and} \quad \Delta x_i \equiv x_{i2} - x_{i1};$$

in the second equality of (2.2), all three products of probabilities share the same denominator

$$\{1 + \exp(\tau_1/\sigma + \tilde{c}_i'\tilde{\alpha}/\sigma + x_{i1}'\beta/\sigma + \delta_i/\sigma)\}\cdot$$
$$\{1 + \exp(\tau_2/\sigma + \tilde{c}_i'\tilde{\alpha}/\sigma + x_{i2}'\beta/\sigma + \delta_i/\sigma)\} \qquad (2.3)$$

that drops out in the third equality. Subtract (2.2) from 1 to get

$$P(y_1 = 1, y_2 = 0|y_1 + y_2 = 1) = 1/\{1 + \exp(\Delta\tau + \Delta x'\beta)\}. \qquad (2.4)$$

The iid assumption in (2.1) is essential for (2.2). As already mentioned, because $\tilde{c}_i$ is removed along with δ_i, redefine δ_i as $\tilde{c}_i'\tilde{\alpha} + \delta_i$ to ignore $\tilde{c}_i'\tilde{\alpha}$ unless otherwise noted.

We can allow time-varying slopes in (2.4) by replacing $\Delta x'\beta$ with $x_{i2}'\beta_2 - x_{i1}'\beta_1$. This, however, seems at odds with conditional logit because (2.1) contains a substantial "constancy" assumption: the iid assumption for the error terms, σ not σ_t, and δ_i has no time-varying parameter attached to it. For conditional logit, we will consider either no time-varying parameters at all or only the intercept change over time as we did in (2.2).

Both probabilities in (2.2) and (2.4) are free of δ_i, and we can estimate $\Delta\tau$ and β by maximizing the likelihood function conditional on $y_{i1} + y_{i2} = 1$. Define

$$d_i = 1 \quad \text{if } y_{i1} + y_{i2} = 1, \quad \text{and 0 otherwise.}$$

The log-likelihood function to be maximized wrt $\Delta\tau$ and β corresponding to the regressors 1 and Δx, respectively, is

$$\sum_i d_i[y_{i1} \cdot \ln\{1/(1 + \exp(\Delta\tau + \Delta x_i'\beta))\} \qquad (2.5)$$

$$+ y_{i2} \cdot \ln\{\exp(\Delta\tau + \Delta x_i'\beta)/(1 + \exp(\Delta\tau + \Delta x_i'\beta))\}].$$

The log-likelihood function is almost the same as that for the cross-section logit. With $\Delta y_i \equiv y_{i2} - y_{i1}$,

$$d_i y_{i1} = 1 \Leftrightarrow y_{i1} = 1 \text{ and } y_{i2} = 0 \Leftrightarrow \Delta y_i = -1; \qquad (2.6)$$
$$d_i y_{i2} = 1 \Leftrightarrow y_{i1} = 0 \text{ and } y_{i2} = 1 \Leftrightarrow \Delta y_i = 1.$$

This shows that the log-likelihood function depends on $(x_{i1}, x_{i2}, y_{i1}, y_{i2})$ only through the first-differences Δx_i and Δy_i; conditional logit is an error-differencing type estimator.

The idea is in essence that $\sum_t y_{it}$ is a "sufficient statistic" (for δ_i): given x_{i1} and x_{i2}, the likelihood of (y_{i1}, y_{i2}) does not depend on δ_i when conditioned on $\sum_t y_{it}$; this idea of conditioning on a sufficient statistic appears in Rasch (1961) and Anderson (1970). The approach of conditioning on a sufficient statistic to remove δ_i will appear again later for limited response models other than binary.

Let $\gamma \equiv (\Delta\tau, \beta')'$ and let $g_N \equiv (\Delta\hat{\tau}, \hat{\beta}')'$ denote the conditional logit estimator. Chamberlain (1980) showed $\sqrt{N}(g_N - \gamma) \Rightarrow N(0, C_N)$ where

$$C_N \equiv [(1/N) \sum_i d_i \exp(\Delta\hat{\tau} + \Delta x_i'\hat{\beta})\{1 + \exp(\Delta\hat{\tau} + \Delta x_i'\hat{\beta})\}^{-2} \cdot$$
$$(1, \Delta x_i')'(1, \Delta x_i')]^{-1}. \qquad (2.7)$$

But the asymptotic variance can be estimated differently. To see this, rewrite (2.5) as

$$\sum_i [-d_i(y_{i1} + y_{i2}) \cdot \ln(1 + \exp(\Delta\tau + \Delta x_i'\beta)) + d_i y_{i2} \cdot (\Delta\tau + \Delta x_i'\beta)]$$
$$= \sum_i [-d_i \ln(1 + \exp(\Delta\tau + \Delta x_i'\beta)) + d_i y_{i2}(\Delta\tau + \Delta x_i'\beta)].$$

Differentiate this wrt γ to get the gradient

$$\sum_i [-d_i \exp(\Delta\tau + \Delta x_i'\beta)/(1 + \exp(\Delta\tau + \Delta x_i'\beta)) + d_i y_{i2}] \cdot (1, \Delta x_i')'$$
$$= \sum_i d_i [y_{i2} - \exp(\Delta\tau + \Delta x_i'\beta)/(1 + \exp(\Delta\tau + \Delta x_i'\beta))] \cdot (1, \Delta x_i')'.$$

Define the "score function" $s_i(\gamma)$ to get $\sum_i s_i(g_N) = 0$:

$$s_i(\gamma) \equiv d_i\{y_{i2} - \exp(\Delta\tau + \Delta x_i'\beta)/(1 + \exp(\Delta\tau + \Delta x_i'\beta))\} \cdot (1, \Delta x_i')'$$
$$= d_i\{y_{i2} - \pi(\gamma)\}(1, \Delta x_i')', \qquad (2.8)$$

where

$$\pi(\gamma) \equiv P(y_2 = 1 | d_i = 1, x_{i1}, x_{i2}, \delta_i) = \exp(\Delta\tau + \Delta x_i'\beta)$$
$$/(1 + \exp(\Delta\tau + \Delta x_i'\beta));$$

$s_i(\gamma)$ includes an "error term" $y_{i2} - \pi(\gamma)$. Observe

$$
\begin{aligned}
E\{s(\gamma)s(\gamma)'\} &= E[d\{y_2 - \pi(\gamma)\}^2(1, \Delta x_i')'(1, \Delta x_i')] \\
&= E[d\{y_2 - 2y_2\pi(\gamma) + \pi(\gamma)^2\}(1, \Delta x_i')'(1, \Delta x_i')] \\
&= E[d \cdot \pi(\gamma)\{1 - \pi(\gamma)\}(1, \Delta x_i')'(1, \Delta x_i')];
\end{aligned}
$$

this is the probability limit of the inverse of (2.7), as can be seen by rewriting $\exp(\Delta\tau + \Delta x_i'\beta)/\{1 + \exp(\Delta\tau + \Delta x_i'\beta)\}^2$ in (2.7) as $\{1 - \pi(\gamma)\}\pi(\gamma)$. Hence $\{(1/N) \sum_i s_i(g_N)s_i'(g_N)\}^{-1}$ can be used instead of (2.7). That is, (2.5) may be treated as the usual log-likelihood function in practice, except that no efficiency claim be made.

4.2.2   Remarks and an Empirical Example on Health Care Demand

The dynamics allowed by conditional logit is restricted in two ways. First, using a generic T, $u_{i1}, ..., u_{iT}$ are iid, and thus $v_{it} = \delta_i + u_{it}$, $t = 1, ..., T$, are allowed to be related only through δ_i. This is plausible for cross-section data with a group structure (equicorrelation), but not attractive otherwise because the serial correlation of v_{it} does not change at all over time. Second, u_{it} is independent of $(\delta_i, x_{i1}, ..., x_{iT})$, not just of (δ_i, x_{it}), or just of $(\delta_i, x_{i1}, ..., x_{it})$; using the same terminology as in the preceding chapters, these three independences are of the type EXO (strictly exogenous), CON (contemporaneous), and PRE(predetermined), respectively.

One disadvantage of the EXO in conditional logit is that, by constraining u_{it} to be independent not just of the past but also of the future regressors, we assume away economic agents who adjust the future x_{it} in view of the past u_{is}, $s < t$. Another disadvantage is that the lagged dependent variable $y_{i,t-1}$ is not allowed in x_{it}: if $y_{i,t-1}$ is in x_{it}, then u_{it} cannot be independent of $x_{i1}, ..., x_{iT}$, because y_{it} including u_{it} appears in $x_{i,t+1}$. The EXO assumption implies

$$
P(y_{it} = 1|\delta_i, x_{i1}, ..., x_{iT}) = P(y_{it} = 1|\delta_i, x_{it}). \tag{2.9}
$$

With or without the latent structure (2.1), this is called strict exogeneity, because if we define a "reduced form" error e_{it} as

$$
e_{it} \equiv y_{it} - P(y_{it} = 1|\delta_i, x_{it}), \tag{2.10}
$$

e_{it} is orthogonal to $x_{i1}, ..., x_{iT}$ under (2.9). Viewed somewhat differently, (2.9) is a "static relationship between x_{it} and y_{it} given δ_i": there is no dynamics between x_{it}'s and y_{it}'s once δ_i is fixed.

Chamberlain (1985) presents a conditional logit with $T \geq 4$ where the lagged dependent variable $y_{i,t-1}$ appears as the *only* regressor, which implies that y_{it} may depend on time invariants but not on time variants other than $y_{i,t-1}$. An empirical application appears in Corcoran and Hill (1985) on whether the current unemployment y_{it} depends on the past unemployment $y_{i,t-1}$ "truly or spuriously"; recall the discussion on dynamic models in the preceding chapter. A generalization of the conditional logit with a lagged response and other time-variants as regressors will be shown in the next section.

Now we present an empirical example using a data set from Health and Retirement Study. This data set, provided in the data appendix, is an abridged version of the data used in Lee and Kobayashi (2001). The sample of $N = 8484$ is for years 1992 and 1994 ($T = 2$), and for people born between 1931 and 1941 and their partners; see Lee and Kobayashi (2001) for more detail. The response variables are zero or positive hospitalization days (y_1), and zero or positive number of visits to doctor offices (y_2) per year. Table 4.1 shows the summary statistics for the regressor wave at 1:

TABLE 4.1 Summary Statistics for Regressor Wave at 1

	MEAN	SD	MIN	LQ	MED	UQ	MAX
age	55.31	5.49	23	52	55	59	82
job	0.69	0.46	0	0	1	1	1
income($1000, inc)	55.72	48.78	0	26.5	46.0	71.5	625
married (mar)	0.83	0.38	0	1	1	1	1
medicare ($care$)	0.058	0.23	0	0	0	0	1
medicaid ($caid$)	0.031	0.17	0	0	0	0	1
blue-hmo ($blue$)	0.722	0.45	0	1	1	0	1

In Table 4.1, LQ (UQ) is the lower (upper) quartile, job is a dummy variable (1 if working and 0 otherwise), married is a dummy for being married, and medicare, medicaid and blue-hmo are all health insurance dummies. Because $age_{i2} - age_{i1} = 2$ over the 2-year span for all i, we drop age_{it}; the regressor 1 then picks up $\Delta\tau + 2\beta_{age}$.

The conditional logit results for y_1 and y_2 are as follows:

	y_1: estimate (t-value)	y_2: estimate (t-value)
$\Delta\tau + 2\beta_{age}$	0.735 (12.06)	1.110 (19.09)
ln(inc)	0.062 (1.62)	0.044 (1.25)
job	−0.530 (−3.42)	0.236 (1.61)
mar	0.438 (1.59)	0.344 (1.17)
care	0.208 (1.00)	0.521 (1.55)
caid	0.111 (0.39)	0.368 (1.07)
blue	0.028 (0.14)	0.411 (2.54)
log-likelihood:	−848.628	−949.705

In the table, $\ln(\text{inc}_{it})$ is replaced by 0 if $\text{inc}_{it}=0$. For hospital days, *job* is significant at the 5% level with a negative effect, which may be biased due to the hospital days affecting *job*. For doctor visits, *blue* is significant. All insurance dummies gain in magnitude compared with hospital days, probably because there is more room for choice in doctor visits than in hospitalization. In $\Delta \tau + 2\beta_{\text{age}}$, it is likely that $2\beta_{\text{age}}$ is dominant.

One reason many estimates are not significant is that, despite the large N, not many variables including the response variables exhibit sufficient variations over the two years. Only 16% of the sample satisfy $y_1 + y_2 = 1$, and the proportion of the regressors changing over time is (the proportion that satisfy $y_1 + y_2 = 1$ additionally is in parentheses):

Note that mar, care, and caid have particularly small variations. Another application for conditional logit appears in the last section of this chapter.

4.2.3 Review of Kernel Nonparametric Estimation

Let h be a positive scalar depending on N. Assuming that $x_1, ..., x_N$ are iid random variables (rv) with density function $f(x)$, consider a $B(N, \pi)$ rv (binomial with N trials and π success probability):

$$\sum_{i=1}^{N} 1[|x_i - x_o| < h] \quad \text{where } \pi \equiv P(|x - x_o| < h) = P(x_o - h < x < x_o + h).$$
(2.11)

Then,

$$E(\sum_{i=1}^{N} 1[|x_i - x_o| < h]) = N \cdot \pi, \quad V(\sum_{i=1}^{N} 1[|x_i - x_o| < h]) = N \cdot \pi (1 - \pi).$$
(2.12)

Define

$$f_N(x_o) \equiv (1/N) \sum_{i=1}^{N} h^{-1} 1[|x_i - x_o|/h < 1]/2.$$

This is a nonparametric estimator for $f(x_o)$; in fact, this is just a "histogram" around x_o with the interval size $2h$.

Equation (2.12) implies

$$E\{f_N(x_o)\} = /2h, \quad V\{f_N(x_o)\} = (1-)/(4Nh^2)$$
$$= (/2h)(1-)(2Nh)^{-1}. \quad (2.13)$$

Let F denote the distribution function of x, three times continuously differentiable. With $\pi = F(x_o + h) - F(x_o - h)$, Taylor's expansion yields

$$\pi/2h \cong \{F(x_o) + f(x_o) \cdot h + f'(x_o) \cdot h^2/2 + f''(x_o)h^3/6\}/2h$$
$$-\{F(x_o) - f(x_o) \cdot h + f'(x_o) \cdot h^2/2 - f''(x_o)h^3/6\}/2h$$
$$= f(x_o) + f''(x_o) \cdot h^2/6. \quad (2.14)$$

Substitute this into (2.13) to get

$$E\{f_N(x_o)\} \cong f(x_o) + f''(x_o) \cdot h^2/6 \tag{2.15}$$
$$V\{f_N(x_o)\} \cong \{f(x_o) + f''(x_o) \cdot h^2/6\} \cdot (1 - \pi) \cdot (2Nh)^{-1}.$$

If $h \to 0$ and $Nh \to \infty$ as $N \to \infty$, then as $N \to \infty$,

$$E\{f_N(x_o)\} \to f(x_o), \quad V\{f_N(x_o)\} \to 0; \tag{2.16}$$

$h \to 0$ makes the bias $E\{f_N(x_o)\} - f(x_o)$ disappear, whereas $Nh \to \infty$ makes the variance disappear. This implies

$$f_N(x_o) \overset{p}{=} f(x_o). \tag{2.17}$$

The role of the indicator function $1[|x_i - x_o|/h < 1]$ in $f_N(x_o)$ is weighting the i-th observation: the weight is 1 if x_i falls within the h-distance from x_o and 0 otherwise. Generalizing this weighting idea, we can think of a smooth weight depending on $|x_i - x_o|$. Let x be now a $k \times 1$ vector; in this case, h-distance becomes h^k-distance (for example, the two dimensional analog of $1[|x_i - x_o| < h]$ is the rectangle of size $(2h)^2 = 4h^2$). A "kernel (nonparametric) density estimator" is based on the smooth weighting idea:

$$f_N(x_o) \equiv (Nh^k)^{-1} \sum_{i=1}^{N} K((x_i - x_o)/h) \tag{2.18}$$

where K (called a "kernel") is a smooth multivariate density symmetric about 0 such as the $N(0, I_k)$ density. Equation (2.18) includes the preceding $f_N(x_o)$ as a special case when $k = 1$ and $K(\cdot) = 1[|\cdot| < 1]/2$. Doing analogously to (2.14) to (2.17), we can show that $f_N(x_o) \overset{p}{=} f(x_o)$ for (2.18). Furthermore, if $Nh^k \to \infty$ and $Nh^{k+4} \to 0$ as $N \to \infty$, then

$$(Nh^k)^{1/2}\{\hat{f}(x_o) - f(x_o)\} \Rightarrow N(0, \ f(x_o) \int K^2(z)dz), \tag{2.19}$$

which can be used to construct (point-wise) confidence intervals for $f(x_o)$.
Other than the $1[\cdot]$ and $N(0, 1)$ kernel,

$$(3/4) \cdot (1 - z^2) \cdot 1[|z| < 1]: \text{ (trimmed) quadratic kernel,}$$
$$(15/16) \cdot (1 - z^2)^2 1[|z| < 1]: \text{ quartic or biweight kernel} \tag{2.20}$$

are popular univariate kernels. For $k > 1$, "product kernels" consisting of copies of univariate kernels, such as $\prod_{j=1}^{k} \phi(z_j)$ with ϕ being the $N(0, 1)$ density, are often used.

The scalar h is called a "bandwidth" or "smoothing parameter," whose role is analogous to that of the interval size in a histogram. If h is too small, there is no grouping (averaging), and $f_N(x_o)$ will be too jagged as x_o varies (small bias but large variance). If h is too large, $f_N(x_o)$ will show little variation (large bias but small variance). As in the interval size, there is no best rule for choosing h in practice. But a practical rule of thumb for choosing h is $h \cong \nu \cdot N^{-1/(k+4)}$ with, say, $0.5 \leq \nu \leq 2.5$ if k is 1 or 2 with all components of x standardized; for example., if $K(t) = \prod_{j=1}^{k} \phi(t_j)$ where $t = (t_1, ..., t_k)'$ is used, then,

$$K((x_i - x_o)/h) = \prod_{j=1}^{k} \phi((x_{ij} - x_{oj})/\{SD(x_j)\nu N^{-1/(k+4)}\}).$$

More discussion on choosing K and h is given next.

A kernel regression estimator $r_N(x_o)$ for $\rho(x_o)$ in $y_i = \rho(x_i) + u_i$ with $E(u|x) = 0 \Leftrightarrow E(y|x) = \rho(x)$ is

$$
\begin{aligned}
r_N(x_o) &\equiv (Nh^k)^{-1} \sum_{i=1}^{N} K((x_i - x_o)/h)y_i / \\
&\quad (Nh^k)^{-1} \sum_{i=1}^{N} K((x_i - x_o)/h) \qquad (2.21) \\
&= g_N(x_o)/f_N(x_o),
\end{aligned}
$$

where the numerator of $r_N(x_o)$ is defined as $g_N(x_o)$. Rewrite $r_N(x_o)$ as

$$\sum_{i=1}^{N} \{K((x_i - x_o)/h)/ \sum_{i=1}^{N} K((x_i - x_o)/h)\} \cdot y_i \qquad (2.22)$$

to see that $r_N(x_o)$ is a weighted average of y_i's where the weight is large if x_i is close to x_o and small otherwise.

Doing analogously for $f_N(x_o) \overset{p}{=} f(x_o)$, it can be shown that

$$g_N(x_o) \overset{p}{=} E(y|x_o) \cdot f(x_o), \qquad (2.23)$$

which implies, when combined with $f_N(x_o) \overset{p}{=} f(x_o)$,

$$r_N(x_o) \overset{p}{=} \rho(x_o). \qquad (2.24)$$

Analogously to (2.19),

$$(Nh^k)^{0.5}\{r_N(x_o) - \rho(x_o)\} \Rightarrow N(0, \ V(u|x_o) \int K(z)^2 dz/f(x_o)); \qquad (2.25)$$

$V(u|x_o) = E(y^2|x_o) - \{E(y|x_o)\}^2$ and $E(y^2|x_o)$ can be estimated replacing y_i in $r_N(x_o)$ with y_i^2.

To implement kernel estimation, one has to choose K and h. As for K, it is known that the choice of kernel makes little difference. But the story is quite different for h, for the choice of h makes a huge difference. When $k = 1$ or 2, other than the above rule of thumb, a good practical method to choose h is drawing $f_N(x)$ or $r_N(x)$ over a reasonable range for x and choosing h such that the curve estimate is not too smooth (if h is too big) nor too jagged (if h is too small).

If $k > 2$, this balancing act is hard to use. In this case, it is advisable to choose h such that

$$\sum_i \{y_i - r_{Ni}(x_i)\}^2 \tag{2.26}$$

is minimized where

$$r_{Ni}(x_i) \equiv \sum_{j=1, j \neq i}^{N} K((x_j - x_i)/h)y_j / \sum_{j=1, j \neq i}^{N} K((x_j - x_i)/h), \tag{2.27}$$

which is a "leave-one-out" estimator for $\rho(x_i)$. This method of choosing h is called a "cross-validation," which works well in practice. For $f(x)$, y_i is irrelevant, and a cross-validation minimand for h is

$$(N^2 h^k)^{-1} \sum_i \sum_j K^{(2)}((x_i - x_j)/h) - 2(N^2 h^k)^{-1} \sum_{i \neq j} K((x_i - x_j)/h), \tag{2.28}$$

where $K^{(2)}(a) \equiv \int K(a - m)K(m)dm$. The evaluation point x_o in $r_N(x_o)$ is arbitrary, whereas x_i is used for the evaluation point in $r_{Ni}(x_i)$.

4.3 CONDITIONAL LOGIT FOR $T \geq 3$

Continuing Section 4.2 on conditional logit with $T = 2$, this section discusses conditional logit with $T \geq 3$. With $T \geq 3$, there are at least three ways to proceed. The first is extending the conditional logit for $T = 2$ on $y_{i1} + y_{i2} \neq 0, 2$ to the conditional logit on $\sum_t y_{it} \neq 0, T$ (Chamberlain, 1980); that is, only the observations with y_{it} varying at least once across t are used. We call this "genuine" conditional logit for $T \geq 3$. The second is estimating each pair of two-periods separately and then imposing the restriction later with a MDE that the same parameter is estimated for each pair; this was in fact shown more or less in the preceding chapter. The third is setting up a single objective function consisting of all two-period conditional logit log-likelihoods. Also discussed in this section is Honoré and Kyriazidou's (2000b) conditional logit for $T \geq 4$ allowing for a lagged response in regressors.

4.3.1 Genuine Conditional Logit for $T \geq 3$

Assume $T = 3$ and $\tau_t = \tau$ for all t for a while, and define

$$d_{i1} \quad = \quad 1 \quad \text{if} \quad \sum_t y_{it} = 1, \quad \text{and 0 otherwise,} \tag{3.1}$$

$$d_{i2} \quad = \quad 1 \quad \text{if} \quad \sum_t y_{it} = 2, \quad \text{and 0 otherwise,}$$

$$x_i \quad \equiv \quad (x_{i1}, x_{i2}, x_{i3}) \Rightarrow \underset{3 \times 1}{x_i' \beta} = (x_{i1}'\beta, x_{i2}'\beta, x_{i3}'\beta)',$$

where x_{it}, $t = 1, 2, 3$, do not include any time-invariant components.

Given $d_{i1} = 1$, there are three possibilities for $y_i' \equiv (y_{i1}, y_{i2}, y_{i3})$:

$$(1, 0, 0), \quad (0, 1, 0), \quad (0, 0, 1). \tag{3.2}$$

Doing analogously to (2.2) and (2.3), the probability of observing a particular y_i given x_i, δ_i, and $d_{i1} = 1$ is

$$\begin{aligned} &\exp(y_i' \cdot x_i'\beta)/[\exp\{(1, 0, 0) \cdot x_i'\beta\} + \exp\{(0, 1, 0) \cdot x_i'\beta\} \\ &\qquad\qquad + \exp\{(0, 0, 1) \cdot x_i'\beta\}] \\ = \;&\exp(y_i' \cdot x_i'\beta)/\{\exp(x_{i1}'\beta) + \exp(x_{i2}'\beta) + \exp(x_{i3}'\beta)\}. \end{aligned} \tag{3.3}$$

Doing analogously, the conditional probability of observing a particular y_i given x_i, δ_i, and $d_{i2} = 1$ is

$$\begin{aligned} &\exp(y_i' \cdot x_i'\beta)/[\exp\{(1, 1, 0) \cdot x_i'\beta\} \\ &\qquad + \exp\{(1, 0, 1) \cdot x_i'\beta\} + \exp\{(0, 1, 1) \cdot x_i'\beta\}] \\ = \;&\exp(y_i' \cdot x_i'\beta)/\{\exp((x_{i1} + x_{i2})'\beta) \\ &\qquad + \exp((x_{i1} + x_{i3})'\beta) + \exp((x_{i2} + x_{i3})'\beta)\}. \end{aligned} \tag{3.4}$$

Hence, the conditional log-likelihood function to maximize for β is

$$\sum_i [d_{i1} \ln[\exp(y_i' \cdot x_i'\beta)/\{\exp(x_{i1}'\beta) + \exp(x_{i2}'\beta) + \exp(x_{i3}'\beta)\}] \tag{3.5}$$

$$+ d_{i2} \ln[\exp(y_i' \cdot x_i'\beta)/ \\ \{\exp((x_{i1} + x_{i2})'\beta) + \exp((x_{i1} + x_{i3})'\beta) + \exp((x_{i2} + x_{i3})'\beta)\}]].$$

From this, the score function s_i for β that is analogous to (2.8) can be obtained; s_i takes the form $d_{i1}(\cdot) + d_{i2}(\cdot)$. The asymptotic variance for $\sqrt{N}(b_N - \beta)$ with b_N being the estimator can be consistently estimated by $\{(1/N) \sum_i s_i s_i'\}^{-1}$. In practice, one may simply use numerical derivatives for s_i.

Allowing the time-varying intercept τ_t in (3.5) is straightforward: define $\Delta\tau_{21} \equiv \tau_2 - \tau_1$ and $\Delta\tau_{31} \equiv \tau_3 - \tau_1$, and replace $x_{i2}'\beta$ with $\Delta\tau_{21} + x_{i2}'\beta$ and $x_{i3}'\beta$ with $\Delta\tau_{31} + x_{i3}'\beta$. In (2.5), we could have used a log-likelihood analogous to (3.5) with $x'_{i1}\beta$ and $x'_{i2}\beta$ appearing instead of using $(1, \Delta x'_i)$ as the regressors; but $(1, \Delta x'_i)$ was used there for $T = 2$ to have the conditional logit reminiscent of the usual cross-section logit.

For a general $T \geq 3$, the log-likelihood function is

$$\sum_i \ln\{\exp(y'_i \cdot x'_i\beta)/ \sum_{\lambda \in G_i} \exp(\lambda' \cdot x'_i\beta)\} \tag{3.6}$$

where

$$G_i \equiv \{\lambda \equiv (\lambda_1, ..., \lambda_T)' | \lambda_t = 0 \text{ or } 1 \quad \text{and} \quad \sum_t \lambda_t = \sum_t y_{it}\}. \tag{3.7}$$

Here each i is classified depending on $\sum_t y_{it}$. For example, if $\sum_t y_{it} = 1$, then we can think of all possible sequences of $\{\lambda_t\}$ such that $\sum_t \lambda_t = 1$ analogously to (3.2). The denominator $\sum_{\lambda \in G_i} \exp(\lambda' \cdot x'_i\beta)$ is nothing but the sum of the possibilities corresponding to each $\{\lambda_t\}$; recall (3.3) and (3.4). If T is large, getting (3.6) can be cumbersome as one can guess from (3.5) with $T = 3$; for a large T, we study MDE in the following subsection.

4.3.2   MDE with Conditional Logits for $T = 3$

Turning to the second method, set $T = 3$ for a while. Suppose we estimate β twice using $t = 1, 2$ and $t = 2, 3$ respectively. Suppose τ_t is time variant whereas β is not. Then, denoting the slope parameters as μ_1 and μ_2, respectively for $t = 1, 2$ and $t = 2, 3$, we have the restriction

$$\begin{bmatrix} \Delta\tau_{21} \\ \mu_1 \\ \Delta\tau_{32} \\ \mu_2 \end{bmatrix} = \begin{bmatrix} 1 & 0 & 0 \\ 0 & 0 & I_{k_x} \\ 0 & 1 & 0 \\ 0 & 0 & I_{k_x} \end{bmatrix} \begin{bmatrix} \Delta\tau_{21} \\ \Delta\tau_{32} \\ \beta \end{bmatrix}, \tag{3.8}$$

where $\Delta\tau_{21} \equiv \tau_2 - \tau_1$, $\Delta\tau_{32} \equiv \tau_3 - \tau_2$, and k_x is the dimension of x_{it}. Denote the matrix with 1 and I_{k_x} as R, and define $\gamma_o \equiv (\Delta\tau_{21}, \Delta\tau_{32}, \beta')'$.

As explained in the early part of the preceding chapter, γ_o is estimated in MDE by minimizing

$$N \cdot (g_N - R \cdot g_o)' W_N^{-1} (g_N - R \cdot g_o) \tag{3.9}$$

wrt g_o, where g_N is the conditional logit estimator for $\tilde{\gamma} \equiv (\Delta\tau_{21}, \mu'_1, \Delta\tau_{32}, \mu'_2)'$ obtained by applying the conditional logit to the two pairs separately, and W_N is a consistent estimator for the asymptotic variance of $\sqrt{N}(g_N - \tilde{\gamma})$.

Let s_{i1} and s_{i2} denote the score functions for the pair $t = 1, 2$ and $t = 2, 3$, respectively. Then we can use

$$W_N = (1/N) \sum_i \eta_i \eta'_i \quad \text{where } \eta_i \equiv (\eta'_{i1}, \eta'_{i2})', \tag{3.10}$$

$$\eta_{i1} \equiv ((1/N) \sum_i s_{i1} s'_{i1})^{-1} \cdot s_{i1} \quad \text{and} \quad \eta_{i2} \equiv ((1/N) \sum_i s_{i2} s'_{i2})^{-1} \cdot s_{i2}.$$

The solution g_{mde} for (3.9) and its asymptotic distribution are

$$g_{mde} = (R'W_N^{-1}R)^{-1} \cdot R'W_N^{-1}g_N,$$

and

$$\sqrt{N}(g_{mde} - \gamma_o) \Rightarrow N(0, (R'W_N^{-1}R)^{-1}). \qquad (3.11)$$

The minimand evaluated at g_{mde} can be used as a test statistic for $H_o : \mu_1 = \mu_2$ owing to

$$N \cdot (g_N - R \cdot g_{mde})'W_N^{-1}(g_N - R \cdot g_{mde}) \Rightarrow \chi^2_{k_x}. \qquad (3.12)$$

If the intercept is time invariant, then replace (3.8) with

$$\begin{bmatrix} \mu_1 \\ \mu_2 \end{bmatrix} = \begin{bmatrix} I_{k_x} \\ I_{k_x} \end{bmatrix} \cdot \beta, \qquad (3.13)$$

and the rest of the steps are analogous to (3.10) to (3.12).

For a general $T \geq 3$, make many two-period pairs, and estimate $\Delta \tau_{t,t-1}$ and β for each pair. Then (3.8) can be extended adding more $\Delta \tau_{t,t-1}$ and μ_{t-1}. An empirical example with $T = 3$ appears in the last section.

4.3.3 SUM-Type Approach and Remarks

The third way for $T \geq 3$ is a "SUM-type" approach that sums up all two period conditional logit log-likelihoods. Define

$$d_{ist} = 1 \quad \text{if } y_{is} + y_{it} = 1, \text{ and } 0 \text{ otherwise} \quad \forall s < t,$$
$$\Delta \tau_{ts} \equiv \tau_t - \tau_s \quad \text{and} \quad \Delta x_{its} \equiv x_{it} - x_{is}.$$

Maximize

$$\sum_i \sum_{s<t} d_{ist}[y_{is} \cdot \ln\{1/(1 + \exp(\Delta \tau_{ts} + \Delta x'_{its}\beta))\} \qquad (3.14)$$

$$+y_{it} \cdot \ln\{\exp(\Delta \tau_{ts} + \Delta x'_{its}\beta)/(1 + \exp(\Delta \tau_{ts} + \Delta x'_{its}\beta))\}]$$

$$\equiv \sum_i q_i(\gamma)$$

wrt $\gamma \equiv (\Delta \tau_{ts}, \forall s < t, s, t = 1, ..., T, \beta')'$. Following the "extremum estimator" framework (for example, Lee, 1996), this estimator can be shown to be $\sqrt{N}$-consistent and asymptotically normal; the asymptotic variance can be estimated consistently by

$$\{(1/N) \sum_i q_{i\gamma\gamma}(\hat{\gamma})\}^{-1} \cdot (1/N) \sum_i q_{i\gamma}(\hat{\gamma})q_{i\gamma}(\hat{\gamma})' \cdot \{(1/N) \sum_i q_{i\gamma\gamma}(\hat{\gamma})\}^{-1}, \qquad (3.15)$$

where

$$q_{i\gamma}(\hat{\gamma}) \equiv \partial q_i(\gamma)/\partial\gamma|_{\gamma=\hat{\gamma}} \quad \text{and} \quad q_{i\gamma\gamma}(\hat{\gamma}) \equiv \partial q_i(\gamma)/\partial\gamma\,\partial\gamma'|_{\gamma=\hat{\gamma}}.$$

For unbalanced panel with varying $T_i, i = 1, ..., N$, Honoré and Kyriazidou (2000a) have suggested a weighting by T_i^{-1} for the SUM type objective function; for (3.14), this idea translates into

$$\sum_i q_i(\gamma)/T_i. \tag{3.16}$$

The reasoning for this can be seen by comparing two individuals with $T_1 = 2$ and $T_2 = 3$: whereas the first person contributes only one term to $q_i(\gamma)$ for the time sequence $1 < 2$, the second person contributes three terms for $1 < 2$, $1 < 3$ and $2 < 3$. Dividing $q_i(\gamma)$ by T_i will alleviate this type of "unfair" treatment. Pursuing the idea further, because a person with T_i observations will be used $\binom{T_i}{2}$ times, one may choose to use

$$\sum_i q_i(\gamma)/\binom{T_i}{2}. \tag{3.17}$$

The three methods for $T \geq 3$ have pros and cons. The first method is likely to be the most efficient, but also the most inconvenient for a large T because we have to consider all possible combinations for a given value of $\sum_t y_{it}$. The third is likely to be the least efficient, because the score functions are summed up, resulting in a SUM type moment condition; also note that the same segments of $\tau_t - \tau_1$ are repeatedly estimated as $\Delta\tau_{ts}$ $\forall s < t$. But the third may be the most convenient: there is no grouping of the data depending on $\sum_t y_{it}$ as in the first and no second step as in the second. The second is likely to be intermediate both in terms of efficiency and convenience. In the last empirical section of this chapter, the second MDE method will be used.

Chamberlain (1984) applied conditional logit to married females' work decision using a sample with $N = 924$ and $T = 4$ from the Panel Study of Income Dynamics (PSID). The time-variant regressors are the number of preschool children and the number of children younger than age 18 living in the family unit. He found that, compared with the cross-section logit, conditional logit gives larger estimates in magnitude, which is somewhat surprising because controlling for δ_i usually reduces the magnitude of estimates as noted in the preceding chapter for long-run (for cross-section) versus short-run (for panel) effects.

For panel ODR, the MDE as in the second method can be employed. For example, if y_{it} takes $0, 1, 2$, then collapse y_{it} into binary responses: $(0, 1)$ to 0 and 2 to 1, or 0 to 0 and $(1, 2)$ to 1. We can estimate the parameters for each binary response, and then impose the restriction that the same slope parameters are estimated for each binary response model. It is easy to show that δ_i does not drop out as in (2.2) for ODR under logistic distribution; namely, there is no "conditional ordered logit for related effect."

4.3.4 Lagged Response as a Regressor

Earlier we mentioned that Chamberlain (1985) showed conditional logit with a lagged response as the only regressor when $T \geq 4$. Honoré and Kyriazidou

(2000b) proposed a conditional logit under $T \geq 4$ that allows other regressors as well by conditioning on

$$y_{i2} + y_{i3} = 1 \quad and \quad x_{i3} = x_{i4}.$$

But the estimator requires u_{it} to be iid logistic over time and be independent of $y_{i0}, \delta_i, \tilde{c}_i$, and $x_{i1}, ..., x_{iT}$.

To see the main idea, let

$$P(y_{i1} = 1|x_{i2}, ..., x_{iT}, \delta_i) \equiv p_1; \quad for \ t = 2, ..., T,$$
$$P(y_{it} = 1|x_{i2}, ..., x_{iT}, \delta_i, y_{i1}, ..., y_{i,t-1})$$
$$= \exp(\alpha y_{i,t-1} + x'_{it}\beta + \delta_i)/\{1 + \exp(\alpha y_{i,t-1} + x'_{it}\beta + \delta_i)\},$$

where the first period model is not specified. Now consider two events

$$A \equiv \{y_{i1} = d_1, y_{i2} = 0, y_{i3} = 1, y_{i4} = d_4\}$$

and

$$B \equiv \{y_{i1} = d_1, y_{i2} = 1, y_{i3} = 0, y_{i4} = d_4\};$$

the two events differ only in the middle two variables y_{i2} and y_{i3}, and this points to a sort of conditional logit using $x_{i3} - x_{i2}$ and $y_{i3} - y_{i2}$. Observe

$$P(A|x_{i2}, ..., x_{iT}, \delta_i) = p_1^{d_1}(1 - p_1)^{1-d_1} \cdot 1/\{1 + \exp(\alpha d_1 + x'_{i2}\beta + \delta_i)\} \cdot$$
$$\exp(x'_{i3}\beta + \delta_i)/\{1 + \exp(x'_{i3}\beta + \delta_i)\} \cdot$$
$$\exp(d_4(\alpha + x'_{i4}\beta + \delta_i))/\{1 + \exp(\alpha + x'_{i4}\beta + \delta_i)\},$$

which has four terms on the right-hand side. The first term is for y_{i1}, the second term is for $(y_{i2} = 0)|y_{i1}$, the third term is for $(y_{i3} = 1)|(y_{i2} = 0)$, and the fourth term is for $y_{i4}|(y_{i3} = 1)$. Analogously, observe

$$P(B|x_{i2}, ..., x_{iT}, \delta_i) = p_1^{d_1}(1 - p_1)^{1-d_1} \cdot$$
$$\exp(\alpha d_1 + x'_{i2}\beta + \delta_i)/\{1 + \exp(\alpha d_1 + x'_{i2}\beta + \delta_i)\} \cdot$$
$$1/\{1 + \exp(\alpha + x'_{i3}\beta + \delta_i)\} \cdot$$
$$\exp(d_4(x'_{i4}\beta + \delta_i))/\{1 + \exp(x'_{i4}\beta + \delta_i)\}.$$

The conditional logit proceeds with $P(A|x_{i2}, ..., x_{iT}, \delta_i, A \cup B)$ and $P(B|x_{i2}, ..., x_{iT}, \delta_i, A \cup B)$, but there is a problem. Recall (2.2) and (2.3) where the probabilties share the same denominator which then drops out in the conditioning. Define A_0, A_1, B_0, and B_1 such that $P(A|x_{i2}, ..., x_{iT}, \delta_i) = A_0/A_1$ and $P(B|x_{i2}, ..., x_{iT}, \delta_i) = B_0/B_1$. Although $A_1 \neq B_1$, if $x_{i3} = x_{i4}$, then $A_1 = B_1$, which is the key idea. Under $x_{i3} = x_{i4}$, we just have to look at $A_0/(A_0 + B_0)$ and $B_0/(A_0 + B_0)$ consisting of the numerators only; in the two ratios, δ_i drops out, and we get

$$P(A|x_{i2}, ..., x_{iT}, \delta_i, A \cup B, x_{i3} = x_{i4}) = 1/\{1 + \exp(\alpha(d_1 - d_4) + (x_{i2} - x_{i3})'\beta)\}.$$

Hence, Honoré and Kyriazidou's (2000b) logit is conditioned on $x_{i3} = x_{i4}$ as well as on $y_{i2} + y_{i3} = 1$.

When x_{it} is discrete, the estimator maximizes

$$\sum_i 1[y_{i2} + y_{i3} = 1] \cdot 1[x_{i3} = x_{i4}] \cdot \ln[\exp\{a(y_{i1} - y_{i4}) \qquad (3.18)$$

$$+ (x_{i2} - x_{i3})'b\}^{y_{i2}} / \{1 + \exp(a(y_{i1} - y_{i4}) + (x_{i2} - x_{i3})'b)\}]$$

wrt $g \equiv (a, b')'$. It is $\sqrt{N}$-consistent for $\gamma \equiv (\alpha, \beta')'$ and asymptotically normal. The asymptotic variance can be found doing analogously to the conditional logit with $T = 2$; in practice, the score function s_i can be obtained with numerical derivatives, and $\{(1/N) \sum_i s_i s_i'\}^{-1}$ can be used for the asymptotic variance.

When x_{it} is continuous, however, $P(x_{i3} = x_{i4}) = 0$. In this case, they propose to maximize

$$\sum_i 1[y_{i2} + y_{i3} = 1] \cdot K((x_{i3} - x_{i4})/h) \cdot \ln[\exp\{a(y_{i1} - y_{i4}) \quad (3.19)$$

$$(x_{i2} - x_{i3})'b\}^{y_{i2}} / \{1 + \exp(a(y_{i1} - y_{i4}) + (x_{i2} - x_{i3})'b)\}],$$

where $K(\cdot)$ is a k-variate kernel (to simplify notations, assume x_{it} is a $k \times 1$ vector only in this paragraph) and h is a bandwidth. The resulting estimator is $(Nh^k)^{1/2}$-consistent with the asymptotic variance matrix $J^{-1}VJ^{-1}$: defining $x_{i34} \equiv x_{i3} - x_{i4}$ and $z_i \equiv (y_{i1} - y_{i4}, (x_{i2} - x_{i3})')'$ and denoting the density for x_{i34} as $f(\cdot)$,

$$J \equiv f(0) \cdot E\{1[y_2 \neq y_3] \cdot \exp(z'\gamma)/(1 + \exp(z'\gamma))^2 \cdot \qquad (3.20)$$

$$zz'|x_{34} = 0\},$$

$$V \equiv \int K^2(v)dv \cdot f(0) \cdot E[1[y_2 \neq y_3] \cdot$$

$$\{y_2 - \exp(z'\gamma)/(1 + \exp(z'\gamma))\}^2 \cdot zz'|x_{34} = 0].$$

Consistent estimates of J and V are, respectively,

$$J_N \equiv (Nh^k)^{-1} \sum_i K(x_{i34}/h) \cdot 1[y_{i2} \neq y_{i3}] \cdot$$

$$\exp(z_i'g_N)/(1 + \exp(z_i'g_N))^2 \cdot z_i z_i', \qquad (3.21)$$

$$V_N \equiv (Nh^k)^{-1} \sum_i K^2(x_{i34}/h) \cdot 1[y_{i2} \neq y_{i3}]$$

$$\{y_{i2} - \exp(z_i'g_N)/(1 + \exp(z_i'g_N))\}^2 z_i z_i'.$$

For (3.18) or (3.19) to work, $x_{i3} - x_{i4}$ should have some probability mass around 0, which rules out time dummies as well as age in x_{it}. Honoré and Kyriazidou (2000b) have also proposed a semiparametric version based upon Manski's (1987) estimator, whose asymptotic distribution is not available, however. They also showed an extension for panel multinomial choice where the current choice depends on the previous choice. An application appears in Chintagunta *et al.* (2001).

4.4 PANEL PROBIT

The preceding section introduced conditional logit. In this section, we study panel probit for related effect. There are a couple of different versions for panel probit, but we will examine closely Chamberlain's (1980, 1984) MDE-based estimator under strict exogeneity in Subsection 4.4.1, and we will then take a quick look at other panel probits of Avery *et al.* (1983) in Subsection 4.4.2, and Arellano and Carrasco (1999) in Subsection 4.4.3. The reader may want to review the section on MDE for related effect in Chapter 3 before reading Subsection 4.4.1. Unlike conditional logit, where the logit form was essential to get rid of δ_i by conditioning, the normality assumption does not play a key role in panel probit; it can be easily replaced by another known distribution.

Before we embark on the task, recall the cross-section binary response model in the beginning of Subsection 4.2.1 with the error term distribution replaced by

$$P(u_i/\sigma \leq \lambda) = \Phi(\lambda)$$

where

$\Phi(\cdot)$ is the $N(0, 1)$ distribution function, $\sigma = \mathrm{SD}(u_i)$.

Because

$$P(y_i = 1|x_i) = P(u_i/\sigma \geq -x_i'\beta/\sigma) = P(u_i/\sigma \leq x_i'\beta/\sigma) = \Phi(x_i'\beta/\sigma),$$

we maximize the probit log-likelihood function

$$\sum_i [(1 - y_1) \ln\{1 - \Phi(x_i'a)\} + y_i \ln\{\Phi(x_i'a)\}]$$

wrt a to obtain the cross-section probit for $\alpha \equiv \beta/\sigma = (\beta_1/\sigma, ..., \beta_k/\sigma)'$.

4.4.1 Panel Probit with MDE

Turning to panel probit, assume that

$$\delta_i = \zeta_o + \tilde{c}_i'\zeta_{\tilde{c}} + x_{i1}'\zeta_1 + \cdots + x_{iT}'\zeta_T + \varepsilon_i, \qquad (4.1)$$

and that ε_i follows a normal distribution independently of $(\tilde{c}_i, x_{i1}, ..., x_{iT})$; the unit-specific effect is a linear function of the regressors. Insert (4.1) into (1.1) to get

$$y_{it}^* = \tau_t + \zeta_o + \tilde{c}_i'(\tilde{\alpha} + \zeta_{\tilde{c}}) + x_{it}'(\beta + \zeta_t) + \sum_{j \neq t} x_{ij}'\zeta_j + \varepsilon_i + u_{it}. \qquad (4.2)$$

Divide both sides by $\sigma_t \equiv \mathrm{SD}(\varepsilon_i + u_{it})$ to get

$$y_{it}^*/\sigma_t = (\tau_t + \zeta_o)/\sigma_t + \tilde{c}_i'(\tilde{\alpha} + \zeta_{\tilde{c}})/\sigma_t + x_{it}'(\beta + \zeta_t)/\sigma_t \qquad (4.3)$$
$$+ \sum_{j \neq t} x_{ij}'\zeta_j/\sigma_t + (\varepsilon_i + u_{it})/\sigma_t.$$

Assuming a joint normality for $v_{it} \equiv \varepsilon_i + u_{it}$, $t = 1, ..., T$, which are independent of $(\tilde{c}_i, x_{i1}, ..., x_{iT})$, one can apply a multivariate probit MLE to estimate all parameters at the same time. If $u_{i1}, ..., u_{iT}$ are independent, then the probit MLE is not difficult to implement, because $v_{i1}, ..., v_{iT}$ are independent given the regressors and ε_i, and ε_i is taken care of by one-dimensional integration of the conditional log-likelihood function wrt ε_i. If $u_{i1}, ..., u_{iT}$ are dependent, however, then the probit MLE is computationally burdensome even for $T = 3$. In this case, each wave can be estimated by cross-section probit, and MDE can be invoked to impose cross-equation restrictions. We explain this convenient approach in the following. Unless otherwise mentioned, we will use the term "panel probit" for this version with MDE, whereas "probit MLE" will be used for the computationally burdensome multivariate probit MLE.

Set $T = 2$ for a while and denote the probit parameters for 1, $\tilde{c}_i$, x_{i1}, and x_{i2} in the t-th wave as χ_{t1}, $\chi_{t\tilde{c}}$, π_{t1}, and π_{t2}, respectively:

$$
\begin{aligned}
\chi_{11} &= (\tau_1 + \zeta_o)/\sigma_1, & \chi_{1\tilde{c}} &= (\tilde{\alpha} + \zeta_{\tilde{c}})/\sigma_1, & (4.4) \\
\chi_{21} &= (\tau_2 + \zeta_o)/\sigma_2, & \chi_{2\tilde{c}} &= (\tilde{\alpha} + \zeta_{\tilde{c}})/\sigma_2, \\
\pi_{11} &= (\beta + \zeta_1)/\sigma_1, & \pi_{12} &= \zeta_2/\sigma_1, \\
\pi_{21} &= \zeta_1/\sigma_2, & \pi_{22} &= (\beta + \zeta_2)/\sigma_2.
\end{aligned}
$$

Call χ_{t1}, $\chi_{t\tilde{c}}$ and π_{tj}, $j, t = 1, 2$, the "reduced form" parameters.
Observe

$$
\pi_{11} + \pi_{12} = (\beta + \zeta_1 + \zeta_2)/\sigma_1 \quad \text{and} \quad \pi_{21} + \pi_{22} = (\beta + \zeta_1 + \zeta_2)/\sigma_2. \quad (4.5)
$$

The ratio of a component in $\pi_{11} + \pi_{12}$ and the corresponding component in $\pi_{21} + \pi_{22}$ identifies

$$
\rho \equiv \sigma_2/\sigma_1.
$$

Also observe

$$
\begin{aligned}
\chi_{21}\rho &= (\tau_2 + \zeta_o)/\sigma_1, & \pi_{11} - \pi_{21}\rho &= \beta/\sigma_1, \\
\pi_{21}\rho &= \zeta_1/\sigma_1, & \pi_{12} &= \zeta_2/\sigma_1. & (4.6)
\end{aligned}
$$

Define the identified "structural form" parameters in the MDE:

$$
\vartheta \equiv (\rho, (\tau_1 + \zeta_o)/\sigma_1, (\tau_2 + \zeta_o)/\sigma_1, (\tilde{\alpha} + \zeta_{\tilde{c}})'/\sigma_1, \beta'/\sigma_1, \zeta_1'/\sigma_1, \zeta_2'/\sigma_1)'.
$$
$$(4.7)$$

Although we identified ρ using the reduced-form coefficients of time variants, we can identify ρ also by using a ratio of an element in $\chi_{1\tilde{c}}$ and the corresponding element in $\chi_{2\tilde{c}}$.

Rewrite (4.4) into a vector equation with the identified parameters ϑ:

$$
\theta \equiv
\begin{bmatrix}
\chi_{11} \\
\chi_{1\tilde{c}} \\
\pi_{11} \\
\pi_{12} \\
\chi_{21} \\
\chi_{2\tilde{c}} \\
\pi_{21} \\
\pi_{22}
\end{bmatrix}
=
\begin{bmatrix}
(\tau_1 + \zeta_o)/\sigma_1 \\
(\tilde{\alpha} + \zeta_{\tilde{c}})/\sigma_1 \\
(\beta + \zeta_1)/\sigma_1 \\
\zeta_2/\sigma_1 \\
\{(\tau_2 + \zeta_o)/\sigma_1\}/\rho \\
\{(\tilde{\alpha} + \zeta_{\tilde{c}})/\sigma_1\}/\rho \\
(\zeta_1/\sigma_1)/\rho \\
\{(\beta + \zeta_2)/\sigma_1\}/\rho
\end{bmatrix}
\equiv \psi(\vartheta). \tag{4.8}
$$

Set $\sigma_1 = 1$ ($\Rightarrow \rho = \sigma_2$) to simplify notations from now on.
The MDE for ϑ is obtained by minimizing

$$
N \cdot \{\theta_N - \psi(\hat{\vartheta})\}' \Omega_N^{-1} \{\theta_N - \psi(\hat{\vartheta})\} \tag{4.9}
$$

wrt $\hat{\vartheta}$ where $\sqrt{N}(\theta_N - \theta) \Rightarrow N(0, \Omega_N)$. Then we get

$$
\sqrt{N}(\hat{\vartheta} - \vartheta) \Rightarrow N(0, \{\psi_\vartheta(\vartheta)' \Omega_N^{-1} \psi_\vartheta(\vartheta)\}^{-1}),
$$
$$
\text{with } \psi_\vartheta(\vartheta) \equiv \partial\psi(\hat{\vartheta})/\partial\hat{\vartheta}'|_{\hat{\vartheta}=\vartheta}; \tag{4.10}
$$

the matrix $\psi_\vartheta' = (\partial\psi/\partial\rho, \partial\psi/\partial(\tau_1 + \zeta_o), ..., \partial\psi/\partial\zeta_2')'$ is (to prevent any confusion, we show the dimensions of all zero matrices)

$$
\begin{bmatrix}
0 & 0_{1 \times k_{\tilde{c}}} & 0_{1 \times k_x} & 0_{1 \times k_x} & -\tau_2/\rho^2 & -(\tilde{\alpha} + \zeta_{\tilde{c}})'/\rho^2 & -\zeta_1'/\rho^2 & -(\beta + \zeta_2)'/\rho^2 \\
1 & 0_{1 \times k_{\tilde{c}}} & 0_{1 \times k_x} & 0_{1 \times k_x} & 0 & 0_{1 \times k_{\tilde{c}}} & 0_{1 \times k_x} & 0_{1 \times k_x} \\
0 & 0_{1 \times k_{\tilde{c}}} & 0_{1 \times k_x} & 0_{1 \times k_x} & 1/\rho & 0_{1 \times k_{\tilde{c}}} & 0_{1 \times k_x} & 0_{1 \times k_x} \\
0_{k_{\tilde{c}} \times 1} & I_{k_{\tilde{c}}} & 0_{k_{\tilde{c}} \times k_x} & 0_{k_{\tilde{c}} \times k_x} & 0_{k_{\tilde{c}} \times 1} & I_{k_{\tilde{c}}}/\rho & 0_{k_{\tilde{c}} \times k_x} & 0_{k_{\tilde{c}} \times k_x} \\
0_{k_x \times 1} & 0_{k_x \times k_{\tilde{c}}} & I_{k_x} & 0_{k_x \times k_x} & 0_{k_x \times 1} & 0_{k_x \times k_{\tilde{c}}} & 0_{k_x \times k_x} & I_{k_x}/\rho \\
0_{k_x \times 1} & 0_{k_x \times k_{\tilde{c}}} & I_{k_x} & 0_{k_x \times k_x} & 0_{k_x \times 1} & 0_{k_x \times k_{\tilde{c}}} & I_{k_x}/\rho & 0_{k_x \times k_x} \\
0_{k_x \times 1} & 0_{k_x \times k_{\tilde{c}}} & 0_{k_x \times k_x} & I_{k_x} & 0_{k_x \times 1} & 0_{k_x \times k_{\tilde{c}}} & 0_{k_x \times k_x} & I_{k_x}/\rho
\end{bmatrix}.
$$
$$\tag{4.11}$$

To see the minimization process, rewrite the minimand as

$$
\theta_N' \Omega_N^{-1} \theta_N + \psi(\hat{\vartheta})' \Omega_N^{-1} \psi(\hat{\vartheta}) - \psi(\hat{\vartheta})' \Omega_N^{-1} \theta_N - \theta_N' \Omega_N^{-1} \psi(\hat{\vartheta}).
$$

Differentiate this wrt $\hat{\vartheta}$ to get the first-order condition

$$
2 \cdot \psi_\vartheta(\hat{\vartheta})' \Omega_N^{-1} \psi(\hat{\vartheta}) - 2 \cdot \psi_\vartheta(\hat{\vartheta})' \Omega_N^{-1} \theta_N = 2\psi_\vartheta(\hat{\vartheta})' \Omega_N^{-1} \cdot \{\psi(\hat{\vartheta}) - \theta_N\} = 0
$$
$$
\Leftrightarrow \psi_\vartheta(\hat{\vartheta})' \Omega_N^{-1} \{\psi(\vartheta) + \psi_\vartheta(\vartheta^*)(\hat{\vartheta} - \vartheta) - \theta_N\} = 0
$$

where ψ_ϑ is continuous and $\vartheta^* \in (\hat{\vartheta}, \vartheta)$. Solve this for $\hat{\vartheta}$ to get

$$
\hat{\vartheta} = \vartheta + \{\psi_\vartheta(\hat{\vartheta})' \Omega_N^{-1} \psi_\vartheta(\vartheta^*)\}^{-1} \cdot \psi_\vartheta(\hat{\vartheta})' \Omega_N^{-1} \{\theta_N - \psi(\vartheta)\}. \tag{4.12}
$$

From this, an iterative algorithm follows:

$$
\vartheta_1 = \vartheta_0 + \{\psi_\vartheta(\vartheta_0)' \Omega_N^{-1} \psi_\vartheta(\vartheta_0)\}^{-1} \cdot \psi_\vartheta(\vartheta_0)' \Omega_N^{-1} \{\theta_N - \psi(\vartheta_0)\}; \tag{4.13}
$$

update ϑ_0 and repeat this until convergence (for example, until the change in the minimand becomes negligible). (4.12) also shows the rationale for (4.10):

$$
\begin{aligned}
\sqrt{N}(\hat{\vartheta} - \vartheta) &= \{\psi_\vartheta(\hat{\vartheta})'\Omega_N^{-1}\psi_\vartheta(\vartheta^*)\}^{-1} \cdot \psi_\vartheta(\hat{\vartheta})'\Omega_N^{-1}\sqrt{N}\{\theta_N - \theta\} \\
&= \{\psi_\vartheta(\vartheta)'\Omega_N^{-1}\psi_\vartheta(\vartheta)\}^{-1} \cdot \psi_\vartheta(\vartheta)'\Omega_N^{-1}\sqrt{N}\{\theta_N - \theta\} + o_p(1) \\
&\Rightarrow N(0, \{\psi_\vartheta(\vartheta)'\Omega_N^{-1}\psi_\vartheta(\vartheta)\}^{-1})
\end{aligned}
\tag{4.14}
$$

Analogously to (4.7), when $T = 3$, the MDE identifies

$$
\rho_2, \rho_3, (\tau_t + \zeta_o)/\sigma_1, t = 1, 2, 3, (\alpha + \zeta_c)/\sigma_1, \beta/\sigma_1, \zeta_1/\sigma_1, \zeta_2/\sigma_1, \zeta_3/\sigma_1
\tag{4.15}
$$

where $\rho_2 \equiv \sigma_2/\sigma_1$ and $\rho_3 \equiv \sigma_3/\sigma_1$. Setting $\sigma_1 = 1$ ($\Rightarrow \rho_2 = \sigma_2$ and $\rho_3 = \sigma_3$) and redefining τ_t as $\tau_t + \zeta_o$, the analog for (4.4) is

$$
\begin{bmatrix}
\chi_{11} & \chi_{1\bar{c}}' & \pi_{11}' & \pi_{12}' & \pi_{13}' \\
\chi_{21} & \chi_{2\bar{c}}' & \pi_{21}' & \pi_{22}' & \pi_{23}' \\
\chi_{31} & \chi_{3\bar{c}}' & \pi_{31}' & \pi_{32}' & \pi_{33}'
\end{bmatrix} =
$$

$$
\begin{bmatrix}
\tau_1 & (\tilde{\alpha} + \zeta_{\bar{c}}) & (\beta + \zeta_1)' & \zeta_2' & \zeta_3' \\
\tau_2/\rho_2 & (\tilde{\alpha} + \zeta_{\bar{c}})/\rho_2 & \zeta_1'/\rho_2 & (\beta + \zeta_2)'/\rho_2 & \zeta_3'/\rho_2 \\
\tau_3/\rho_3 & (\tilde{\alpha} + \zeta_{\bar{c}})/\rho_3 & \zeta_1'/\rho_3 & \zeta_2'/\rho_3 & (\beta + \zeta_3)'/\rho_3
\end{bmatrix}.
$$

The last three columns of the matrix on the right-hand side can be written as

$$
\text{diag}(1, \rho_2^{-1}, \rho_3^{-1}) \cdot \{I_3 \otimes \beta' + 1_3 \cdot (\zeta_1', \zeta_2', \zeta_3')\}.
\tag{4.16}
$$

Turning back to the $T = 2$ case, the practical difficulty of the MDE stems from the fact that $\psi(\vartheta)$ in (4.8) is a nonlinear function of ϑ. The algorithm (4.13) is based on a linear approximation; a poor linear approximation can lead to an unstable result. The source of the nonlinearity is ρ (or σ_2) residing in the denominators. In the empirical application section at the end of this chapter, we discuss how to avoid this problem.

In the probit MLE using all waves together, $COR(v_{i1}, v_{i2})$ is identified in addition to ϑ, because the variance matrix for v_{i1} and v_{i2} ought to be estimated along with ϑ; in both the probit MLE and the panel probit with MDE, the coefficients of time invariants are not identified. The panel probit with MDE is not efficient, for its first-stage cross-section probit is not efficient ignoring $COR(v_{i1}, v_{i2})$.

Chamberlain (1984) applied panel probit to the same data set to which conditional logit was applied. In the preceding chapter, we mentioned that estimators controlling for δ_i are likely to be smaller in magnitude than those that do not. This indeed was the case in the Chamberlain's application of panel probit, whereas the opposite happened for conditional logit as already mentioned.

In Lechner (1995), a binary response equation for being self-employed or not is estimated by panel probit with $N = 1926$ and $T = 6$ from the German

Socio-Economic Panel; Lechner (1995) also suggested specification tests for panel probit. Jakubson (1988) estimated a censored (observed if positive and 0 otherwise) female labor supply equation with a MLE ("tobit") after specifying δ_i as a linear function of all period regressors plus a normal error term as in (4.1). Generalizing (4.1), Newey (1994) allowed δ_i to depend on all-time regressors with an unknown functional form instead of the linear form in (4.1).

4.4.2 Panel Probit with Nonlinear GMM

For (1.1) but with unrelated effect, assuming normality for $v_{i1}, \dots, v_{iT}$, Avery *et al.* (1983) did a nonlinear GMM using orthogonality conditions between

$$\varepsilon_{it} \equiv y_{it} - \Phi(w'_{it}\gamma_t) \quad \text{and} \quad w_{is}, \tag{4.17}$$

where $\gamma_t = (\tau_t, \tilde{\gamma}')'$ is the parameter vector for the t-th wave corresponding to w_{it}; nonlinear GMM for cross-section data is reviewed in the beginning of the next chapter. Avery *et al.* proposed the GMM to alleviate the computational problem for the multivariate panel probit. As in the preceding chapters, for GMM, we can think of SUM, CON, PRE, and EXO type moment conditions. If we pool the waves together and maximize

$$\sum_i \sum_t [y_{it} \cdot \ln\{\Phi(w'_{it}g_t)\} + (1 - y_{it}) \cdot \ln\{1 - \Phi(w'_{it}g_t)\}], \tag{4.18}$$

wrt $g_1, \dots, g_T$, then we will be using a SUM type moment condition; this is analogous to the third method to extend the two-period conditional logit to more than two periods. Avery *et al.* used EXO; they proposed a test for EXO using two estimators, one using CON and the other using EXO. They estimated a married female work (or not) decision equation using a data drawn from PSID with $N = 500$ and $T = 5$.

Bertschek and Lechner (1998) reviewed GMM estimators for (4.17) allowing for related effect under (4.1), and they proposed an optimal version using nonparametric instruments suggested in Newey (1993); see also Lee (1996, p. 116). They applied the GMM estimators to an innovation equation (whether a product innovation takes place or does not take place in a year) with the main regressors of interest being imports and foreign direct investment; they used German data with $N = 1270$ and $T = 5$.

Conditional logit and the panel probit estimators introduced so far have certain pros and cons. The advantage of panel probit is that it allows correlations across t in u_{it}'s, which is ruled out in conditional logit. Usually data over time exhibit some type of dynamics, which is captured, other than by δ_i, either by including lagged dependent variables in the regressors or by allowing serial correlations for the error terms. The conditional logit in Honoré and Kyriazidou (2000b) allows a lagged dependent variable, whereas panel probit allows serial correlations of the error terms.

A disadvantage of panel probit is the assumption that the unit-specific effect is a linear function of all-period regressors plus a normally distributed error term. Although this assumption may look reasonable, if δ_i is related to all-period regressors, then we need indeed "all" periods even outside the available panel periods. But we will hardly ever have all the periods, and the excluded period regressors will become part of ε_i, making the independence of ε_i from $(\tilde{c}_i, x_{i1}, ..., x_{iT})$ implausible for a small T. On the other hand, if T is too large, then there will be too many regressors in a single cross-section probit, which is also a nontrivial problem. This weakness of panel probit is quite critical that we may advocate conditional logit over panel probit.

One practical alternative for panel probit could be not using δ_i and doing panel probit with $y_{i,t-1}$ (and $x_{i,t-1}$) in the regressors; here the presumption is that $y_{i,t-1}$ captures the related effect. This is motivated by the discussion on dynamic linear models of the preceding chapter where $y_{i,t-1}$ (and $x_{i,t-1}$) is included on the right-hand side to remove δ_i. In this dynamic panel probit, each wave can be estimated using cross-section probit with $y_{i,t-1}$ and w_{it} (and $x_{i,t-1}$) as regressors, and then the estimates across the waves can be combined using MDE. One critical assumption for the dynamic panel probit, however, is that u_{it} should be independent over time; otherwise, u_{it} will be related to the regressor $y_{i,t-1}$. Also assumptions should be imposed on y_{i1} (say, y_{i1} being a constant); see, for example, Chintagunta et al. (2001, p.125).

4.4.3   Panel Probit with Predeterminedness

Arellano and Carrasco (1999) have suggested a panel probit using only PRE-type moments. They have shown a couple of different estimators, but we will present the one that fits our method-of-moment framework best. Assume

$$y_{it} = 1[\tau_t + \tilde{c}_i'\tilde{\alpha} + x_{it}'\beta + \delta_i + u_{it} > 0], \qquad (4.19)$$

$$(\delta_i + u_{it})|W_{it} \sim N(E(\delta_i|W_{it}), \sigma_t^2)$$

where x_{it} may include $y_{i,t-1}$, and $\sigma_t \equiv SD(\delta_i + u_{it}|W_{it})$ is assumed not to be a function of W_{it}, with

$$W_{it} \equiv (\tilde{c}_i', x_{i1}', ..., x_{it}', y_{i1}, ..., y_{i,t-1})'.$$

From this,

$$P(y_{it} = 1|W_{it}) = \Phi\{(\tau_t + \tilde{c}_i'\tilde{\alpha} + x_{it}'\beta + E(\delta_i|W_{it}))/\sigma_t\}. \qquad (4.20)$$

Invert Φ and multiply both sides by σ_t to get

$$\Phi^{-1}\{P(y_{it} = 1|W_{it})\} \cdot \sigma_t - \tau_t - \tilde{c}_i'\tilde{\alpha} - x_{it}'\beta = E(\delta_i|W_{it}). \qquad (4.21)$$

First-difference this to get the key equation

$$\Phi^{-1}\{P(y_{it} = 1|W_{it})\}\sigma_t - \Phi^{-1}\{P(y_{i,t-1} = 1|W_{i,t-1})\}\sigma_{t-1}$$
$$-\Delta\tau_t - \Delta x_{it}'\beta = \epsilon_{it}, \qquad (4.22)$$

where

$$\Delta\tau_t \equiv \tau_t - \tau_{t-1}, \quad \Delta x_{it} \equiv x_{it} - x_{i,t-1}, \quad \epsilon_{it} \equiv E(\delta_i|W_{it}) - E(\delta_i|W_{i,t-1}).$$
$$(4.23)$$

The error term ε_{it} satisfies

$$E(\varepsilon_{it}|W_{i,t-1}) = 0, \qquad (4.24)$$

which is the main conditional moment condition to use.

Let $P_N(y_{it} = 1|W_{it})$ denote a kernel nonparametric estimator for $P(y_{it} = 1|W_{it})$. The moments to be used in practice are

$$(1/N)\sum_i [\Phi^{-1}\{P_N(y_{it} = 1|W_{it})\}\sigma_t/\sigma_2 -$$

$$\Phi^{-1}\{P_N(y_{i,t-1} = 1|W_{i,t-1})\}\sigma_{t-1}/\sigma_2 \qquad (4.25)$$

$$-\Delta\tau_t/\sigma_2 - \Delta x'_{it}\beta/\sigma_2]\cdot g(W_{i,t-1}), \quad t = 3, ..., T,$$

where $g(W_{i,t-1})$ is a vector of functions of $W_{i,t-1}$, and the parameters to estimate are

$$\lambda \equiv (\Delta\tau_3/\sigma_2, ..., \Delta\tau_T/\sigma_2, \beta'/\sigma_2, \sigma_3/\sigma_2, ..., \sigma_T/\sigma_2)'. \qquad (4.26)$$

Because $W_{i,t-1}$ is allowed to have $y_{i,t-2}$, the time index t in (4.25) starts from $t = 3$.

The scale normalization for the panel binary model is done by σ_2; at $t = 3$, $\sigma_{t-1}/\sigma_2 = 1$, which "anchors" the scale factor. With (4.25), one can do GMM for panel linear models, for the moment condition is linear in parameters. One complication is the infinite dimensional first-stage estimators $P_N(y_{it} = 1|W_{it})$ and $P_N(y_{i,t-1} = 1|W_{i,t-1})$, which affect the GMM asymptotic variance, but this effect can be accounted for by using techniques in Newey (1994) and Lee (1996, chapter 10).

4.5 ROOT-Nh CONSISTENT ESTIMATORS

Panel probits and conditional logit for binary response require known error term distributions, violation of which makes the estimators inconsistent in general. Manski (1987) proposed a panel maximum score estimator (PME) for a binary response two-period panel without specifying the distribution of the error terms but imposing other assumptions instead. In this section, we review PME and its smoothed version, which is then followed by a brief empirical example. As will be noted later, the estimators require a good deal of computational effort and a fairly large sample to get the asymptotic properties realized. Because PME is an error-differencing estimator, redefine Δ_i as $\Delta_i + \tilde{c}'_i\tilde{\alpha}$ and ignore $\tilde{c}'_i\tilde{\alpha}$.

Recall (1.1) with $T = 2$. Let $\Delta x_i \equiv (1, x'_{i2} - x'_{i1})'$, and denote the j-th component of Δx_i as Δx_{ij}; that is, with k denoting the row dimension of Δx_i,

$$\Delta x_i \equiv (\Delta x_{i1}, \Delta x_{i2}, ..., \Delta x_{ik})', \quad \Delta x_{i1} = 1 \quad \text{for all } i \qquad (5.1)$$
$$= (\Delta x'_{ic}, \Delta x_{ik})' \quad \text{where } \Delta x_{ic} \equiv (\Delta x_{i1}, ..., \Delta x_{i,k-1})'.$$

Also let

$$\Delta y_i \equiv y_{i2} - y_{i1} \quad \text{and} \quad \beta = (\beta_1, ..., \beta_k)' = (\beta_c', \beta_k)'$$
$$\text{where } \beta_1 = \tau_2 - \tau_1 \text{ and } \beta_c \equiv (\beta_1, ..., \beta_{k-1})'.$$

Assume

$u_{i1}|(\delta_i, x_{i1}, x_{i2})$ and $u_{i2}|(\delta_i, x_{i1}, x_{i2})$ follow the same "marginal" distribution on R^1 for all $(\delta_i, x_{i1}, x_{i2})$;

$E(\Delta x_i \Delta x_i')$ is p.d., $\beta_k \neq 0$, and $\Delta x_{ik}|\Delta x_{ic}$ has an everywhere positive density for all Δx_{ic}. $\qquad (5.2)$

Although the marginal distribution is restricted to be the same, there is no restriction on the relationship between u_{i1} and u_{i2}; also, heteroskedasticity across i is allowed. Because β is identified only up to a positive scale, divide β by $|\beta_k|$ to identify

$$\beta_1/|\beta_k|, ..., \beta_{k-1}/|\beta_k|, \text{sgn}(\beta_k)$$

where $\text{sgn}(A) = 1$ if $A \geq 0$ and -1 otherwise. We will, however, denote this scaled version just as β to save notations.

PME is obtained by maximizing

$$(1/N) \sum_i \Delta y_i \cdot 1[\Delta x_i' b > 0] \qquad (5.3)$$

wrt b, and its consistency is based on

$$\text{Med}(\Delta y_i | \delta_i, x_{i1}, x_{i2}, \Delta y_i \neq 0) = \text{sgn}(\Delta x_i' \beta). \qquad (5.4)$$

To see how (5.4) holds, first observe that Δy_i takes only 1 and -1 given $\Delta y_i \neq 0$. Then the median is 1 iff

$$P(\Delta y_i = 1 | \delta_i, x_{i1}, x_{i2}, \Delta y_i \neq 0) \geq P(\Delta y_i = -1 | \delta_i, x_{i1}, x_{i2}, \Delta y_i \neq 0)$$
$$\Leftrightarrow \ P(y_{i1} = 0, y_{i2} = 1 | \delta_i, x_{i1}, x_{i2}) / P(\Delta y_i \neq 0 | \delta_i, x_{i1}, x_{i2})$$
$$\geq P(y_{i1} = 1, y_{i2} = 0 | \delta_i, x_{i1}, x_{i2}) / P(\Delta y_i \neq 0 | \delta_i, x_{i1}, x_{i2})$$
$$\Leftrightarrow \ P(y_{i1} = 0, y_{i2} = 1 | \delta_i, x_{i1}, x_{i2}) \geq P(y_{i1} = 1, y_{i2} = 0 | \delta_i, x_{i1}, x_{i2}). \qquad (5.5)$$

Adding $P(y_{i1} = 1, y_{i2} = 1 | \delta_i, x_{i1}, x_{i2})$ to both sides, (5.5) becomes

$$P(y_{i2} = 1 | \delta_i, x_{i1}, x_{i2}) \geq P(y_{i1} = 1 | \delta_i, x_{i1}, x_{i2}) \qquad (5.6)$$
$$\Leftrightarrow \ P(u_{i2} > -\tau_2 - x_{i2}'\beta - \delta_i | \delta_i, x_{i1}, x_{i2})$$
$$\geq P(u_{i1} > -\tau_1 - x_{i1}'\beta - \delta_i | \delta_i, x_{i1}, x_{i2})$$
$$\Leftrightarrow \ \Delta x_i'\beta \geq 0.$$

Likewise, we can show that the median is -1 if $\Delta x_i'\beta < 0$. Putting these two cases together renders (5.4).

PME is consistent but the asymptotic distribution is unknown due to the nonsmooth maximand; PME is likely to be $N^{1/3}$-consistent in view of Kim and Pollard (1990). To get an asymptotic distribution, Charlier *et al.* (1995) smooth PME as Horowitz (1992) smooths the cross-section version of PME in Manski (1985). In the following discussion, we introduce another smoothed PME in Lee (1998) that seems to behave better in computation while having the same first order asymptotic distribution as the smoothed PME in Charlier *et al.* (1995). The main practical advantage in Lee's (1998) smoothing scheme over that in Charlier *et al.* (1995) is that the bandwidth may be chosen with cross-validation as shown next.

Suppose $\text{sgn}(\beta_k) = 1$. Then

$$
\begin{aligned}
E(\Delta y \cdot 1[\Delta x > 0]) &= E(\Delta y \cdot 1[\Delta x_k > -\Delta x_c' \beta_c]) \\
&= E\{\Delta y \cdot E(1[\Delta x_k > -\Delta x_c' \beta_c] | \Delta x_c, \Delta y)\} \\
&= E[\Delta y \cdot S(-\Delta x_c' \beta_c | \Delta x_c, \Delta y)], \\
&\qquad \text{where } S(p|\Delta x_c, \Delta y) \equiv P(\Delta x_k > p|\Delta x_c, \Delta y).
\end{aligned}
$$

A sample analog for this is

$$
(1/N) \sum_i \Delta y_i \cdot S_N(-\Delta x_{ic}' b_c | \Delta x_{ic}, \Delta y_i), \tag{5.7}
$$

where $S_N(-\Delta x_{ic}' b_c | \Delta x_{ic}, \Delta y_i)$ is a kernel nonparametric estimator for $S(-\Delta x_{ic}' b_c | \Delta x_{ic}, \Delta y_i)$:

$$
\begin{aligned}
S_N(-\Delta x_{ic}' b_c | \Delta x_{ic}, \Delta y_i) &\equiv \{(N-1)h^{k-2}\}^{-1} \\
&\quad \sum_{j, j \neq i} K_{ji} 1_{ji} \bar{\kappa}((\Delta x_{jk} + \Delta x_{ic}' b_c)/h)/\psi_N(\Delta x_{ic}, \Delta y_i),
\end{aligned}
$$

K is a $(k-2)$-variate kernel, h is a bandwidth,

$$
\kappa \text{ is a univariate kernel for } \bar{\kappa}(\cdot) \equiv \int^{\cdot} \kappa(t)dt,
$$

$$
K_{ji} \equiv K((\Delta x_{j2} - \Delta x_{i2})/h, ..., (\Delta x_{j,k-1} - \Delta x_{i,k-1})/h),
$$

$$
1_{ji} \equiv 1[\Delta y_j = \Delta y_i], \quad \psi_N(x_{ic}, \Delta y_i) \equiv \{(N-1)h^{k-2}\}^{-1} \sum_{j, j \neq i} K_{ji} 1_{ji}.
$$

Differently from (5.3), (5.7) is smooth in b_c. If $\text{sgn}(\beta_k) = -1$, multiply x_k by -1; in practice, because $\text{sgn}(\beta_k)$ is unknown, both $\text{sgn}(\beta_k) = 1$ and $\text{sgn}(\beta_k) = -1$ (that is, $-x_k$) should be tried, and (5.7) corresponding to the two cases should be compared in order to pick the better one.

The main issue in implementing the estimator is the bandwidth choice. For this, the following practical scheme is useful. First, estimate β_c with any easy-to-use estimator such as conditional logit; the estimate should be normalized so that the coefficient of β_k be ± 1. With this estimate as b_c, the bandwidth can be chosen minimizing

$$(1/N)\sum_i \{1[\Delta x_{ik} > -\Delta x'_{ic}b_c] - S_N(-\Delta x'_{ic}b_c | \Delta x_{ic}, \Delta y_i)\}^2$$

wrt h over some range, which is a cross-validation.
Define

$$g(\Delta x_k | \Delta x_c) \text{ as a density for } \Delta x_k | \Delta x_c,$$
$$f(\Delta x_k | \Delta x_c, \Delta y) \text{ as a density for } \Delta x_k | (\Delta x_c, \Delta y),$$
$$f'(\Delta x_k | \Delta x_c, \Delta y) \equiv \partial f(\Delta x_k | \Delta x_c, \Delta y)/\partial \Delta x_k.$$

For the asymptotic distribution, $\text{sgn}(\beta_k)$ is as good as known, for it can be estimated much faster than β_c. Denoting the estimator for β_c in $\beta = (\beta'_c, \beta_k)'$ as b_{cN}, under some regularity conditions, we have

$$(Nh)^{1/2}(b_{cN} - \beta_c) \Rightarrow N(0, \ H^{-1} \cdot M \cdot H^{-1}), \qquad (5.8)$$

$$M \equiv E[\Delta x_c \Delta x'_c \cdot 1[\Delta y \neq 0] \cdot g(-\Delta x'_c \beta_c | \Delta x_c)] \cdot \int \kappa(t)^2 dt,$$

$$H \equiv -E[\Delta x_c \Delta x'_c \cdot \Delta y \cdot f'(-\Delta x'_c \beta_c | \Delta x_c, \Delta y)].$$

It is not recommended that one use the outer product of the gradient of (5.7) to estimate M; it seems better to estimate M by replacing $g(-\Delta x'_c \beta_c | \Delta x_c)$ with a nonparametric estimate to avoid the problem of too small standard errors (Gerfin, 1996, Horowitz, 1993, Melenberg and Van Soest, 1996).

Compared with the parametric methods, PME imposes a rather weak assumption on the error term distribution in the first part of (5.2). But the assumption on the regressors in the second part of (5.2) is rather strong; it may not be easy to find a regressor with unbounded support conditional on all the other regressors. This kind of trade-off of assumptions is often seen in semiparametric methods. Probably the biggest problem with PME is its computation: the maximand (5.3) tends to have many local maxima, although this problem is alleviated in the smoothed version (5.7). Also note that both PME and its smoothed version still fall short of being $\sqrt{N}$-consistent.

Rewrite (5.3) as

$$(1/N)\sum_i (1[\Delta y_i > 0] - 1[\Delta y_i < 0]) \cdot 1[\Delta x'_i b > 0] \qquad (5.9)$$

$$= (1/N)\sum_i \{1[\Delta y_i > 0] \cdot 1[\Delta x'_i b > 0] - 1[\Delta y_i < 0] \cdot (1 - 1[\Delta x'_i b < 0])\}$$

$$= (1/N)\sum_i \{1[\Delta y_i > 0] \cdot 1[\Delta x'_i b > 0] + 1[\Delta y_i < 0] \cdot 1[\Delta x'_i b < 0] - 1[\Delta y_i < 0]\}.$$

Dropping the last term, maximizing (5.3) is equivalent to maximizing

$$(1/N) \sum_i \{1[\Delta y_i > 0] \cdot 1[\Delta x_i'b > 0] + 1[\Delta y_i < 0] \cdot 1[\Delta x_i'b < 0]\}. \quad (5.10)$$

Abrevaya (2000) generalized this into

$$(1/N) \sum_i \{H(y_{i2}, y_{i1}) \cdot 1[\Delta x_i'b > 0] + H(y_{i1}, y_{i2}) \cdot 1[\Delta x_i'b < 0]\} \quad (5.11)$$

where $H(v_2, v_1)$ is nondecreasing in v_2 and nonincreasing in v_1; (5.10) is a special case with $H(v_2, v_1) = 1[v_2 > v_1]$. This generalization allows y_{it}^* to be generated nonlinearly or with many related effects so long as $\Delta x_i'\beta > (<)0$ translates into $y_{i2} > (<)y_{i1}$: for example,

$$y_{it}^* = F(x_{it}'\beta, \delta_i, u_{it}) \quad \text{or} \quad y_{it}^* = \delta_{1i}(x_{it}'\beta)^{\delta_{2i}} + \delta_{3i} + u_{it}, \quad (5.12)$$

where $F(v_1, v_2, v_3)$ is increasing in v_1 and v_3, and δ_{1i}, δ_{2i} and δ_{3i} are related effects with $\delta_{1i} > 0$ and $\delta_{2i} > 0$.

Charlier *et al.* (1995) applied their smoothed PME to the female (of age 18 to 65) labor market participation decision; "participation" means having or looking for a job. They use a Dutch data, the Socio-Economic Panel, with $N = 3174$, which is unbalanced with the maximum $T = 5$ (1984–1988); about 43% of the respondents have $y_{it} = 1$. The time-variant regressors include

LOI: log of one plus after-tax family income net of the female's
HM: husband's hours worked
NCH: number of children younger than 18
DCH6: dummy for children younger than 6
IEM: dummy for husband working or not

Using LOI as the normalizing variable, part of their Table 3 is presented in Table 4.2 (standard errors in parenthesis).

Table 4.2 Female Labor Market Participation Decision Equation

	Panel probit	PME	Smoothed PME	$|b_N| = 1$	Cond. logit
LOI	.003(.002)	-1	-1	$-.057(.007)$	.046(.044)
HM	$-.05$ (.002)	-0.228	$-0.127(.023)$	$-.007(.001)$	$-.010(.03)$
NCH	$-.144(.030)$	0.552	2.914(.563)	.166(.022)	$-.109(.055)$
DCH6	$-.160(.060)$	-14.219	$-15.895(3.13)$	$-.905(.016)$	$-.837(.085)$
IEM	.165(.109)	9.463	4.762(.823)	.271(.034)	.488(.155)

The result for panel probit and conditional logit is based on the balanced sub-sample with 1017 individuals. For PME, setting the coefficient for LOI at 1 gave the maximand 957, whereas setting it at -1 gave 991; thus, the estimates corresponding to -1 were chosen. The column $|b_N| = 1$ is the smoothed PME with the normalization $|b_N| = 1$, which is to compare smoothed PME to conditional logit at the last column with the same normalization.

Comparing PME and the smoothed PME, the only big difference is in NCH (about five-fold difference). Comparing signs of estimates in panel probit with those in (smoothed) PME, NCH lowers the tendency to participate in the labor market for panel probit, whereas the opposite is true for (smoothed) PME. Because different normalizations are used across panel probit and (smoothed) PME, we can compare only ratios of estimates if interested in their magnitude. For example, the ratios for IEM/HM and DCH6/IEM for the three estimators are, respectively,

$$
\begin{array}{llll}
\text{IEM/HM:} & -3.300, & 41.504, & -37.496; \\
\text{DCH6/IEM:} & -0.970, & -1.503, & -3.338;
\end{array}
$$

the ratios in panel probit are quite different from those in (smoothed) PME; Charlier *et al.* (1995) rejected normality and independence between error terms and regressors through some specification tests.

Comparing the last two columns ($|b_N| = 1$ and conditional logit), LOI is insignificant in conditional logit; this is unfortunate, for LOI was used as the normalizing variable for (smoothed) PME. A rather disconcerting aspect is that standard errors of smoothed PME are three or four times smaller than those of conditional logit.

4.6 A ROOT-N CONSISTENT ESTIMATOR

So far we have introduced some parametric estimators and one semiparametric estimator for panel binary response. Although the semiparametric estimator, panel maximum score (PME), does not specify the error term distribution, PME is slower-than-$\sqrt{N}$ consistent and imposes a restriction on regressors. This section introduces Lee's (1999) semiparametric estimator that is $\sqrt{N}$-consistent at the cost of imposing stronger restrictions on regressors; it is bandwidth-free, although estimating its asymptotic variance requires nonparametric techniques. Recently, Honoré and Lewbel (2002) proposed another $\sqrt{N}$-consistent semiparametric estimator under PRE, $T = 2$, $E(x_{i1}z_i') \neq E(x_{i2}z_i')$ for an instrument vector z_i, and the independence of v_{it} from a regressor with a large support.

As in the preceding section, $\delta_i + \tilde{c}_i'\tilde{\alpha}$ is redefined as δ_i. Recall (1.1) with $T = 2$. Define in this section, with k denoting the row dimension of x_{it},

$$
\begin{aligned}
\Delta x_i &\equiv x_{i2} - x_{i1} = (\Delta x_{i1}, ..., \Delta x_{i,k-1}, \Delta x_{ik})' \\
&= (\Delta x_{ic}', \Delta x_{ik})', \quad \Delta x_{ic} = (\Delta x_{i1}, ..., \Delta x_{i,k-1})'; \\
\Delta y_i &\equiv y_{i2} - y_{i1} \quad \text{and} \\
\beta &= (\beta_1, ..., \beta_k) = (\beta_c', \beta_k)' \quad \text{where } \beta_c = (\beta_1, ..., \beta_{k-1})';
\end{aligned}
$$

as will be seen shortly, τ_t's as well as $\tilde{\alpha}$ are not identified in the Lee's (1999) estimator. Because β is identified only up to a positive scale, divide β by $|\beta_k|$ to identify

$$\beta_1/|\beta_k|, \ldots, \beta_{k-1}/|\beta_k|, \mathrm{sgn}(\beta_k).$$

We will denote this scaled version simply as β to save notations.

Lee's (1999) estimator b_N is obtained by maximizing

$$\{N(N-1)\}^{-1} \sum_{i \neq j} \mathrm{sgn}(\Delta x_i' b - \Delta x_j' b) \cdot (\Delta y_i - \Delta y_j) \cdot (\Delta y_i)^2 (\Delta y_j)^2 \quad (6.1)$$

$$= \binom{N}{2}^{-1} \sum_{i < j, \Delta y_i \neq \Delta y_j, \Delta y_i \neq 0, \Delta y_j \neq 0} \mathrm{sgn}(\Delta x_i' b - \Delta x_j' b) \cdot (\Delta y_i - \Delta y_j).$$

The consistency of b_N is based on the key equation

$$\mathrm{Med}(\Delta y_i - \Delta y_j | \delta_i, x_{i1}, x_{i2}, \delta_j, x_{j1}, x_{j2}, \Delta y_i \neq 0, \Delta y_j \neq 0, \Delta y_i \neq \Delta y_j)$$
$$= 2 \cdot \mathrm{sgn}(\Delta x_i' \beta - \Delta x_j' \beta).$$

Although $\Delta y_i - \Delta y_j$ can take five different values $(0, \pm 1, \pm 2)$, it can take only ± 2 given $\Delta y_i \neq 0$, $\Delta y_j \neq 0$, and $\Delta y_i \neq \Delta y_j$, for which $(\Delta y_i - \Delta y_j)(\Delta y_i)^2(\Delta y_j)^2$ appears in (6.1).

For a latent linear cross-section model

$$z_i^* = w_i' \beta + u_i, \ z = \lambda(z^*) \text{ with } \lambda \text{ being a nondecreasing transformation,}$$

Han's (1987) "maximum rank correlation estimator" (RCE) maximizes

$$\{N(N-1)\}^{-1} \sum_{i \neq j} 1[w_i' b > w_j' b] \cdot 1[z_i > z_j]$$

wrt b under the independence of u and w. The summand in (6.1) takes ± 2 depending on whether the sign of $\Delta x_i' b - \Delta x_j' b$ agrees with that of $\Delta y_i - \Delta y_j$ given $\{\Delta y_i \neq 0, \Delta y_j \neq 0\}$. Adding 2 to the summand and dividing it by 4, the summand takes 1 or 0. Then maximizing (6.1) is equivalent to maximizing

$$\{N(N-1)\}^{-1} \sum_{i \neq j} 1[\Delta x_i' b > \Delta x_j' b] \cdot 1[\Delta y_i > \Delta y_j] \cdot (\Delta y_i)^2 (\Delta y_j)^2 :$$

the estimator for (6.1), b_N, may be viewed as a panel analog of RCE.

The main assumptions for b_N are

(6.2) $E(\Delta x \Delta x')$ is p.d., $\beta_k \neq 0$, and $\Delta x_k | \Delta x_c$ has an everywhere positive density for all Δx_c.

(6.3) $(u_1, u_2)|\delta$ is independent of $(x_1', x_2')|\delta$, and the support of $(u_1, u_2)|\delta$ is R^2 for all δ.

(6.4) $P(\Delta y = 1 | \Delta x' \beta)$ is an increasing function of $\Delta x' \beta$ and $P(\Delta y = -1 | \Delta x' \beta)$ is a decreasing function of $\Delta x' \beta$.

(6.5) "Index increment sufficiency" of $(x_1' \beta, \delta)$: $P(x_1' \beta, \delta | \Delta x) = P(x_1' \beta, \delta | \Delta x' \beta)$ for all Δx where $P(\cdot | \cdot)$ denotes the conditional distribution function.

Note that (6.3), which includes an EXO type condition, allows a relation between u_1 and u_2 as well as between $(u_1, u_2)'$ and δ; u_1 and u_2 can have heteroskedasticity of an unknown form where the conditional variance depends only on δ; (6.3) does not allow a lagged y_t in the regressor. For (6.4), observe

$$\Delta y_i = 1 \Leftrightarrow y_{i2} = 1 \text{ and } y_{i1} = 0$$
$$\Leftrightarrow \tau_2 + x'_{i2}\beta + \delta_i + u_{i2} > 0 \quad \text{and} \quad \tau_1 + x'_{i1}\beta + \delta_i + u_{i1} \leq 0.$$

This shows that (6.4) is plausible, because as $\Delta x'\beta$ increases, either $x'_2\beta$ increases or $x'_1\beta$ decreases (or a combination of both); (6.4) is verifiable with a nonparametric method once β is estimated.

As for (6.5), because $\Delta x = (\Delta x'_c, \Delta x_k)'$ is one-to-one to $(\Delta x_c, \Delta x'\beta)'$, rewrite (6.5):

for the left-hand side: $P(x'_1\beta, \delta|\Delta x) = P(x'_1\beta|\delta, \Delta x_c, \Delta x'\beta) \cdot P(\delta|\Delta x_c, \Delta x'\beta)$;

for the right-hand side: $P(x'_1\beta, \delta|\Delta x'\beta) = P(x'_1\beta|\delta, \Delta x'\beta) \cdot P(\delta|\Delta x'\beta)$.

Hence, a sufficient condition for (6.5) is

$$\delta \text{ is independent of } \Delta x_c \text{ given } \Delta x'\beta, \text{ and} \tag{6.6}$$

$$x'_1\beta \text{ is independent of } \Delta x_c \text{ given } (\delta, \Delta x'\beta). \tag{6.7}$$

Although (6.6) is not so restrictive because δ is time-invariant, (6.7) is so because essentially it allows a relation between Δx_c and $x'_1\beta$ only through δ and $\Delta x'\beta$. This aspect—that (6.5) is impossible to verify whereas (6.7) is restrictive—seems to be the main drawback of b_N, which has otherwise good properties, being $\sqrt{N}$-consistent, semiparametric, and bandwidth-free.

A simple sufficient condition for (6.7) is

$$x_2 = x_1 + \varepsilon_2 \quad \text{and} \quad \varepsilon_2 \text{ is independent of } x_1 \text{ given } \delta; \tag{6.8}$$

$\Delta x = \varepsilon_2$ is independent of x_1 given δ. For continuous regressors, a multidimensional random walk satisfies (6.8); correlations among the components of ε_2, however, are allowed. For discrete regressors, (6.8) cannot hold in general, analogously to the errors-in-variable problem for discrete variables; an exception is ε_2 being deterministic as in age. This problem for discrete regressors can be avoided by maximizing (6.1) on cells formed by support points of the discrete regressors; in this case, the coefficients of the discrete regressors are not identified.

In typical microeconometric applied works using middle-age people, we often have age, job experience, income, and (demographic) dummy variables in the data. Age satisfies (6.8) and so does job experience so long as the subjects stay employed for the two periods. Log(income) satisfies (6.8) if income grows by a certain percentage of the base-period income, which is often the case. Thus by conditioning on cells formed by the (demographic) dummies, we can consistently estimate the coefficient of age, job experience, or income. Also in panels with aggregate variables (country-wide or region-wide panels), many variables (or their transformations) may satisfy (6.8) closely; for those panels, the fact that

(6.3) allows dependence in u_1 and u_2 helps in allowing for dynamics. Griliches and Mairesse (1998, p. 180) noted that "many economic variables evolve in a random-walk-like fashion at the microeconomic level"; that is, their growth rates (or log differences) are only weakly serially correlated.

Turning to the asymptotic distribution, as in the smoothed version for PME, $\text{sgn}(\beta_k)$ is as good as known for the asymptotic distribution of $\sqrt{N}(b_{cN} - \beta_c)$, which is normal with the asymptotic variance $4A^{-1}BA^{-1}$ where

$$
\begin{aligned}
A \;\equiv\; & -8 \cdot E[\{\Delta x_c - E(\Delta x_c | \Delta x' \beta)\}\{\Delta x_c - E(\Delta x_c | \Delta x' \beta)\}' && (6.9) \\
& \cdot g_o(\Delta x' \beta) \cdot \eta(\Delta x' \beta)], \\
B \;\equiv\; & 16 \cdot E[\{\Delta x_c - E(\Delta x_c | \Delta x' \beta)\}\{\Delta x_c - E(\Delta x_c | \Delta x' \beta)\}' \\
& \cdot g_o(\Delta x' \beta)^2 \cdot P(\Delta y = -1 | \Delta x' \beta) P(\Delta y = 1 | \Delta x' \beta) \\
& \cdot \{P(\Delta y = -1 | \Delta x' \beta) + P(\Delta y = 1 | \Delta x' \beta)\}],
\end{aligned}
$$

$g_o(\cdot)$ is a density of $\Delta x' \beta$,

$$
\begin{aligned}
\eta(\Delta x' \beta) \equiv\; & P'(\Delta y = 1 | \Delta x' \beta) \cdot P(\Delta y = -1 | \Delta x' \beta) \\
& - P'(\Delta y = -1 | \Delta x' \beta) \cdot P(\Delta y = 1 | \Delta x' \beta),
\end{aligned}
$$

and $P'(\cdot | \Delta x' \beta) = dP(\cdot | \Delta x' \beta)/d(\Delta x' \beta)$. The second order matrix A is n.d. because it can be shown that

$$
P'(z = 1 | w' \beta) > 0 > P'(z = -1 | w' \beta) \tag{6.10}
$$

where

$$
z_i \equiv \Delta y_i \quad \text{and} \quad w_i \equiv \Delta x_i \; (= (w_{ic}', w_{ik})').
$$

The asymptotic variance of RCE for the cross-section binary response model $z_i = 1[z_i^* > 0] = 1[w_i' \beta + u_i > 0]$ takes the same form as (6.9): what Sherman (1993, p. 134) shows is essentially equivalent to

$$
\begin{aligned}
A \;=\; & -4 \cdot E[\{w_c - E(w_c | w' \beta)\}\{w_c - E(w_c | w' \beta)\}' \cdot g_o(w' \beta) && (6.11) \\
& \cdot P'(z = 1 | w' \beta)], \\
B \;=\; & 16 \cdot E[\{w_c - E(w_c | w' \beta)\}\{w_c - E(w_c | w' \beta)\}' \cdot g_o(w' \beta)^2 \\
& \cdot P(z = 0 | w' \beta) P(z = 1 | w' \beta) \cdot \{P(z = 0 | w' \beta) + P(z = 1 | w' \beta)\}]
\end{aligned}
$$

where $g_o(w' \beta)$ is a density for $w' \beta$. Equation (6.11) is almost the same as (6.9) except at four aspects. First, $z = 0$ in RCE whereas $z = -1$ in panel data. Second, $P(z = 0 | w' \beta) + P(z = 1 | w' \beta) = 1$ for RCE, whereas $P(z = -1 | w' \beta) + P(z = 1 | w' \beta) < 1$ for panel data, which is a normalizing factor because only $\Delta y = \pm 1$ is used for (6.1). Third, $P'(z = 1 | w' \beta)$ appears in RCE instead of $\eta(w' \beta)$. To see how $\eta(w' \beta)$ becomes $P'(z = 1 | w' \beta)$ for RCE, replace $z = -1$ in $\eta(w' \beta)$ with $z = 0$ to get

$$
\begin{aligned}
\eta(w' \beta) \;=\; & P'(z = 1 | w' \beta) P(z = 0 | w' \beta) - P'(z = 0 | w' \beta) P(z = 1 | w' \beta) && (6.12) \\
=\; & P'(z = 1 | w' \beta)\{P(z = 0 | w' \beta) + P(z = 1 | w' \beta)\} = P'(z = 1 | w' \beta)
\end{aligned}
$$

due to $P'(z = 1|w'\beta) = -P'(z = 0|w'\beta)$ in the cross-section binary response. Fourth, A in (6.11) has 4 whereas A in (6.9) has $8 = 4 \times 2$; the number 4 for the RCE's asymptotic distribution is an error that should be 8 (see Cavanagh and Sherman, 1998, Theorem 3).

Compared with the parametric methods, the estimator maximizing (6.1) imposes a rather weak assumption on the error term distribution in (6.3). But the assumption on the regressors and the unit-specific effect seems strong, as can be seen in (6.7). Compared with PME, the maximand (6.1) behaves better in computation due to the double sum in (6.1), and the estimator is $\sqrt{N}$-consistent; both are advantages over PME. However, the estimator restricts the relationship between regressors and the unit-specific effect, whereas PME does not.

4.7   AN EMPIRICAL EXAMPLE FOR PANEL PROBIT AND CONDITIONAL LOGIT

In this section, we apply conditional logit and the MDE-based panel probit to the data used in Vella and Verbeek (1998) with $N = 545$ (all males) and $T = 8$ (1980–1987); the data set only with $t = 2, 3, 6, 7, 8$ is in the data appendix. See Vella and Verbeek (1998) for the details on the data including the descriptive statistics. They used an unrelated-effect model with a lagged dependent variable $y_{i,t-1}$ as a regressor to explain a binary response y_{it}, union membership. Their motivation for $y_{i,t-1}$ was that there are nonpecuniary benefits and potential seniority concerns for staying in the union. But $y_{i,t-1}$ can also represent other factors; for example, some individuals may prefer labor union membership for a psychological reason (the sense of "belonging"). If this is related to x_{it}, then a related-effect model would be more appropriate.

Vella and Verbeek specified the error distribution fully to do MLE for all periods together without using MDE. We will do four estimations:

$$
\begin{aligned}
&\text{(a) panel probit with MDE using wave 7 and 8;} \\
&\text{(b) conditional logit using wave 7,8;} \\
&\text{(c) conditional logit using wave 6,7,8;} \\
&\text{(d) no-}\delta_i\text{ probit with } y_{i,t-1} \text{ as a regressor for wave 6,7,8.}
\end{aligned}
\quad (7.1)
$$

None of the semiparametric methods for panel binary response seems suitable for the data, because there are some thirty plus variables in the data with the majority being dummy variables.

The regressors are 1,

edu: years of schooling
exr: job experience computed as age-6-edu
exredu: interaction between exr and edu (exr times edu)
blc: race dummy for black
hisp: race dummy for Hispanic
mar: dummy for married
rur: dummy for living in a rural area
sou: dummy for living in south

The other regressors used are industry dummies: agr (agriculture), bus (business and repair service), cst (construction), fin (finance), man (manufacturing), pro (professional), pub (public administration), trad (trade), and tran (transportation); more regressors were used in Vella and Verbeek (1998). Although only 1, edu, blc, and hisp are the true time invariants in the data, many time variants show little variation over time; for example, only 3% of agr is 1, which means that even if agr varies over time, the variation will be minuscule. For the panel probit, we will treat only mar, rur, and sou as time variants. For conditional logit, as will be shown later in Table 4.4, different variables are used as time variants; the reason for this is given later as well.

Turning to the data analysis, first, we applied cross-section probit to all waves. Table 4.3 shows the results for waves 2, 3, 7, and 8 along with the t-values for wave 3 and wave 8; the choice of regressors and waves is due to the fact that some dummies show almost no across-individual variation in certain waves. The main reason for showing Table 4.3 is to alert the reader of a pitfall in panel data: the parameters tend to change over time, which is evident in the estimates for edu, blc and rur. Also they indicate that two adjacent waves are similar at least in significant estimates, whereas the pair 2 and 3 seems to differ from the pair 7 and 8.

In Table 4.4, four columns are the estimation results corresponding to (a) to (d) in (7.1). Only waves 6, 7, and 8 are used in view of the parameter nonconstancy just mentioned. Because the first step of the MDE panel probit is cross-section probit, the panel probit needs cross-section variation in the regressors, whereas conditional logit needs temporal variation. This explains why we could not use the same set of regressors for both panel probit and conditional logit. The last column for the probit with $y_{i,t-1}$ is a no-δ_i model using only the time invariants and the contemporaneous time variants. Vella and Verbeek (1998) were able to use more regressors, for they estimated all periods together using both cross-section and temporal variation in the regressors under the parameter constancy assumption.

Comparing the first two columns, the estimates for panel probit and conditional logit are very different, as are their t-values, which is rather disconcerting. The MDE specification test (the bottom line) for the panel probit does not reject the over-identifying restrictions. The estimate for σ_2 is 1.296; after all, because the wave 7-th standard deviation is set at 1, it is natural not to have σ_2 too different from 1 given the one year gap. Because the standard error for σ_2 is 0.339, $H_o : \sigma_2 = 1$ is not rejected.

Comparing the second and third column, there is not much difference. The MDE test in the third column at the bottom does not reject the parameter constancy. Comparing the first and the last column, the two panel probits are rather different but they do not differ as much as the first two columns do. The lagged dependent variable $y_{i,t-1}$ has a big highly significant estimate. Because the parameters in probit are normalized, the fact that the coefficient of $y_{i,t-1}$ is greater than 1 should not be alarming. The MDE test at the bottom of the fourth column rejects the slope constancy across the two pairs (6,7) and (7,8). Comparing the first and fourth column to Vella and Verbeek (1998), there is much difference. One reason is that different regressors are used. Another reason is the time-varying parameter problem.

In getting the MDE in the first column, the first four iterations resulted in the following minimand and σ_2 values:

$$
\begin{array}{lcccc}
\text{minimand:} & 427607, & 174, & 12563, & 3243433 \\
\sigma_2: & 0.247, & 37, & 29.8, & 24.6
\end{array}
\tag{7.2}
$$

After the four iterations, the computation algorithm blew off as can be seen in the fourth minimand value. The main culprit for this is σ_2; estimating components of a variance matrix is almost always the main source of numerical optimization troubles. Thus we modified the program such that σ_2 is fixed at each grid point over $[0.5, 2]$. For each fixed σ_2, the routine converged within a couple of iterations. The choice of the range $[0.5, 2]$ reflects the notion that σ_1 and σ_2 are unlikely to differ much, and indeed the final estimate for σ_2 was 1.296 in Table 4.4. Equation (7.2) shows a danger of an automatic blindfolded application of the MDE in nonlinear problems.

TABLE 4.3 Cross−section Probit for Waves 2, 3, 7, and 8

Variable	Wave 2	Wave 3 ($t-$value)	Wave 7	Wave 8 ($t-$value)
one	1.389	3.793 (2.27)	6.657	6.438 (2.42)
edu	−0.235	−0.433 (−3.04)	−0.797	−0.724 (−3.12)
exr	−0.606	−0.897 (−3.08)	−0.895	−0.721 (−3.09)
exredu	0.064	0.081 (3.12)	0.091	0.068 (3.23)
blc	0.345	0.427 (2.08)	0.586	0.763 (4.02)
hisp	0.024	0.204 (1.15)	0.425	0.175 (0.96)
agr	−0.390	−0.408 (−0.75)	0.355	1.090 (1.91)
bus	−0.120	−0.446 (−1.05)	−0.435	−0.148 (−0.32)
cst	−0.264	−0.648 (−1.04)	−0.790	−0.256 (−0.45)
fin	0.209	0.542 (1.48)	−0.205	0.614 (1.41)
man	0.463	0.468 (1.45)	0.293	0.575 (1.42)
pro	0.227	0.019 (0.05)	1.072	0.815 (1.80)
pub	−0.174	0.184 (1.11)	−0.057	−0.083 (−0.51)
trad	0.006	0.018 (0.05)	−0.017	0.226 (0.55)
tran	0.763	0.986 (2.58)	1.067	0.934 (2.14)
mar	0.055	0.275 (2.01)	0.153	0.131 (0.94)
rur	0.851	0.886 (2.00)	1.123	1.294 (2.91)
sou	−0.190	−0.094 (−0.64)	−0.269	−0.019 (−0.14)

TABLE 4.4 Panel Probit and Conditional Logit: estimate (t−value)

	Pro (wave 7,8)	Logit (wave 7,8)	Logit (wave 6,7,8)	Pro (wave 6,7,8)
σ_2	1.296 (3.82)			y_{t-1}: 1.890 (14.9)
τ_1	3.918 (1.62)		$\Delta\tau_1$: −0.49(−1.43)	τ_1: 0.169 (0.08)
τ_2	3.833 (1.59)	$\Delta\tau_2$: 0.96 (3.37)	$\Delta\tau_2$: 0.96(3.45)	τ_2: 0.384 (0.18)
edu	−0.519 (−2.52)			−0.224 (−1.19)
exr	−0.537 (−2.40)			−0.201 (−1.01)
exredu	0.056 (2.78)			0.022 (1.25)
blc	0.691 (3.58)			0.599 (3.86)
hisp	0.309 (1.84)			0.255 (2.15)
agr	0.345 (0.76)			0.678 (1.31)
bus	−0.626 (−1.73)	0.857 (0.53)	0.461 (0.37)	0.067 (0.16)
cst	0.076 (0.21)			0.286 (0.76)
fin	−0.705 (−1.22)			0.239 (0.40)
man	0.197 (0.70)	0.936 (1.52)	0.921 (1.75)	0.392 (1.12)
pro	0.872 (2.50)	2.471 (1.86)	2.336 (2.09)	0.925 (2.52)
pub	−0.088 (−0.53)	−1.358 (−0.89)	−1.190 (−1.15)	−0.114 (−0.84)
trad	−0.124 (−0.42)	0.121 (0.14)	0.268 (0.37)	0.190 (0.54)
tran	0.787 (2.41)	0.392 (0.40)	0.371 (0.44)	0.559 (1.51)
mar	0.068 (0.27)	2.504 (1.64)	1.459 (1.80)	0.259 (2.14)
rur	0.626 (1.59)	0.949 (0.71)	1.271 (1.26)	0.935 (2.28)
sou	−0.017(−0.02)			−0.190 (−1.70)
mar1	0.457 (1.50)			
rur1	0.214 (0.63)			
sou1	0.115 (0.17)			
mar2	−0.330 (−1.27)			
rur2	0.435 (1.37)			
sou2	−0.299 (−0.42)			
	log−likelihood: −44.518			
MDE−test(p−value):	23.21 (0.108)		3.580 (0.893)	31.45 (0.036)

In summary, the followings can be said. First, conditional logit yields rather different estimates from panel probit; it is hard to say which requires weaker assumptions, but the former is truer to pure related effect than the latter is, and, on this ground, conditional logit may be preferred to panel probit. More discussion on this point appears at the end of Section 6.4 after we cover more first-difference estimators and estimators specifying the form dependence of δ_i on regressors. Second, depending on the estimator, different regressors may be used, not by choice, but by necessity due to the regressors' limited temporal and cross-sectional variation; this makes comparing estimators more difficult than it would be otherwise. Third, time-varying parameters should be considered for a long panel; long panels are not necessarily a boon.

5

PANEL DATA ESTIMATORS FOR
LIMITED RESPONSES

5.1 INTRODUCTION

The preceding chapter reviewed estimators for panel binary response models. This chapter examines estimators for panel limited response models other than binary; specifically, count response, censored response, and multinomial response will be covered. Other than count responses, only a few applications have appeared in the literature. Panel sample selection, which presents yet another important limited response problem, will be discussed in the following chapter. As in the previous chapters, our focus is on error-differencing (or first-differencing type) estimators allowing for related effect (that is, unit-specific error δ_i related to regressors). Also as in the previous chapters, our focus is on estimators based on weak assumptions rather than on heavily parametric ones.

Section 5.2 reviews nonlinear generalized methods of moment (GMM) for cross-section data as a preparation for studying panel GMM for count responses; nonlinear GMM was mentioned briefly for panel probit in the preceding chapter. Section 5.3 presents nearly parametric methods (conditional Poisson and conditional negative binomial) in Hausman *et al.* (1984) for panel count response with multiplicative related effect. Section 5.4 introduces moment-based estimators for panel count response, drawing on Chamberlain (1992), Wooldridge (1997, 1999), and Blundell *et al.* (2002). Section 5.5 examines Honoré's (1992) estimator for panel censored response. Section 5.6 introduces conditional logit for panel multinomial choice. Section 5.7 presents an empirical example on patents and research and development (R&D) for conditional Poisson and GMM. The sections in this chapter can be read selectively, depending on the reader's interest.

5.2 REVIEW OF CROSS-SECTION NONLINEAR IVE AND GMM

Consider a $v \times 1$ vector moment condition nonlinear in parameters:

$$E\rho(\omega, \beta) = 0 \qquad (2.1)$$

where $\omega \equiv (y, x')'$ is a random vector and β is a $k \times 1$ ($k \le v$) parameter vector. The GMM efficient under (2.1) is obtained by minimizing

$$(1/\sqrt{N}) \sum_i \rho(\omega_i, b)' \cdot \{V[(1/\sqrt{N}) \sum_i \rho(\omega_i, \beta)]\}^{-1} \cdot (1/\sqrt{N}) \sum_i \rho(\omega_i, b)$$
$$(2.2)$$

with respect to (wrt) b; the weighting matrix $V[\cdot]$ should be replaced by a consistent estimate; for example., under iid for $\omega_1, \dots, \omega_N$,

$$C_N = (1/N) \sum_i \rho(\omega_i, b_N) \cdot \rho(\omega_i, b_N)', \qquad (2.3)$$

where b_N is any $\sqrt{N}$-consistent estimator such as the inefficient GMM with I_v as the weighting matrix. See Hansen (1982), Newey and McFadden (1994), and Lee (1996) for more on GMM as explained in this section. In nonlinear GMM, basically, we deal with the linearized version.

Define a $k \times v$ matrix

$$\rho_b(\omega, \beta) \equiv \partial \rho(\omega, b)/\partial b|_{b=\beta}.$$

Then, denoting the GMM as b_{gmm},

$$\sqrt{N}(b_{gmm} - \beta) \Rightarrow N(0, [E\rho_b(\omega, \beta) \cdot \{V[(1/\sqrt{N}) \sum_i \rho(\omega_i, \beta)]\}^{-1} \cdot$$
$$E\rho_b(\omega, \beta)']^{-1}). \qquad (2.4)$$

For the GMM overidentification (over-id) test, for iid $\omega_1, \dots, \omega_N$, we have

$$(1/\sqrt{N}) \sum_i \rho(\omega_i, b_{gmm})' \cdot \{(1/N) \sum_i \rho(\omega_i, b_{gmm}) \cdot \rho(\omega_i, b_{gmm})'\}^{-1}$$
$$\cdot (1/\sqrt{N}) \sum_i \rho(\omega_i, b_{gmm}) \Rightarrow \chi^2_{v-k}; \qquad (2.5)$$

from now on, assume that $\omega_1, \dots, \omega_N$ are iid.

Instead of the unconditional moment condition $E\rho(\omega, \beta) = 0$, suppose we have the conditional moment condition

$$E\{\rho(\omega, \beta)|x\} = 0. \qquad (2.6)$$

Under $E\rho(\omega, \beta)^2 < \infty$, this is equivalent to

$$E\{\rho(\omega, \beta) \cdot h(x)\} = 0 \quad \text{for any function } h(x) \text{ with } E\{h(x)^2\} < \infty. \qquad (2.7)$$

Because $h(x)$ can be approximated arbitrarily well by polynomial functions of components of x on a compact set for x, we may replace (2.7) with

$$E\{\rho(\omega, \beta) \cdot x_j^m\} = 0, \quad j = 1, ..., J, \quad m = 0, 1, 2, ..., \qquad (2.8)$$

where $x = (x_1, x_2, ..., x_J)'$. Thus (2.6) renders far more moment conditions than (2.1). But we can stack the moment conditions in (2.8) and redefine $\rho(\omega, \beta)$ for the stacked version. Hence, there is a GMM using unconditional moments that is efficient under (2.6) (Chamberlain, 1987).

We may also use a second-order information: the functional form of

$$\sigma(x, \gamma)^2 \equiv E\{\rho(\omega, \beta)\rho(\omega, \beta)'|x\} \qquad (2.9)$$

is known up to an unknown parameter γ. But this can be rewritten as

$$E\{\rho(\omega, \beta)\rho(\omega, \beta)' - \sigma(x, \gamma)^2|x\} = 0, \qquad (2.10)$$

which is a conditional moment condition as in (2.6). Hence, in short, GMM for the first order moment conditions is general enough to deal with conditional or high-order moment conditions.

An iteration algorithm for the nonlinear GMM under (2.1) is

$$
b_1 = b_0 - s \cdot [\sum_i \rho_b(\omega, b_0) \cdot C_{N0}^{-1} \cdot \sum_i \rho_b(\omega, b_0)']^{-1} \qquad (2.11)
$$
$$
\sum_i \rho_b(\omega, b_0) \cdot C_{N0}^{-1} \cdot \sum_i \rho(\omega_i, b_0),
$$

where b_0 is an initial estimate, b_1 is a new one, s is a step-size (a value, typically, between 0 and 1), and

$$C_{N0} \equiv (1/N) \sum_i \rho(\omega_i, b_0) \cdot \rho(\omega_i, b_0)'.$$

The algorithm can be repeated until convergence, which can be defined as almost no change in the minimand (2.5) or in the normalized estimates. If the step size is too small, the algorithm moves too slowly; if it is too big, the optimum may be missed. The iteration may be done only for some components of β, while the other components are fixed at grid points for which grid search is done. Also, "squeezing" may help: if b_1 is not an improvement over b_0, $(b_0 + b_1)/2$ is used instead of b_1; if $(b_0 + b_1)/2$ is not an improvement either, move further toward b_0, say, with $b_0/2 + \{(b_0 + b_1)/2\}/2$.

Despite the generality, nonlinear GMM has a couple of problems. First, there may be multiple parameters satisfying (2.1), which is an identification problem, and (2.11) can easily yield multiple local minima. Second, instruments can be weak. Third, the weighting matrix estimate may be poor. There is not much one can do for the first problem. We will examine the second and third problems in the following discussion.

If the instruments are many but weak, then the asymptotic theory for instrumental variable estimator (IVE) and GMM, linear or nonlinear, may not work well. The literature suggests that, in linear models, IVE is biased toward the least squares estimator (LSE), and the bias gets bigger with more instruments. Suppose y_2 and w are, respectively, the endogenous and exogenous regressor in an equation of interest, and z is an instrument for y_2. Although the relation between z and the equation error u cannot be checked out, to see the relation between z and y_2, the LSE of y_2 on z is often done in practice; Shea (1997) proposed an improvement that amounts to the LSE of the residual of y_2 from w on the residual of z from w, removing the effect of w. But Hall et al. (1996) showed that the instruments looking good in the sample tend to be related to u. The sample splitting idea of Angrist and Krueger (1995) avoids this problem, but suffers from higher standard errors; "Jackknife IVE" suggested by Angrist et al. (1999) overcomes the standard error problem as well. But, overall, it is not clear yet how useful the procedures put forward for weak instruments are. For one thing, there are Monte Carlo designs favoring those procedures but one can come up with other designs against them. Also, most theoretical findings are derived from limited settings such as "local-to-zero" for moment conditions or instrument relevance (Staiger and Stock, 1997, Stock and Wright, 2000, and Wang and Zivot, 1998). Interested readers can start with these references.

For (2.11), the most troublesome is C_{N0}, which may come out almost singular. A remedy is to replace C_{N0} with I_ν to get an inefficient GMM, from which doing (2.11) only once is enough asymptotically although repeating (2.11) may lead to a further improvement. A better idea may be replacing C_{N0} with $\text{diag}(c_1, ..., c_\nu)$, where c_j is the j-th diagonal element of C_{N0} to remove different scales in the moments. Once this iteration converges, one can take only one step to the efficient GMM or repeat (2.11) from there. As in linear GMM, the efficient GMM may perform more poorly than the I_ν-weighted GMM in small samples.

As Hansen et al. (1996) showed, GMM can be implemented differently from (2.11): one way is to use the I_ν-weighted GMM for C_{N0} and keep this C_{N0} at all iterations, and another way is minimizing (2.2) with β in the middle matrix replaced by b. Also, in "empirical-likelihood"-based ideas (see Imbens, 1997,

Qin and Lawless, 1994, Owen, 2001, and the references therein), probabilities p_i, $i = 1, ..., N$, are estimated along with β in

$$\max_{b, p_1, ..., p_N} \sum_i \ln(p_i) \quad \text{subject to } p_i \geq 0, \quad \sum_i p_i = 1, \quad \sum_i p_i \rho(\omega_i, b) = 0.$$

The last restriction is that the moment conditions hold exactly for the "profile likelihood" where $P(\omega = \omega_i) = p_i$, whereas $P(\omega = \omega_i) = 1/N$ in the empirical likelihood. The GMM estimator obtained this way avoids the issue of the weighting matrix but still follows (2.4).

As an empirical example, consider a stochastic differential equation for an interest rate $y(t)$:

$$dy(t) = \{\beta_1 - \beta_2 y(t)\} \cdot dt + \sigma \cdot y(t)^\eta \cdot dw(t), \tag{2.12}$$

where β_1, β_2, σ, and η are positive parameters, and $w(t)$ is a standard Brownian motion or Wiener process: $w(0) = 0$, $w(t)$ is continuous, and for all $q \leq s < t$,

$w(t) - w(s)$ follows $N(0, t - s)$ and is independent of $w(q)$.

Equation (2.12) can be approximated in discrete time by

$$\begin{aligned}
y_t &\cong y_{t-1} + (\beta_1 - \beta_2 y_{t-1}) \cdot \Delta t + \sigma y_{t-1}^\eta \cdot (\Delta t)^{1/2} \varepsilon_t, \tag{2.13} \\
&\quad \{\varepsilon_t\} \text{ is iid } N(0, 1) \\
&= y_{t-1} + \beta_2 (\beta_1/\beta_2 - y_{t-1}) \cdot \Delta t + \sigma y_{t-1}^\eta \cdot (\Delta t)^{1/2} \varepsilon_t.
\end{aligned}$$

The stationary level for y_t (with $\varepsilon_t = 0$) is β_1/β_2. The second term on the right-hand side makes y_t revert to β_1/β_2 ("mean-reversion"), and β_2 is the speed of adjustment.

With $\Delta t = 1$, (2.13) becomes

$$y_t = \beta_1 + (1 - \beta_2) \cdot y_{t-1} + \sigma y_{t-1}^\eta \varepsilon_t. \tag{2.14}$$

If we set Δt differently, say $\Delta t = c$, then this decreases β_1 and β_2 by c times and σ by $\sqrt{c}$ times as can be seen by rewriting the right-hand side of (2.13):

$$y_{t-1} + (\beta_1/c - (\beta_2/c) \cdot y_{t-1}) \cdot c\Delta t + (\sigma/\sqrt{c}) \cdot (c\Delta t)^{1/2} \cdot y_{t-1}^\eta \varepsilon_t.$$

With this point understood, we will use (2.14) from now on to estimate the four parameters $\gamma \equiv (\beta_1, \beta_2, \sigma, \eta)'$ with GMM; instead of σ, σ^2 may be estimated if one desires equivariance for Δt. See Ahn and Gao (1999) and the references therein for the literature of (2.12) on interest rate.

Define, from (2.14),

$$\begin{aligned}
u_t &\equiv \sigma y_{t-1}^\eta \cdot \varepsilon_t = y_t - y_{t-1} - (\beta_1 - \beta_2 y_{t-1}), \quad v_t \equiv u_t^2 - \sigma^2 y_{t-1}^{2\eta} \\
&\Rightarrow E(u_t | y_1, ..., y_{t-1}) = 0 \quad \text{and} \quad E(v_t | y_1, ..., y_{t-1}) = 0. \tag{2.15}
\end{aligned}$$

Because this gives too many moment conditions, we will use only the following six unconditional moment conditions for illustration:

$$E(u_t) = 0, \quad E(u_t y_{t-1}) = 0, \quad E(u_t y_{t-2}) = 0, \qquad (2.16)$$
$$E(v_t) = 0, \quad E(v_t y_{t-1}) = 0, \quad E(v_t y_{t-2}) = 0.$$

The main source of difficulty in this GMM is η, the identification of which becomes almost impossible when σ is close to zero.

Using the U.S. 3-month treasury bill rates (in percentages) monthly from January 1982 to December 1999 ($N = 216$), (2.11) failed to work. Instead, η is fixed over grid points 0.7 to 1.5, and then the inefficient GMM with the nonscalar diagonal matrix was carried out with $(0.1, 0.1, 0.1)$ as the initial values for $(\beta_1, \beta_2, \sigma)$; numerical derivatives were used for the derivative of the moment conditions. Comparing the GMM minimands over the η-grid points, $\eta = 1.24$ gave the minimum, and $(0.162, 0.029, 0.024)$ was the estimate for $(\beta_1, \beta_2, \sigma)$. Taking one step (2.11) from these values did not change the estimates but gave the t-values; the final estimates with t-values in $(\cdot)$ are

β_1	β_2	σ	η	
0.162	0.029	0.024	1.24	(2.17)
(2.13)	(2.18)	(2.58)	(6.47)	

The over-id test statistic and p-value from $\chi^2_{6-4} = \chi^2_2$ are

$$\text{Test statistic} = 5.858, \quad p\text{-value} = 0.053, \qquad (2.18)$$

indicating a possible misspecification. The steady state rate is $0.162/0.029 = 5.33\%$, which looks reasonable. As noted already, the estimation is sensitive to η, a contentious parameter in the literature. Although GMM provides a unifying theme for econometrics, nonlinear GMM does not behave computationally as well as it is made out to behave; often algorithms as in (2.11) converge to different local minima, depending on the weighting matrices.

5.3   NEARLY PARAMETRIC METHODS FOR COUNT RESPONSE

When a response variable y_{it} takes integer values 0, 1, 2, ..., y_{it} is called a "count response." In this section, first we review parametric unrelated-effect estimators in Subsection 5.3.1, and then examine their related-effect versions in Subsection 5.3.2. For the latter, we draw extensively on Hausman, Hall, and Griliches (1984, HHG for the rest of this section), who employ the idea of conditioning on a sufficient statistic for the unit-specific effect δ_i as in conditional logit. Subsection 5.3.3 provides an empirical example with the health data that was used already in the preceding chapter. In the next section, GMM for related-effect count responses are presented. For the related-effect panel estimators, δ_i should be taken as $\tilde{c}_i'\tilde{\alpha} + \delta_i$ as has been done in other sections already where $\tilde{c}_i$ refers to the time-invariant regressors.

5.3.1 Poisson and Negative Binomial

Suppose $(y_{it}, w_{it}')'$, $t = 1, ..., T$, $i = 1, ..., N$, are iid, where w_{it} is a vector of regressors including both time variants and time invariants. Assume that $y_{it}|w_{it}$ follows Poisson with parameter λ_{it}:

$$P(y_{it} = y|w_{it}) = \lambda_{it}^{y} \cdot \exp(-\lambda_{it})/y!, \quad \lambda_{it} = \exp(w_{it}'\gamma), \quad \text{for } y = 0, 1, ...$$

Then the parameter γ can be estimated by maximizing the log-likelihood

$$\sum_{i=1}^{N}\sum_{t=1}^{T}\{y_{it}w_{it}'g - \exp(w_{it}'g) - \ln(y_{it}!)\}$$

wrt g; drop $\ln(y_{it}!)$ for the actual maximization. The score function for individual i is

$$\sum_{t=1}^{T}\{y_{it} - \exp(w_{it}'g)\}w_{it} = \sum_{t=1}^{T}\{y_{it} - E(y_{it}|w_{it})\}w_{it},$$

showing that the Poisson maximum likelihood estimator (MLE) uses a summation (SUM) type moment condition

$$E[\sum_{t=1}^{T}\{y_{it} - E(y_{it}|w_{it})\}w_{it}] = 0.$$

The Poisson assumption includes the critical restriction

$$E(y_{it}|w_{it}) = \lambda_{it} = V(y_{it}|w_{it}),$$

which is usually violated in practice, for the variance tends to be greater than the mean ("overdispersion" problem). In this case, because $V(y_{it}|w_{it})$ is underestimated, the resulting standard deviations of the estimators are underestimated, resulting in too large t-values. Other than the overdispersion problem, the Poisson model is also restrictive in that the iid assumption across t for a given i does not allow any dynamic feature in the model. HHG propose estimating $E(\varepsilon_i \varepsilon_i')$ to check out the iid assumption, where $\varepsilon_i \equiv (\varepsilon_{i1}, ..., \varepsilon_{iT})'$ and $\varepsilon_{it} \equiv (y_{it} - \lambda_{it})/(\lambda_{it})^{1/2}$, $t = 1, ..., T$: under the Poisson and iid assumption, $E(\varepsilon_i \varepsilon_i') = I_T$ should hold.

To overcome the overdispersion problem of Poisson, maintain the restrictive iid assumption across i and t, but introduce an "unobserved heterogeneity" ε_{it} such that

$$y_{it}|(w_{it}, \varepsilon_{it})$$

follows Poisson with parameter

$$\hat{\lambda}_{it} \equiv \exp(w_{it}'\gamma + \varepsilon_{it}), \quad \text{where} \quad E(\exp(\varepsilon_{it})|w_{it}) = 1.$$

Then

$$E(y_{it}|w_{it}) = \exp(w'_{it}\gamma) \cdot E(\exp(\varepsilon_{it})|w_{it}) = \exp(w'_{it}\gamma);$$
$$V(y_{it}|w_{it}) = E(y_{it}^2|w_{it}) - \{E(y_{it}|w_{it})\}^2 = E(y_{it}^2|w_{it}) - \exp(2w'_{it}\gamma).$$

Observe

$$
\begin{aligned}
E(y_{it}^2|w_{it}) &= E\{E(y_{it}^2|w_{it}, \varepsilon_{it})|w_{it}\} \\
&= E\{V(y_{it}|w_{it}, \varepsilon_{it}) + (E(y_{it}|w_{it}, \varepsilon_{it}))^2|w_{it}\} \\
&= E\{\exp(w'_{it}\gamma + \varepsilon_{it}) + \exp(2w'_{it}\gamma + 2\varepsilon_{it})|w_{it}\} \\
&= \exp(w'_{it}\gamma) + \exp(2w'_{it}\gamma) \cdot E(\exp(2\varepsilon_{it})|w_{it}).
\end{aligned}
$$

Substitute this into $V(y_{it}|w_{it})$ to get

$$
\begin{aligned}
V(y_{it}|w_{it}) &= \exp(w'_{it}\gamma) + \exp(2w'_{it}\gamma) \cdot \\
&\quad \{E(\exp(2\varepsilon_{it})|w_{it}) - 1\} > \exp(w'_{it}\gamma) \\
&= E(y_{it}|w_{it})
\end{aligned}
$$

because

$$
\begin{aligned}
E\{\exp(2\varepsilon_{it})|w_{it}\} - 1 &= E\{(\exp(\varepsilon_{it}))^2|w_{it}\} - \{E(\exp(\varepsilon_{it})|w_{it})\}^2 \\
&= V(\exp(\varepsilon_{it})|w_{it}) > 0.
\end{aligned}
$$

Hence the presence of ε_{it} causes overdispersion.

In the preceding derivation, two aspects deserve comments in relation to linear models. Let $w_{it} = (1, w_{it2}, ..., w_{itk})'$ and $\gamma = (\gamma_1, \gamma_2, ..., \gamma_k)'$ so that w_{it} includes 1 and the first component of γ_1 is the intercept. First, the assumption $E(\exp(\varepsilon_{it})|w_{it}) = 1$ is analogous to $E(\varepsilon_{it}|w_{it}) = 0$; just imagine $\varepsilon_{it} = 0$ in both equations. In the former, if $E(\exp(\varepsilon_{it})|w_{it}) = \mu$, an unknown constant, then

$$E(y_{it}|w_{it}) = \exp(w'_{it}\gamma) \cdot \exp(\ln \mu) = \exp\{(\gamma_1 + \ln \mu) + w'_{it2}\gamma_2 + , ..., + w_{itk}\gamma_k\}:$$

the intercept shifts by $\ln \mu$. Hence with 1 included in w_{it}, the slopes are identified so long as $E(\exp(\varepsilon_{it})|w_{it})$ is a constant. If this is a function of w_{it}, say $m(w_{it}) > 0$, then $E(y_{it}|w_{it}) = \exp(w'_{it}\gamma + \ln(m(w_{it})))$; γ is not identified in general. In the linear model, say $y_{it} = w'_{it}\gamma + u_{it}$, an analogy holds: if $E(u_{it}|w_{it}) = \mu$, then the slopes are identified whereas the intercept is not because μ is absorbed into the intercept; if $E(u_{it}|w_{it}) = m(w_{it})$, then the slopes are not identified in general. Second, in the Poisson assumption with ε_{it}, two separate "error terms" appear in the model:

$$u_{it} \equiv y_{it} - E(y_{it}|w_{it}, \varepsilon_{it}) \Leftrightarrow y_{it} = \exp(w'_{it}\gamma + \varepsilon_{it}) + u_{it}.$$

In contrast, in the linear model, they get merged: $y_{it} = w'_{it}\gamma + v_{it}$, $v_{it} \equiv \varepsilon_{it} + u_{it}$.

Because ε_{it} is unobserved, it should be removed to estimate γ; this can be done by specifying its distribution. Suppose

$$\exp(\varepsilon_{it})|w_{it} \text{ follows Gamma } (\pi_{it}, \pi_{it}), \quad \pi_{it} \equiv \alpha^{-1}\lambda_{it}^{\kappa}$$
$$= \alpha^{-1}\exp(\kappa \cdot w_{it}'\gamma), \quad \alpha > 0$$

where Gamma (c, d) denotes Gamma distribution with parameters c and d, α is a parameter to estimate whereas κ is estimated or often set at 0 or 1, and λ_{it} was defined already for Poisson. Because Gamma (c, c) distribution has mean 1, the condition $E(\exp(\varepsilon_{it})|w_{it}) = 1$ is met by the Gamma specification. Integrating ε_{it} out, $y_{it}|w_{it}$ follows a "negative binomial " distribution: with $\Gamma(s) \equiv \int_0^\infty z^{s-1}e^{-z}dz$ for $s > 0$,

$$P(y_{it} = y|w_{it}) = [\Gamma(y + \pi_{it})/\{\Gamma(\pi_{it}) \cdot \Gamma(y + 1)\}]$$
$$\cdot \{\pi_{it}/(\lambda_{it} + \pi_{it})\}^{\pi_{it}} \cdot \{\lambda_{it}/(\lambda_{it} + \pi_{it})\}^y, \quad \text{for } y = 0, 1, \ldots$$

Define $p \equiv \pi_{it}/(\lambda_{it} + \pi_{it})$, which falls between 0 and 1, and suppose π_{it} is an integer. Then, using $\Gamma(n) = (n - 1)!$ for an integer n, we get a negative binomial (NB) distribution with parameters (p, π_{it}) :

$$P(y_{it} = y|w_{it}) = (y + \pi_{it} - 1)!/\{(\pi_{it} - 1)!y!\} \cdot p^{\pi_{it}-1}(1 - p)^y \cdot p.$$

If we repeat a binary experiment until we get π_{it} successes (π_{it} is fixed), then the probability of getting y-many failures before we reach π_{it} successes is given by this formula: there should be $\pi_{it} - 1$ successes and y failures in the total $y + \pi_{it} - 1$ trials, with the last additional trial being a success. If $\pi_{it} = 1$, the experiment lasts only until the first success, and the NB is called "geometric." This experiment is where NB appears usually. For our purpose, however, this interpretation is of no particular use.

NB allows for overdispersion:

$$E(y_{it}|w_{it}) = \lambda_{it} \quad \text{and} \quad V(y_{it}|w_{it}) = \lambda_{it} + \alpha \cdot \lambda_{it}^{2-\kappa};$$

the variance is greater than the mean. Poisson is included as a limiting case as $\alpha \to 0$. The log-likelihood function for α, γ (and κ) is

$$\sum_{i=1}^{N}\sum_{t=1}^{T}[\ln\{\Gamma(y_{it} + \pi_{it})\} - \ln\{\{\Gamma(\pi_{it})\} - \ln\{\Gamma(y_{it} + 1)\}$$
$$\pi_{it} \cdot \{\ln(\pi_{it}) - \ln(\lambda_{it} + \pi_{it})\} + y_{it} \cdot \{\ln(\lambda_{it}) - \ln(\lambda_{it} + \pi_{it})\}];$$

drop $\ln\Gamma(y_{it} + 1)$ for the actual maximization.

Although κ can be estimated, we will set $\kappa = 0$ from now on to get $\pi_{it} \equiv 1/\alpha$, and $V(y_{it}|w_{it}) = \lambda_{it} + \alpha\lambda_{it}^2$, which is quadratic in λ_{it}. One reason for $\kappa = 0$ is to avoid a possible identification problem: κ is not identified well if $\alpha \simeq 0$. Besides, $\kappa = 0$ is particularly attractive because the information matrix of the MLE becomes blockdiagonal for γ and α (see, for example, Cameron and Trivedi, 1998), which means that γ can be estimated "independently" (or "adaptively") for α as follows.

The score function for γ for individual i is

$$\sum_{t=1}^{T}\{(y_{it}-\lambda_{it})/(1+\alpha\lambda_{it})\}w_{it} = \sum_{t=1}^{T}\{(y_{it}-\lambda_{it})/(\lambda_{it}+\alpha\lambda_{it}^2)\}\lambda_{it}w_{it} = 0. \quad (3.1)$$

If we estimate γ by minimizing $\sum_i \sum_t (y_{it} - \lambda_{it})^2$, then the first order condition is equivalent to

$$\sum_i \sum_t (y_{it} - \lambda_{it})\lambda_{it}w_{it} = 0,$$

showing that the preceding score function is a weighted version of $\sum_t (y_{it} - \lambda_{it})\lambda_{it}w_{it}$, with the weight being $\lambda_{it} + \alpha\lambda_{it}^2$. In general, the ideal weighting function is the conditional variance of the "error term" in the first-order condition (as in generalized LSE for linear models): in (3.1), the ideal weight is used, for $V(y_{it}-\lambda_{it}|w_{it}) = \lambda_{it}+\alpha\lambda_{it}^2$. If there is a $\sqrt{N}$-consistent estimator for α, then it can be plugged into the score function, which then can be used to estimate γ. Even when the wrong weighting function is used because α is not $\sqrt{N}$-consistent or because the weighting function is misspecified, still the MLE for γ using the score function is consistent, although the asymptotic variance is no longer valid. This is the main reason why setting $\kappa = 0$ is a reasonable thing to do.

5.3.2 Conditional Poisson and Conditional Negative Binomial

NB in the preceding subsection introduced ε_{it} to allow overdispersion. But then, to eliminate ε_{it}, which may be related to w_{it}, a Gamma distribution was imposed on $\exp(\varepsilon_{it})|w_{it}$ and the relationship between ε_{it} and w_{it} was spelled out; note, however, that, if $\kappa = 0$, ε_{it} becomes independent of w_{it}. This is too restrictive. In panel data, if unobserved heterogeneity is time invariant, we can do without such restrictive assumptions.

HHG use Poisson distribution conditional on x_{it} and δ_i:

$$P(y_{it}|x_{it},\delta_i) = e^{-\tilde{\lambda}_{it}}(\tilde{\lambda}_{it})^{y_{it}}/y_{it}!$$

where

$$\tilde{\lambda}_{it} \equiv \exp(x_{it}'\beta + \delta_i) = \exp(\delta_i) \cdot \exp(x_{it}'\beta),$$

and assume strict exogeneity (EXO):

$$P(y_{it}|x_{i1}, ..., x_{iT}, \delta_i) = P(y_{it}|x_{it}, \delta_i). \quad (3.2)$$

Then, under the independence assumption

$$y_{i1}, ..., y_{iT} \text{ are independent given } (x_{i1}, ..., x_{iT}) \text{ and } \delta_i, \quad (3.3)$$

$\sum_t y_{it}|(x_{i1}, ..., x_{iT}, \delta_i)$ follows a Poisson distribution with parameter

$$\sum_t \tilde{\lambda}_{it} = \exp(\delta_i) \cdot \sum_t \exp(x'_{it}\beta). \tag{3.4}$$

This is simply due to a property of the Poisson distribution: a sum of independent Poisson random variables follows a Poisson distribution with the parameter being the sum of the individual parameters.

It can be shown that (3.2) to (3.4) imply that

$$(y_{i1}, ..., y_{iT})|(\sum_t y_{it}, x_{i1}, ..., x_{iT}, \delta_i)$$

follows the multinomial distribution: the number of trials is $\sum_t y_{it}$, there are T-many distinct events with the t-th event occurring y_{it} times, and the probability for the t-th event occurring in a given trial is $\tilde{\lambda}_{it}/\sum_t \tilde{\lambda}_{it}$. The multinomial probability distribution is

$$(\sum_t y_{it})! \cdot (\prod_t y_{it}!)^{-1} \cdot \prod_t (\tilde{\lambda}_{it}/\sum_t \tilde{\lambda}_{it})^{y_{it}}$$
$$= (\sum_t y_{it})! \cdot (\prod_t y_{it}!)^{-1} \cdot \prod_t \{(\tilde{\lambda}_{it}/\tilde{\lambda}_{i1})/\sum_t (\tilde{\lambda}_{it}/\tilde{\lambda}_{i1})\}^{y_{it}}$$
$$= (\sum_t y_{it})! \cdot (\prod_t y_{it}!)^{-1} \cdot \prod_t \{\exp(\Delta x'_{it1}\beta)/\sum_s \exp(\Delta x'_{is1}\beta)\}^{y_{it}},$$

where

$$\Delta x_{it1} \equiv x_{it} - x_{i1}.$$

Note the similarity to conditional logit in conditioning on $\sum_t y_{it}$ and in how δ_i is removed.

The log-likelihood function for all observations is (the iid assumption across i of Poisson is maintained although the iid acrss t is replaced by (3.3))

$$\sum_i [\ln\{(\sum_t y_{it})!\} - \sum_t \ln(y_{it}!) \tag{3.5}$$
$$+ \sum_t y_{it} \cdot \{\Delta x'_{it1}b - \ln(\sum_s \exp(\Delta x'_{is1}b))\}]$$

to be maximized for b. The score function for the i-th individual is

$$\sum_t y_{it}\{\Delta x_{it1} - \sum_s \Delta x_{is1} \exp(\Delta x'_{is1}\beta)/\sum_s \exp(\Delta x'_{is1}\beta)\}; \tag{3.6}$$

note $\Delta x_{it1} = 0$ for $t = 1$. The rest of the conditional Poisson MLE is straightforward; call the MLE "CPOI" (conditional Poisson).

To give a method-of-moment interpretation to CPOI, rewrite the score function as

$$
\begin{aligned}
&\sum_t y_{it} \Delta x_{it1} - \sum_t y_{it} \sum_s \Delta x_{is1} \exp(\Delta x'_{is1}\beta) / \sum_s \exp(\Delta x'_{is1}\beta) \\
=\;&\sum_t y_{it} \Delta x_{it1} - \sum_s y_{is} \sum_t \Delta x_{it1} \exp(\Delta x'_{it1}\beta) / \sum_s \exp(\Delta x'_{is1}\beta) \\
=\;&\sum_t \Delta x_{it1}[y_{it} - \{\exp(\Delta x'_{it1}\beta) / \sum_s \exp(\Delta x'_{is1}\beta)\} \sum_s y_{is}]. \quad (3.7)
\end{aligned}
$$

Define the weight ω_{it}:

$$
\omega_{it} \equiv \exp(\Delta x'_{it1}\beta) / \sum_s \exp(\Delta x'_{is1}\beta) \quad \text{where } \sum_t w_{it} = 1
$$

to rewrite the error term in the score function as

$$
y_{it} - \omega_{it} \sum_s y_{is} : \quad (3.8)
$$

y_{it} is "predicted" with a fraction ω_{it} of the sum $\sum_t y_{it}$. As it is clear from $\sum_t$ in the score function, a SUM-type moment condition is used.

CPOI has a couple of restrictions. The first is the EXO. The second is the independence assumption in (3.3) ruling out dynamics operating through relations among y_{it}'s given $\delta_i, x_{i1}, ..., x_{iT}$. The third is the overdispersion problem for the restriction

$$
E(y_{it}|x_{it}, \delta_i) = V(y_{it}|x_{it}, \delta_i); \quad (3.9)
$$

HHG provide an extension using a negative binomial to alleviate this problem, as to be seen shortly.

The overdispersion problem makes CPOI underestimate the standard errors and thus give too large t-values; this is simply because CPOI imposes (3.9). One remedy to this problem is using a more flexible parametric model not requiring (3.9) as shown later in (3.12), but a simpler solution is to take the CPOI likelihood as a "pseudo-likelihood" not requiring (3.9) and use the usual extremum estimator asymptotic variance

$$
H^{-1} \cdot C \cdot H^{-1} \quad (3.10)
$$

instead of C^{-1} where H is the second-order derivative matrix of the log-likelihood and C is the sum of the outer products of score functions. For this, the second-order matrix for (3.5) is needed:

$$
\begin{aligned}
-\sum_i \sum_t y_{it}[&\sum_s \Delta x_{is1} \Delta x'_{is1} \exp(\Delta x'_{is1}\beta) / \sum_s \exp(\Delta x'_{is1}\beta) \quad (3.11) \\
&-\{\sum_s \Delta x_{is1} \exp(\Delta x'_{is1}\beta) / \sum_s \exp(\Delta x'_{is1}\beta)\} \\
&\cdot\{\sum_s \Delta x'_{is1} \exp(\Delta x'_{is1}\beta) / \sum_s \exp(\Delta x'_{is1}\beta)\}].
\end{aligned}
$$

A formal justification for the pseudo-MLE will appear later under a different name, and an alternative form for (3.11) will be seen there. The pseudo-MLE works well computationally, and this is the one we advocate for panel count response so long as the strict exogeneity (3.2) is plausible.

Finally, HHG provide "conditional negative binomial" under (a) EXO (3.2), (b) the independence (3.3), and (c)

$$y_{it}|(x_{it}, \delta_i) \text{ follows negative binomial with parameters } (p_i, \tilde{\lambda}_{it}). \quad (3.12)$$

The conditional log-likelihood function to be maximized for b is

$$\sum_i (\sum_t [\ln\{\Gamma(y_{it} + \lambda_{it})\} - \ln\{\Gamma(\lambda_{it})\} - \ln\{\Gamma(y_{it} + 1)\} \quad (3.13)$$

$$\ln\{\Gamma(\sum_t \lambda_{it})\} + \ln\{\Gamma(1 + \sum_t y_{it})\} - \ln\{\Gamma(\sum_t \lambda_{it} + \sum_t y_{it})\}]);$$

both δ_i and p_i drop out in the conditioning. The conditional NB is not so attractive because it requires (3.3) and (3.12) which are not needed in the aforementioned pseudo-MLE.

5.3.3 An Empirical Example on Health Care Demand

Recall the Health and Retirement Study data set used for conditional logit: the sample of $N = 8484$ is for years 1992 and 1994 ($T = 2$), and for people born between 1931 and 1941. Now y_{it} is the number of doctor office visits per year. Lee and Kobayashi (2001) used more than 60 variables to explain y_{it}, but we present only part of their results for some regressors. Table 5.1 shows the summary statistics for wave 1.

TABLE 5.1 Summary Statistics for Wave 1

	MEAN	SD	MIN	MED	MAX
y_{it}	3.64	6.01	0	2	80
age	55.31	5.49	23	55	82
job	0.69	0.46	0	1	1
income($1000, inc)	55.72	48.78	0	46.0	625
married (mar)	0.83	0.38	0	1	1
schooling (edu)	12.19	3.18	0	12	17
medicare ($care$)	0.058	0.23	0	0	1
medicaid ($caid$)	0.031	0.17	0	0	1
blue-hmo ($blue$)	0.722	0.45	0	1	1

Table 5.2 shows part of the estimation results (t-values in ($\cdot$)).

Table 5.2 Doctor Office Visit Equation

	Poisson	NB ($\kappa = 0$)	CPOI
age/10	0.297 (1.40)	0.172 (1.35)	−3.141 (−1.69)
age²/100	−0.038 (−1.99)	−0.025 (−2.14)	0.042 (0.51)
edu	0.010 (2.15)	0.013 (4.87)	
male	−0.102 (−3.50)	−0.154 (−9.62)	
mar	−0.050 (−1.58)	−0.008 (−0.39)	−0.081 (−0.74)
job	0.009 (0.09)	−0.005 (−0.08)	−0.024 (−0.14)
ln(inc)	0.009 (0.83)	0.009 (1.87)	0.012 (1.00)
care	0.230 (5.03)	0.280 (9.96)	−0.076 (−1.07)
caid	0.318 (5.76)	0.346 (8.83)	0.015 (0.15)
blue	0.149 (4.94)	0.178 (9.95)	0.079 (1.17)

The t-values for Poisson and CPOI were obtained using a (3.10)-like formula, not the inverse of the outer product of the score functions. For Poisson, this means assuming only $E(y_{it}|w_{it}) = \exp(w'_{it}\gamma)$, not the full Poisson assumption. As for CPOI, as to be seen in the next section, this means an analogous relaxation of an assumption.

The parameters for time invariants, edu and male, are identified only in Poisson and NB: the effect of education is positive and significant, whereas the effect of being male is negative and significant. Poisson differs little from NB, but differs much from CPOI. The effect of marriage is negative but not significant. The insignificant insurance dummy estimates for CPOI are likely to be due to small temporal variation in the dummy variables.

In these estimators, zeros are treated more or less in the same way as other numbers of visits. But it may be more plausible that the initial decision to visit a doctor (that is, zero or positive) is made by an individual, whereas the follow-up visits (that is, the number of visits given it is positive) are mostly determined by the doctor. In this scenario, the zero-or-not decision may be modeled as a binary response depending on one set of parameters whereas positive numbers of visits are modeled with another set of parameters (Pohlmeier and Ulrich, 1995).

5.4 MOMENT-BASED ESTIMATORS FOR COUNT RESPONSES

This section reviews method-of-moment estimators for panel count responses; Chamberlain (1992) and Wooldridge (1997) in Subsection 5.4.1, Blundell *et al.* (2002) in Subsection 5.4.2, and Wooldridge (1999) in Subsection 5.4.3. They are presented as semiparametric alternatives to the nearly parametric methods in the preceding section; little is assumed in the semiparametric estimators, which are also not difficult to implement.

5.4.1 GMM without Additive Lagged Response

It holds in conditional Poisson (CPOI) that, with a time-varying intercept τ_t in now,

$$E(y_{it}|\delta_i, w_{it}) = \exp(\delta_i) \cdot \exp(\tau_t + \tilde{c}_i'\tilde{\alpha} + x_{it}'\beta) \ (= \tilde{\lambda}_{it});$$

here we are using $w_{it} \equiv (1, \tilde{c}_i', x_{it}')'$ to make the presence of $\tilde{c}_i$ explicit. Taking this equality as a nonlinear regression model without the Poisson distributional assumption gives the following semiparametric method that allows dependence among $y_{i1}, ..., y_{iT}$ given $w_{i1}, ..., w_{iT}$ and δ_i, which was not the case in CPOI. Suppose

$$
\begin{aligned}
E(y_{it}|\delta_i, w_{i1}, ..., w_{it}) &= E(y_{it}|\delta_i, w_{it}) & (4.1)\\
&= \exp(\delta_i) \cdot \exp(\tau_t + \tilde{c}_i'\tilde{\alpha} + x_{it}'\beta) \\
\Leftrightarrow \quad y_{it} &= \tilde{\lambda}_{it} + u_{it}, \\
u_{it} &\equiv y_{it} - \tilde{\lambda}_{it}, E(u_{it}|\delta_i, w_{i1}, ..., w_{it}) = 0.
\end{aligned}
$$

Here, u_{it} is orthogonal only to the past and current regressors but is allowed to influence future regressors. This allows feedback from the past errors (and thus from the past responses) to future x_{it}; that is, predeterminedness (PRE) type moment conditions can be used.

To simplify notations, define

$$W_{it} \equiv (w_{i1}, ..., w_{it})', \quad Y_{it} \equiv (y_{i1}, ..., y_{it})' \quad \text{and} \quad \lambda_{it} \equiv \exp(\tau_t + x_{it}'\beta).$$

Chamberlain (1992) and Wooldridge (1997) proposed a GMM based on the conditional moment condition: with $s < t$,

$$
\begin{aligned}
E\{y_{is} - y_{it}(\lambda_{is}/\lambda_{it})|W_{is}\} &= E\{E(y_{is}|\delta_i, W_{is})|W_{is}\} & (4.2)\\
-E[E\{y_{it}(\lambda_{is}/\lambda_{it})|\delta_i, W_{it}\}|W_{is}] &= E\{\tilde{\lambda}_{is} - \tilde{\lambda}_{it}(\tilde{\lambda}_{is}/\tilde{\lambda}_{it})|W_{is}\} = 0.
\end{aligned}
$$

This implies, for any (square-integrable) function $g(W_{is})$,

$$E[g(W_{is}) \cdot \{y_{is} - y_{it}\exp(\tau_s - \tau_t + (x_{is} - x_{it})'\beta)\}] = 0. \quad (4.3)$$

Although only $x_{is} - x_{it}$ appears as regressors, $\tilde{c}_i$ may be used in $g(W_{is})$, which is why we are using the notation w_{it} not x_{it}.

To implement the GMM with (4.3), define

$$
\begin{aligned}
\gamma &\equiv (\tau_2 - \tau_1, \tau_3 - \tau_2, ..., \tau_T - \tau_{T-1}, \beta')', \\
r_{it}(\gamma) &\equiv y_{it} - y_{i,t+1}\exp(-(\tau_{t+1} - \tau_t) - (x_{i,t+1} - x_{it})'\beta), \\
t &= 1, ..., T - 1.
\end{aligned}
$$

When the GMM error term $r_{it}(\cdot)$ is evaluated at the true value, we will sometimes omit the argument. Also define

$$
r_i(\gamma) \equiv \begin{bmatrix} r_{i1}(\gamma) \\ r_{i2}(\gamma) \\ \vdots \\ r_{i,T-1}(\gamma) \end{bmatrix} \qquad M_i \equiv \begin{bmatrix} M_{i1} & 0 & 0 & \cdots & 0 \\ 0 & M_{i2} & 0 & \cdots & 0 \\ \vdots & \vdots & \vdots & & \vdots \\ 0 & 0 & 0 & \cdots & M_{i,T-1} \end{bmatrix},
$$

where M_{it} is an $L_t \times 1$ instrument vector for r_{it} consisting of functions of $w_{i1}, ..., w_{it}$; M_i is a $(\sum_{t=1}^{T-1} L_t) \times (T - 1)$ matrix. With these, the moment condition to be used is

$$
E(M_i r_i) = 0. \tag{4.4}
$$

The GMM using this condition minimizes

$$
(1/N) \sum_i \{M_i r_i(g)\}' \cdot \Omega_N^{-1} \cdot (1/N) \sum_i \{M_i r_i(g)\} \tag{4.5}
$$

wrt g, where Ω_N is a consistent estimator for $E\{M_i r_i(\gamma) r_i(\gamma)' M_i'\}$. An iterative algorithm for this is

$$
\begin{aligned}
g_1 &= g_0 - [\sum_i \{M_i \partial r_i(g_0)/\partial g\}' \cdot \Omega_N^{-1} \cdot \sum_i \{M_i \partial r_i(g_0)/\partial g\}]^{-1} \tag{4.6} \\
&\quad \cdot \sum_i \{M_i \partial r_i(g_0)/\partial g\}' \cdot \Omega_N^{-1} \cdot \sum_i M_i r_i(g_0),
\end{aligned}
$$

which is to be updated and repeated until convergence. The derivative $\partial r_i(g_0)/\partial g$ can be computed numerically; or if desired, the following analytic derivative can be used (to speed up the algorithm):

$$
\begin{aligned}
\partial r_{it}(\gamma)/\partial(\tau_{t+1} - \tau_t) &= y_{i,t+1} \exp(-(\tau_{t+1} - \tau_t) - (x_{i,t+1} - x_{it})'\beta), \\
&\qquad t = 1, ..., T - 1, \\
\partial r_{it}(\gamma)/\partial\beta &= \{y_{i,t+1} \cdot \exp(-(\tau_{t+1} - \tau_t) - (x_{i,t+1} - x_{it})'\beta)\} \cdot \\
&\qquad (x_{i,t+1} - x_{it}), \\
\partial r_{it}(\gamma)/\partial\gamma &= \{\partial r_{it}(\gamma)/\partial(\tau_{t+1} - \tau_t), t = 1, ..., T - 1, \\
&\qquad \partial r_{it}(\gamma)/\partial\beta'\}'; \\
\partial r_i(\gamma)/\partial\gamma &= (\partial r_{i1}(\gamma)/\partial\gamma, ..., \partial r_{i,T-1}(\gamma)/\partial\gamma)'. \tag{4.7}
\end{aligned}
$$

The GMM is asymptotically normal with the asymptotic variance being

$$
[E\{M_i \partial r_i(\gamma)/\partial g\}' \cdot \{E(M_i r_i(\gamma) r_i(\gamma)' M_i')\}^{-1} \cdot E\{M_i \partial r_i(\gamma)/\partial g\}]^{-1}.
$$

Call the (model for) GMM "CW" for Chamberlain and Wooldridge.

5.4.2 GMM with Additive Lagged Response

Consider an "integer-valued AR(1) process" (see Alzaid and Al-Osh, 1990, and the references therein):

$$y_{it} = \rho \circ y_{i,t-1} + v_{it}, \quad 0 < \rho < 1,$$

where $\rho \circ y_{i,t-1}$ denotes a binomial random variable with the success probability ρ and the number of trials $y_{i,t-1}$, and v_{it} is a Poisson random variable with parameter λ independent of $\rho \circ y_{i,t-1}$; $v_{it}, t = 1, ..., T$, are independent. Here $\rho \circ y_{i,t-1}$ is the "carry-over" from the past, whereas v_{it} is an "innovation" at t. Observe

$$E(y_{it}|y_{i,t-1}) = \rho \cdot y_{i,t-1} + \lambda; \tag{4.8}$$

regressors can be introduced into λ (or into ρ).

Motivated by (4.8), Blundell, Griffith, and Windmeijer (2002) included a lagged dependent variable in the regressors. Recall $W_{it} \equiv (w_{i1}, ..., w_{it})'$, $Y_{it} \equiv (y_{i1}, ..., y_{it})'$, and suppose

$$E(y_{it}|\delta_i, Y_{i,t-1}, W_{it}) = E(y_{it}|\delta_i, y_{i,t-1}, w_{it}) = \rho y_{i,t-1} + \tilde{\lambda}_{it} \tag{4.9}$$

$$\Leftrightarrow \quad y_{it} = \rho y_{i,t-1} + \tilde{\lambda}_{it} + e_{it} \quad \text{where } e_{it} \equiv y_{it} - \rho y_{i,t-1} - \tilde{\lambda}_{it},$$

$$E(e_{it}|\delta_i, Y_{i,t-1}, W_{it}) = 0.$$

Define

$$
\begin{aligned}
s_{it}(\rho, \gamma) &\equiv (y_{it} - \rho y_{i,t-1}) \cdot \lambda_{i,t-1}/\lambda_{it} - (y_{i,t-1} - \rho y_{i,t-2}) \tag{4.10} \\
&= (y_{it} - \rho y_{i,t-1}) \cdot \\
&\quad \exp(-(\tau_t - \tau_{t-1}) - (x_{it} - x_{i,t-1})'\beta) - (y_{i,t-1} - \rho y_{i,t-2});
\end{aligned}
$$

ρ and γ in $s_{it}(\rho, \gamma)$ are often omitted in the following. We have

$$
\begin{aligned}
s_{it} &= (\tilde{\lambda}_{it} + e_{it}) \cdot \tilde{\lambda}_{i,t-1}/\tilde{\lambda}_{it} - (\tilde{\lambda}_{i,t-1} + e_{i,t-1}) \tag{4.11} \\
&= e_{it}\tilde{\lambda}_{i,t-1}/\tilde{\lambda}_{it} - e_{i,t-1}.
\end{aligned}
$$

This yields the main moment condition:

$$
\begin{aligned}
& E(s_{it}|\delta_i, Y_{i,t-2}, W_{i,t-1}) \\
= \ & E\{E(e_{it}\tilde{\lambda}_{i,t-1}/\tilde{\lambda}_{it}|\delta_i, Y_{i,t-1}, W_{it})|\delta_i, Y_{i,t-2}, W_{i,t-1}\} \\
& -E(e_{i,t-1}|\delta_i, Y_{i,t-2}, W_{i,t-1}) \\
= \ & E\{(\tilde{\lambda}_{i,t-1}/\tilde{\lambda}_{it}) \cdot E(e_{it}|\delta_i, Y_{i,t-1}, W_{it})|\delta_i, Y_{i,t-2}, W_{i,t-1}\} - 0 = 0 \\
\Rightarrow \ & E(s_{it}|Y_{i,t-2}, W_{i,t-1}) = 0. \tag{4.12}
\end{aligned}
$$

This looks more general than CW because $\rho = 0$ in s_{it} would lead to (4.2) with $s = t-1$, but that is not always the case. The CW with only $W_{i,t-1}$ in the conditioning set is not nested by (4.9), for the CW does not specify $E(\cdot|Y_{i,t-1}, W_{it})$.

If we use only $W_{i,t-1}$ in the conditioning set for both (4.2) and (4.12), however, the ensuing GMM for (4.12) does include CW as a special case with $\rho = 0$; alternatively, if CW uses lagged responses as regressors as well (thus adding $Y_{i,t-2}$ to the conditioning set), then the GMM with (4.12) includes the CW as a special case.

For any (square-integrable) function $g(Y_{i,t-2}, W_{i,t-1})$,

$$E[g(Y_{i,t-2}, W_{i,t-1}) \cdot \{(y_{it} - \rho y_{i,t-1}) \qquad (4.13)$$
$$\cdot \exp(-(\tau_t - \tau_{t-1}) - (x_{it} - x_{i,t-1})'\beta) - (y_{i,t-1} - \rho y_{i,t-2})\}] = 0.$$

The remaining GMM steps are analogous to that for CW, for which we need the derivatives of $s_{it}(\rho, \gamma)$ wrt ρ and γ:

$$\partial s_{it}/\partial \rho \quad = \quad -y_{i,t-1} \cdot \exp(-(\tau_t - \tau_{t-1})) \qquad (4.14)$$
$$-(x_{it} - x_{i,t-1})'\beta) + y_{i,t-2},$$
$$\partial s_{it}/\partial (\tau_t - \tau_{t-1}) \quad = \quad -(y_{it} - \rho y_{i,t-1}) \cdot \exp(-(\tau_t - \tau_{t-1}))$$
$$-(x_{it} - x_{i,t-1})'\beta),$$
$$\partial s_{it}/\partial \beta \quad = \quad -\{(y_{it} - \rho y_{i,t-1}) \exp(-(\tau_t - \tau_{t-1}))$$
$$-(x_{it} - x_{i,t-1})'\beta)\} \cdot (x_{it} - x_{i,t-1}).$$

An instrument matrix analogous to M_i can be constructed. We will call the (model for) GMM "BGW" for Blundell, Griffith, and Windmeijer (2002). If we define an artificial response variable $z_{it}(\rho) \equiv y_{it} - \rho y_{i,t-1}$, then s_{it} takes the same form as r_{it} for CW. This suggests implementing BGW first by fixing ρ at a value to use (4.6) and then varying ρ.

In fact, BGW's main proposal is not (4.9) but using a presample estimator for δ_i. But because presample information is a luxury not readily available, and also because this raises a whole new issue of optimally utilizing the information, we will stick to a given sample and no more. BGW present a further generalization of (4.9):

$$E(y_{it}|\delta_i, Y_{i,t-1}, W_{it}) \qquad (4.15)$$
$$= \quad E(y_{it}|\delta_i, y_{i,t-p}, ..., y_{i,t-1}, w_{it}) = \sum_{s=1}^{p} \rho_s y_{i,t-s} + \tilde{\lambda}_{it}, \quad 0 < p < t.$$

For this, Y_{t-p-1} and W_{t-1} can be used for instruments. An empirical application of CW and BGW appears in the last section of this chapter.

Because only W_{it}, not W_{iT}, appears in the conditioning set for u_{it} and e_{it} (recall (4.1) and (4.9)), CW and BGW do not require $\{x_{it}\}_{t=1}^{T}$ to be strictly exogenous to $\{u_{it}\}_{t=1}^{T}$ and $\{e_{it}\}_{t=1}^{T}$. This is important, for strict exogeneity rules out a past error term, say u_{is}, affecting a future regressor, say x_{it}, through y_{is}; in patent-R&D relationship with y_{it} being patents, this link is a likely scenario, because the past profitability due to patents means more fund availability for the future R&D.

If one takes the CW model and is interested only in testing for the specification, one may estimate the BGW model and test for $\rho = 0$ using only the CW instruments; call this a "one-step test for CW." This amounts to adding an artificial regressor $y_{i,t-1}$ to CW to detect misspecification. If the BGW model is difficult to implement due to a convergence problem, instead of reestimating γ, one may use the CW estimator for γ and do a grid search over ρ; call this a "two-step test for CW." The power is likely to be higher for the one-step test; for the two-step test, the power depends on the "pseudo-true value" to which CW converges when the CW model is false. The following discussion presents the asymptotic distribution for the two-step test procecure.

In the two-step test for CW, the first stage CW error should be accounted for. Denote the BGW minimand as

$$(1/N) \sum_i \{N_i s_i(\rho_N, \gamma)\}' \cdot A_N^{-1} \cdot (1/N) \sum_i \{N_i s_i(\rho_N, \gamma)\}, \qquad (4.16)$$

where N_i and A_N are, respectively, an instrument matrix and a variance matrix estimate for the BGW moment conditions. Minimizing this wrt ρ_N with γ fixed at g_{cw}, the CW estimate, we get

$$\sqrt{N}(\rho_N - \rho) \Rightarrow N(0, G \cdot C \cdot G'), \qquad (4.17)$$

where G and C are consistently estimable, respectively, by

$$G_N \equiv [(1/N) \sum_i \{N_i \partial s_i(\rho_N, g_{cw})/\partial \rho\}' \cdot A_N^{-1}$$

$$\cdot (1/N) \sum_i \{N_i \partial s_i(\rho_N, g_{cw})/\partial \rho\}]^{-1}$$

$$\cdot (1/N) \sum_i \{N_i \partial s_i(\rho_N, g_{cw}/\partial \rho\}' \cdot A_N^{-1},$$

$$C_N \equiv (1/N) \sum_i \{N_i s_i(\rho_N, g_{cw}) + L_N \eta_{Ni}\} \cdot \{N_i s_i(\rho_N, g_{cw}) + L_N \eta_{Ni}\}',$$

where

$$L_N \equiv (1/N) \sum_i N_i \partial s_i(\rho_N, g_{cw})/\partial g,$$

$$\eta_{Ni} \equiv -[(1/N) \sum_i \{M_i \partial r_i(g_{cw})/\partial g\}' \cdot \Omega_N^{-1} \cdot (1/N) \sum_i \{M_i \partial r_i(g_{cw})/\partial g\}]^{-1}$$

$$\cdot (1/N) \sum_i \{M_i \partial r_i(g_{cw})/\partial g\}' \cdot \Omega_N^{-1} \cdot M_i r_i(g_{cw}).$$

5.4.3 Quasi-Conditional MLE

This sub-section introduces Wooldridge's (1999) "quasi-conditional MLE" interpretation of CPOI for non-negative responses, which can be a binary response, a censored response, a proportion, or a count response. The estimator requires a correctly specified mean function under strict exogeneity, but hardly anything else; even dependence among $y_{i1}, \ldots, y_{iT}$ is allowed given $x_{i1}, \ldots, x_{iT}, \delta_i$. This finding gives a boost to CPOI, for CPOI works well computationally, whereas the preceding GMM for count responses may not.

Let x_{it} be a $k \times 1$ regressor vector and let δ_i include all time invariants, observed or not. Define

$$x_i \equiv (x_{i1}, \ldots, x_{iT})'.$$

Suppose

$$E(y_{it}|\delta_i, x_i) = E(y_{it}|\delta_i, x_{it}) = \exp(x_{it}'\beta + \delta_i).$$

Define the normalized version for $\exp(x_{it}'\beta + \delta_i)$: with $\Delta x_{it1} \equiv x_{it} - x_{i1}$,

$$p_{it}(\beta) \equiv \exp(x_{it}'\beta)/\sum_{s=1}^{T}\exp(x_{is}'\beta) = \exp(\Delta x_{it1}'\beta)/\sum_{s=1}^{T}\exp(\Delta x_{is1}'\beta)$$

in which δ_i drops out; $\sum_t p_{it}(\beta) = 1$ by construction.

The key finding is that

$$
\begin{aligned}
L(b) &\equiv \sum_{i=1}^{N}\sum_{t=1}^{T} y_{it} \ln\{p_{it}(b)\} & (4.18)\\
&= \sum_{i=1}^{N}\sum_{t=1}^{T} y_{it} \ln\{\exp(\Delta x_{it1}'b)/\sum_{s=1}^{T}\exp(\Delta x_{is1}'b)\}
\end{aligned}
$$

is maximized uniquely at $b = \beta$, which does not require any parametric assumptions such as Poisson or negative binomial nor any independence of $y_{i1}, \ldots, y_{iT}$ given x_i and δ_i. Allowing for temporal dependence, however, calls for a modification in the asymptotic variance of CPOI.

The maximand is the same as that for CPOI in (3.5), but the fact that $L(b)$ is maximized at $b = \beta$ holds not just for the exponential function but for other positive function $p_{it}(\beta)$ as well, so long as the restriction $\sum_{t=1}^{T} p_{it}(\beta) = 1$ holds. Let $\nabla(\cdot)$ denote the gradient of $(\cdot)$, and let

$$
\begin{aligned}
L_i(b) &\equiv \sum_{t=1}^{T} y_{it} \ln\{p_{it}(b)\},\\
s_i(b) &\equiv \nabla L_i(b) \equiv \sum_{t=1}^{T} y_{it} \nabla p_{it}(b)/p_{it}(b)\\
&= \sum_t \{\nabla p_{it}(b)/p_{it}(b)\} \cdot \{y_{it} - p_{it}(b)\sum_t y_{it}\} & (4.19)
\end{aligned}
$$

due to $\sum_t \nabla p_{it}(b) = 0$ from $\sum_t p_{it}(b) = 1$; $\nabla p_{it}(b)$ is a column vector. Define

$$u_{it}(b) \equiv y_{it} - p_{it}(b) \sum_t y_{it},$$

which is (3.8) with $\omega_{it} = p_{it}(b)$. Equation (3.7) has $\sum_t \Delta x_{it1}\{y_{it} - \omega_{it} \sum_t y_{it}\}$ which looks different from (4.19), but they are equivalent, because $\nabla p_{it}(b)/p_{it}(b) = \Delta x_{it1} -$(a term not a function of t); when $\sum_t$ is taken on the second term times $y_{it} - p_{it}(b) \sum_t y_{it}$, the second term disappears due to $\sum_t\{y_{it} - p_{it}(b) \sum_t y_{it}\} = 0$.

The moment condition $E\{s_i(\beta)|x_i\} = 0$ holds:

$$E\{u_{it}(\beta)|x_i, \delta_i\} = \exp(x'_{it}\beta + \delta_i) - p_{it}(\beta) \sum_{s=1}^{T} \exp(x'_{is}\beta + \delta_i) = 0 \quad (4.20)$$

because

$$p_{it}(\beta) = \exp(x'_{it}\beta)/ \sum_{s=1}^{T} \exp(x'_{is}\beta) = \exp(x'_{it}\beta + \delta_i)/ \sum_{s=1}^{T} \exp(x'_{is}\beta + \delta_i).$$

Define

$$
\begin{aligned}
p_i(b) &\equiv (p_{i1}(b), ..., p_{iT}(b))', & \nabla p_i(b) &\equiv (\nabla p_{i1}(b), ..., \nabla p_{iT}(b))' \\
y_i &\equiv (y_{i1}, ..., y_{iT})', & u_i(b) &\equiv (u_{i1}(b), ..., u_{iT}(b))', \\
W_i(b) &\equiv \mathrm{diag}(1/p_{i1}(b), ..., 1/p_{iT}(b)),
\end{aligned}
$$

to rewrite the score function as

$$s_i(b) = \nabla p_i(b)' \cdot W_i(b) \cdot u_i(b).$$

Differentiating this wrt b, the asymptotic distribution is

$$\sqrt{N}(b_N - \beta) \Rightarrow N(0, H^{-1}\Omega H^{-1}),$$

where H and Ω can be estimated consistently, respectively, by

$$
\begin{aligned}
H_N &\equiv (1/N) \sum_i \{\nabla p_i(b_N)' W_i(b_N) \nabla p_i(b_N) \cdot \sum_t y_{it}\}, \\
\Omega_N &\equiv (1/N) \sum_i s_i(b_N)s_i(b_N)'.
\end{aligned}
$$

This scheme of estimating the asymptotic variance looks complicated, but it is the same as that in (3.10) and (3.11).

5.5 ROOT-N CONSISTENT ESTIMATOR FOR CENSORED RESPONSE

This section examines a semiparametric $\sqrt{N}$-consistent estimator of Honoré (1992) for a panel related-effect censored response model:

$$y_{it}^* = \tau_t + x_{it}'\beta + \delta_i + u_{it}, \tag{5.1}$$
$$y_{it} = \max(y_{it}^*, 0) = y_{it}^* \cdot 1[y_{it}^* > 0],$$
$$(y_{it}, x_{it}')', \quad i = 1, ..., N, \quad t = 1, 2, \quad \text{are observed, iid across } i,$$

where δ_i contains all time invariants including $\tilde{c}_i$. Honoré proposed LSE and least absolute deviation type estimators for the censored model, but we will examine only the LSE type, for its asymptotic variance is easier to estimate. Honoré also proposed estimators for truncated response panel where $(y_{it}, x_{it}'1[y_{it}^* > 0])'$ is observed.

Let $\Delta x_i \equiv (1, x_{i2}' - x_{i1}')'$, and denote the j-th component of Δx_i as Δx_{ij}; that is,

$$\Delta x_i \equiv (\Delta x_{i1}, ..., \Delta x_{i,k-1}, \Delta x_{ik})', \quad \Delta x_{i1} = 1 \quad \text{for all } i,$$

where k denotes the row dimension of Δx_i. Also let

$$\Delta y_i \equiv y_{i2} - y_{i1} \quad \text{and} \quad \beta = (\beta_1, ..., \beta_k)', \quad \text{where } \beta_1 = \tau_2 - \tau_1.$$

Unlike the binary response models of the preceding chapter, β is now fully identified.

Honoré (1992) assumed that u_1 and u_2 are iid given (δ, x_1, x_2), but a weaker "exchangeability" of $(u_1, u_2)|(\delta, x_1, x_2)$ is sufficient:

$$P(u_1 \le t_1, u_2 \le t_2|\delta, x_1, x_2) = P(u_2 \le t_1, u_1 \le t_2|\delta, x_1, x_2) \quad \forall t_1, t_2, \delta, x_1, x_2. \tag{5.2}$$

The exchangeability implies an identical marginal distribution for $u_1|(\delta, x_1, x_2)$ and $u_2|(\delta, x_1, x_2)$, and it includes the iid assumption as a special case. In fact, Honoré and Kyriazidou (2000a) show that only the same marginal distribution for $u_1|(\delta, x_1, x_2)$ and $u_2|(\delta, x_1, x_2)$ is sufficient for the LSE type estimator reviewed in this section; this type of condition to take care of δ_i appeared in Section 4.5.

Observe

$$u_t > -\tau_t - x_t'\beta - \delta \iff y_t = y_t^* > 0. \tag{5.3}$$

Even when (5.2) holds, the trimmed errors

$$(u_1, u_2)|(\delta, x_1, x_2, u_1 > -\tau_1 - x_1'\beta - \delta, u_2 > -\tau_2 - x_2'\beta - \delta)$$

are not exchangeable: the different trimming points across t make the trimmed errors nonidentically distributed. But if we can impose the additional conditions $u_1 > -\tau_2 - x_2'\beta - \delta$ and $u_2 > -\tau_1 - x_1'\beta - \delta$, then we will get

$$u_t > \max(-\tau_1 - x_1'\beta, -\tau_2 - x_2'\beta) - \delta, \quad t = 1, 2,$$

restoring the exchangeability; the two trimmed errors share the common trimming point.

Observe

$$u_1 > -\tau_2 - x_2'\beta - \delta \quad \Leftrightarrow \quad y_1^* - \tau_1 - x_1'\beta - \delta > -\tau_2 - x_2'\beta - \delta$$
$$\Leftrightarrow \quad y_1^* > -\Delta x'\beta,$$
$$u_2 > -\tau_1 - x_1'\beta - \delta \quad \Leftrightarrow \quad y_2^* - \tau_2 - x_2'\beta - \delta > -\tau_1 - x_1'\beta - \delta$$
$$\Leftrightarrow \quad y_2^* > \Delta x'\beta.$$

Imposing (5.3) on these, replace y_t^* with y_t to get

$$u_1 > -\max(-\tau_1 - x_1'\beta, -\tau_2 - x_2'\beta) - \delta \quad \Leftrightarrow \quad y_1 > -\Delta x'\beta,$$
$$u_2 > -\max(-\tau_1 - x_1'\beta, -\tau_2 - x_2'\beta) - \delta \quad \Leftrightarrow \quad y_2 > \Delta x'\beta.$$

Let $A \equiv \{y_1 > -\Delta x'\beta, y_2 > \Delta x'\beta\}$, and subtract $y_1 = \tau_1 + x_1'\beta + \delta + u_1$ from $y_2 = \tau_2 + x_2'\beta + \delta + u_2$ on A to get $(\Delta y - \Delta x'\beta)1[A] = (u_2 - u_1)1[A]$. The main point is that $(u_2 - u_1)1[A]$ is symmetric about zero given (δ, x_1, x_2) due to the exchangeability; this is proven later. Thus we get

$$E\{(u_2 - u_1)1[A]|x_1, x_2\} = E[E\{(u_2 - u_1)1[A]|\delta, x_1, x_2\}|x_1, x_2] = 0, \quad (5.4)$$

which implies an unconditional moment condition:

$$E\{(\Delta y - \Delta x'\beta) \cdot \Delta x \cdot 1[y_1 > -\Delta x'\beta, y_2 > \Delta x'\beta]\} = 0. \quad (5.5)$$

A convex minimand with (5.5) as the asymptotic first-order condition is

$$(1/N) \sum_i [\{\max(y_{i2}, \Delta x_i'b) - \max(y_{i1}, -\Delta x_i'b) - \Delta x_i'b\}^2 \quad (5.6)$$

$$-2 \cdot 1[y_{i2} < \Delta x_i'b](y_{i2} - \Delta x_i'b)y_{i1} - 2 \cdot 1[y_{i1} < -\Delta x_i'b](y_{i1} + \Delta x_i'b)y_{i2}].$$

The first term becomes $(\Delta y_i - \Delta x_i'b)^2$ when $y_{i2} > \Delta x_i'b$ and $y_{i1} > -\Delta x_i'b$, showing that the estimator is a version of LSE on the first-differenced model. The remaining two terms can be regarded as adjustment terms to make use of the observations with $y_{i1} = 0$ or $y_{i2} = 0$ and to make the minimand smooth when $y_{i2} < \Delta x_i'b$ or $y_{i1} < -\Delta x_i'b$. The estimator b_N is $\sqrt{N}$-consistent and asymptotically normal with the asymptotic variance

$$E^{-1}(1[-y_1 < \Delta x'\beta < y_2] \cdot \Delta x \Delta x') \cdot$$
$$E[\{y_2^2 1[y_1 < -\Delta x'\beta] + y_1^2 1[y_2 < \Delta x'\beta]$$
$$+(\Delta y - \Delta x'\beta)^2 1[-y_1 < \Delta x'\beta < y_2]\} \cdot \Delta x \Delta x'] \cdot \quad (5.7)$$
$$E^{-1}(1[-y_1 < \Delta x'\beta < y_2] \cdot \Delta x \Delta x').$$

where $E^{-1}(\cdot) = \{E(\cdot)\}^{-1}$. A consistent estimator for this is easy to get by replacing $E(\cdot)$ with its sample version and substituting b_N for β.

To show that the exchangeability implies the symmetry of $(u_2 - u_1)|(\delta, x_1, x_2)$ about 0, we need to show

$$P(u_2 - u_1 \leq a | \delta, x_1, x_2) = P(u_2 - u_1 \geq -a | \delta, x_1, x_2)$$

for any a, δ, x_1, and x_2. Denote the conditional density for $(u_1, u_2)|(\delta, x_1, x_2)$ as $f(u_1, u_2)$. Observe

$$
\begin{aligned}
P(u_2 - u_1 \leq a | \delta, x_1, x_2) &= \int 1[u_2 - u_1 \leq a] \cdot f(u_1, u_2) du_1 du_2 \qquad (5.8) \\
&= \int 1[u_2 - u_1 \leq a] \cdot f(u_2, u_1) du_1 du_2 \\
&= \int 1[u_1 - u_2 \leq a] \cdot f(u_1, u_2) du_2 du_1 \\
&= \int 1[u_2 - u_1 \geq -a] \cdot f(u_1, u_2) du_2 du_1 \\
&= P(u_2 - u_1 \geq -a | \delta, x_1, x_2); \qquad (5.9)
\end{aligned}
$$

the second equality is due to the exchangeability, and the third equality is just interchanging integration dummies.

Honoré's estimator minimizes a convex function without any smoothing and thus is straightforward computationally. The error terms are allowed to be serially correlated under the exchangeability, although the regressors should be strictly exogenous. If we try to use unconditional moment conditions other than (5.5) to make a more extensive use of the conditional moment condition (5.4), then we will lose the convex minimand (5.6).

Honoré (1993) extended the estimator to allow for a lagged dependent variable as a regressor, but this comes at the cost of going from a globally convex minimization problem to a nonlinear method-of-moment where the identification of the parameter may not hold. The exchangeability now should hold conditionally on δ_i, x_{i1}, x_{i2}, y_{i0}; here, y_{i0} can spell a trouble for the exchangeability.

Udry (1995) estimated a grain sales equation using Honoré's estimator where censoring occurs due to reporting only important sales; household data from Nigerian farms with $N = 200$ and $T = 3$ were used. Udry (1996) estimated agricultural plot input equations (mostly labor inputs) using Honoré's estimator to see if there are input differences between male-owned plots and female-owned plots; a data set from Burkina Faso with $N = 150$ and $T = 3$ was used.

Hochguertel (1998) analyzed the effect of precautionary motives on household portfolio decisions. He took the ratio of liquid assets to financial wealth as the dependent variable and used a Dutch data with $N = 1915$ and $T = 3$; the data were censored from above at 1 (43% censoring). Unfortunately, the symmetry that followed from the exchangeability was rejected. The exchangeability is that looking backward from the future is the same as looking forward from the past. The irreversible and nonstationary nature of human life many not fit exchangeability well.

5.6 CONDITIONAL LOGIT FOR MULTINOMIAL RESPONSES

This section examines panel multinomial logit (PML) in detail, which is shown in Chamberlain (1980, p. 231) in half a page; but the actual implementation requires more explanation depending on the desired generality level of the PML model in use. Because PML has one more dimension (alternatives to choose from) in addition to N and T, notations in this section will differ somewhat from those in the other sections, and this section may make for fairly hard reading. First we deal with the simplest case, three alternatives with $T = 2$, in detail, and then the general case, which is followed by an empirical example in Börsch-Supan (1990).

Set $T = 2$, and suppose that there are three alternatives ($j = a, b, c$) to choose from. Define

$$y_{ijt} = 1 \text{ if } i \text{ chooses } j \text{ at time } t, \text{ and } 0 \text{ otherwise, } \forall i, j, t,$$
$$y_{it} \equiv (y_{iat}, y_{ibt}, y_{ict})' \quad \forall i, t, \quad \text{and} \quad y_i \equiv (y_{i1}', y_{i2}')' \quad \forall i;$$

for example, if person i chooses b at $t = 1$ and c at $t = 2$, then $y_i = (0, 1, 0, 0, 0, 1)'$.

Suppose that alternative j at time t gives "satisfaction (or utility)" s_{ijt} to i, and the s_{ijt} equation is

$$s_{ijt} = c_{it}'\alpha_j + x_{ijt}'\beta + \delta_{ij} + u_{ijt}, \quad \forall i, j, t, \tag{6.1}$$

where c_{it} and x_{ijt} are regressors with c_{it} being the same for all alternatives, and δ_{ij} and u_{ijt} are error terms. One chooses the alternative giving the maximum satisfaction, and consequently the choice depends only on $s_{ibt} - s_{iat}$ and $s_{ict} - s_{iat}$, with alternative a being the normalizing one. The main feature of PML is that δ_{ij} drops out as δ_i does in the conditional logit. Equation (6.1) can be generalized further, for example, by allowing for β_j; (6.1) is used here to simplify exposition.

Let k_c and k_x denote the row dimension of c_{it} and x_{ijt}, respectively. Define $0_{f \times g}$ as the $f \times g$ zero matrix, and

$$w_{ijt} \equiv (c_{it}', x_{ijt}' - x_{iat}')', \quad \gamma_j \equiv (\alpha_j' - \alpha_a', \beta')' \quad j = a, b, c, \tag{6.2}$$
$$w_{it} \equiv \text{diag}(w_{iat}, w_{ibt}, w_{ict}), \quad \gamma \equiv (\gamma_a', \gamma_b', \gamma_c')',$$
$$\Delta c_i \equiv c_{i2} - c_{i1}, \quad \Delta x_{ij} \equiv x_{ij2} - x_{ij1}$$

where w_{it} is a $3(k_c + k_x) \times 3$ block-diagonal matrix. From this, we get

$$\gamma' w_{it} = (w_{iat}'\gamma_a, w_{ibt}'\gamma_b, w_{ict}'\gamma_c), \tag{6.3}$$
$$w_{ijt}'\gamma_j = c_{it}'(\alpha_j - \alpha_a) + (x_{ijt} - x_{iat})'\beta,$$
$$s_{ijt} - s_{iat} = w_{ijt}'\gamma_j + \delta_{ij} - \delta_{ia} + u_{ijt} - u_{iat},$$
$$w_{ij2}'\gamma_j - w_{ij1}'\gamma_j = \Delta c_i'(\alpha_j - \alpha_a) + (\Delta x_{ij} - \Delta x_{ia})'\beta;$$

note that $w_{iat}'\gamma_a = 0$.

Assume that y_{i1} and y_{i2} are independent given

$$c_{i1}, c_{i2}, x_{ij1}, x_{ij2}, \delta_{ij}, \quad j = a, b, c. \tag{6.4}$$

Although this is restrictive, still y_{i1} and y_{i2} are allowed to be related through the variables in (6.4). Further suppose it holds that

$$P(y_{ijt} = 1|(6.4)) = \exp(c'_{it}\alpha_j + x'_{ijt}\beta + \delta_{ij}) / \sum_{j=a,b,c} \exp(c'_{it}\alpha_j + x'_{ijt}\beta + \delta_{ij}).$$

After the normalization by the first alternative (that is, dividing the numerator and denominator by $\exp(c'_{it}\alpha_a + x'_{iat}\beta + \delta_{ia})$), this becomes

$$P(y_{ijt} = 1|(6.4)) = \exp(w'_{ijt}\gamma_j + \delta_{ij} - \delta_{ia}) / \sum_j \exp(w'_{ijt}\gamma_j + \delta_{ij} - \delta_{ia}). \tag{6.5}$$

For the conditional log-likelihood function, we need to consider three types of alternative changes across the two periods:

$$(a, b) \text{ or } (b, a), \quad (a, c) \text{ or } (c, a), \quad (b, c) \text{ or } (c, b). \tag{6.6}$$

People with no change in their choices are not informative.

Examine (a, b) or (b, a) first. In terms of y_i, (a, b) and (b, a) are

$$(1, 0, 0, 0, 1, 0) \quad \text{and} \quad (0, 1, 0, 1, 0, 0). \tag{6.7}$$

Omitting "$|(6.4)$" and using (6.5), the probability of observing the choice (a, b) given that it is either (a, b) or (b, a) is

$$
\begin{aligned}
P(y_{ia1} &= 1, y_{ib2} = 1|(y_{ia1} = 1, y_{ib2} = 1) \text{ or } (y_{ib1} = 1, y_{ia2} = 1)) \tag{6.8} \\
&= P(y_{ia1} = 1) \cdot P(y_{ib2} = 1)/\{P(y_{ia1} = 1) \cdot P(y_{ib2} = 1) \\
&\quad + P(y_{ib1} = 1) \cdot P(y_{ia2} = 1)\}.
\end{aligned}
$$

The denominator in (6.5) does not matter for this conditional probability, because it appears in all three terms in (6.8); likewise, $\delta_{ib} - \delta_{ia}$ does not matter for (6.8). Also, because choosing a makes the numerator of (6.5) one, $P(y_{ia1} = 1)$ and $P(y_{ia2} = 1)$ can be ignored in (6.8). Hence,

$$
\begin{aligned}
P(y_{ia1} &= 1, y_{ib2} = 1|(y_{ia1} = 1, y_{ib2} = 1) \text{ or } (y_{ib1} = 1, y_{ia2} = 1)) \tag{6.9} \\
&= \exp((1, 0, 0, 0, 1, 0) \cdot (\gamma'w_{i1}, \gamma'w_{i2})') \\
&\quad /\{\exp((1, 0, 0, 0, 1, 0) \cdot (\gamma'w_{i1}, \gamma'w_{i2})') \\
&\quad + \exp((0, 1, 0, 1, 0, 0) \cdot (\gamma'w_{i1}, \gamma'w_{i2})')\} \\
&= \exp(w'_{ib2}\gamma_b)/\{\exp(w'_{ib2}\gamma_b) + \exp(w'_{ib1}\gamma_b)\} \\
&= \exp(w'_{ib2}\gamma_b - w'_{ib1}\gamma_b)/\{\exp(w'_{ib2}\gamma_b - w'_{ib1}\gamma_b) + 1\} \\
&= \exp\{\Delta c'_i(\alpha_b - \alpha_a) + (\Delta x_{ib} - \Delta x_{ia})'\beta\} \\
&\quad /[\exp\{\Delta c'_i(\alpha_b - \alpha_a) + (\Delta x_{ib} - \Delta x_{ia})'\beta\} + 1]. \tag{6.10}
\end{aligned}
$$

Also,

$$P(y_{ib1} = 1, y_{ia2} = 1 | (y_{ia1} = 1, y_{ib2} = 1) \text{ or } (y_{ib1} = 1, y_{ia2} = 1))$$
$$= 1 - (6.10). \quad (6.11)$$

Doing analogously for (a, c) or (c, a), we get

$$P(y_{ia1} = 1, y_{ic2} = 1 | (y_{ia1} = 1, y_{ic2} = 1) \text{ or } (y_{ic1} = 1, y_{ia2} = 1))$$
$$= \exp\{\Delta c_i'(\alpha_c - \alpha_a) + (\Delta x_{ic} - \Delta x_{ia})'\beta\}$$
$$/[\exp\{\Delta c_i'(\alpha_c - \alpha_a) + (\Delta x_{ic} - \Delta x_{ia})'\beta\} + 1]. \quad (6.12)$$

Also,

$$P(y_{ic1} = 1, y_{ia2} = 1 | (y_{ia1} = 1, y_{ic2} = 1) \text{ or } (y_{ic1} = 1, y_{ia2} = 1))$$
$$= 1 - (6.12). \quad (6.13)$$

As for (b, c) or (c, b),

$$P(y_{ib1} = 1, y_{ic2} = 1 | (y_{ib1} = 1, y_{ic2} = 1) \text{ or } (y_{ic1} = 1, y_{ib2} = 1)) \quad (6.14)$$
$$= \exp((0, 1, 0, 0, 0, 1) \cdot (\gamma' w_{i1}, \gamma' w_{i2})')$$
$$/\{\exp((0, 1, 0, 0, 0, 1) \cdot (\gamma' w_{i1}, \gamma' w_{i2})')$$
$$+ \exp((0, 0, 1, 0, 1, 0) \cdot (\gamma' w_{i1}, \gamma' w_{i2})')\}$$
$$= \exp(w_{ib1}'\gamma_b + w_{ic2}'\gamma_c)$$
$$/\{\exp(w_{ib1}'\gamma_b + w_{ic2}'\gamma_c) + \exp(w_{ic1}'\gamma_c + w_{ib2}'\gamma_b)\}$$
$$= 1/[1 + \exp\{-(w_{ic2}'\gamma_c - w_{ic1}'\gamma_c) + (w_{ib2}'\gamma_b - w_{ib1}'\gamma_b)\}].$$

The term in $\exp\{\cdot\}$ is

$$-\{\Delta c_i'(\alpha_c - \alpha_a) + (\Delta x_{ic} - \Delta x_{ia})'\beta\} + \Delta c_i'(\alpha_b - \alpha_a) + (\Delta x_{ib} - \Delta x_{ia})'\beta$$
$$= \Delta c_i'(\alpha_b - \alpha_a - (\alpha_c - \alpha_a)) + (\Delta x_{ib} - \Delta x_{ic})'\beta.$$

Hence,

$$P(y_{ib1} = 1, y_{ic2} = 1 | (y_{ib1} = 1, y_{ic2} = 1) \text{ or } (y_{ic1} = 1, y_{ib2} = 1))$$
$$= 1/[1 + \exp\{\Delta c_i'(\alpha_b - \alpha_a - (\alpha_c - \alpha_a)) + (\Delta x_{ib} - \Delta x_{ic})'\beta\}]. \quad (6.15)$$

Also,

$$P(y_{ic1} = 1, y_{ib2} = 1 | (y_{ib1} = 1, y_{ic2} = 1) \text{ or } (y_{ic1} = 1, y_{ib2} = 1))$$
$$= 1 - (6.15). \quad (6.16)$$

Therefore, the desired log-likelihood function is

$$\sum_i \{y_{ia1}y_{ib2} \ln(6.10) + y_{ib1}y_{ia2} \ln(6.11) \quad (6.17)$$
$$+ y_{ia1}y_{ic2} \ln(6.12) + y_{ic1}y_{ia2} \ln(6.13)$$
$$+ y_{ib1}y_{ic2} \ln(6.15) + y_{ic1}y_{ib2} \ln(6.16)\}.$$

This can be differentiated wrt the identified parameters

$$\zeta \equiv (\alpha'_b - \alpha'_a, \alpha'_c - \alpha'_a, \beta')'$$

for the score function, and with the score function at hand, the rest of the steps are straightforward.

When there are J alternatives and $T \geq 2$, grouping data should be done conditioning on the values $\sum_t y_{ijt}$ can take for all j so long as $\sum_t y_{ijt} \neq 0, T$. For $T = 2$ and $J = 3$ as shown earlier, this boils down to the three groups in (6.6) because only $\sum_t y_{ijt} = 1$, $j = a, b, c$, are informative where each alternative occurs only once. In the following discussion, we will show how things are to be done with $(J = 4, T = 2)$ and $(J = 3, T = 3)$ and then present a general log-likelihood function analogous to the case of $T \geq 3$ in the conditional logit for binary response.

If there are four alternatives (a, b, c, d) and $T = 2$, then we have to consider six groups

$$(a, b) \text{ or } (b, a), \quad (a, c) \text{ or } (c, a), \quad (a, d) \text{ or } (d, a), \quad (6.18)$$
$$(b, c) \text{ or } (c, b), \quad (b, d) \text{ or } (d, b), \quad (c, d) \text{ or } (d, c).$$

If there are three alternatives and $T = 3$, then the following five groups with at least one change in the choices should be considered:

$$
\begin{aligned}
\text{one } a \text{ and two } b's \quad &: \quad (a, b, b), \ (b, a, b), \ (b, b, a); \\
\text{one } a \text{ and two } c's \quad &: \quad (a, c, c), \ (c, a, c), \ (c, c, a); \\
\text{one } b \text{ and two } c's \quad &: \quad (b, c, c), \ (c, b, c), \ (c, c, b); \quad (6.19) \\
\text{one } c \text{ and two } b's \quad &: \quad (c, b, b), \ (b, c, b), \ (b, b, c); \\
\text{one } a, \text{ one } b, \text{ one } c \quad &: \quad (a, b, c), \ (a, c, b), \ (b, a, c), \\
&\qquad (b, c, a), \ (c, a, b), \ (c, b, a).
\end{aligned}
$$

In the general multinomial choice with J alternatives and T, define y_{ijt} as before, and (now use $1, 2, ..., J$ to list the alternatives, not a, b, c)

$$y_{it} \equiv (y_{i1t}, ..., y_{iJt})', \quad y_i \equiv (y'_{i1}, ..., y'_{iT})'. \quad (6.20)$$

The identified parameters are

$$\zeta \equiv (\alpha'_2 - \alpha'_1, ..., \alpha'_J - \alpha'_1, \beta')'. \quad (6.21)$$

Also define

$$w_{ijt} \equiv (c'_{it}, x'_{ijt} - x'_{i1t})', \quad \gamma_j \equiv (\alpha'_j - \alpha'_1, \beta')' \quad \forall j = 2, ..., J, \quad (6.22)$$
$$w_{it} \equiv \text{diag}(w_{ijt}, \ j = 1, ..., J),$$
$$\gamma \equiv (\gamma'_j, \ j = 1, ..., J)'.$$

From this, we get

$$\gamma' w_{it} = (w'_{ijt} \gamma_j, \quad j = 1, ..., J); \tag{6.23}$$

$w'_{i1t} \gamma_1 = 0$ for $\forall t$. The log-likelihood function is

$$\sum_i \ln\{\exp(y'_i(\gamma' w_{i1}, \gamma' w_{i2}, ..., \gamma' w_{iT})') \tag{6.24}$$

$$/ \sum_{\lambda \in G_i} \exp(\lambda'(\gamma' w_{i1}, \gamma' w_{i2}, ..., \gamma' w_{iT})')\}$$

where

$$G_i \equiv \{\lambda \equiv (\lambda_{11}, \lambda_{21}, ..., \lambda_{J1}, \lambda_{12}, \lambda_{22}, ..., \lambda_{J2}, ..., \lambda_{1T}, \lambda_{2T}, ..., \lambda_{JT})'$$

$$|\lambda_{jt} = 0 \text{ or } 1, \sum_j \lambda_{jt} = 1, \sum_t \lambda_{jt} = \sum_t y_{ijt} \; \forall j\}.$$

The denominator $\sum_{\lambda \in G_i} \exp(\cdot)$ is nothing but the sum of the possibilities corresponding to each λ in G_i.

Börsch-Supan (1990) analyzed four housing choices

rented-small (RS, about 14%), rented-large (RL, about 10%),

owned-small (OS, about 22%), owned-large (OL, about 54%),

using 880 families from PSID 1977–1981 ($T = 5$); the regressors are

age of the household head (age), age^2,

household income (inc), number of household members (size),

employed or not (work; mostly 0 for the retired),

housing price (price; imputed from a source other than PSID).

Because all regressors other than price are invariant across j,

$$c_{it} = (\text{age}_{it}, \text{age}^2_{it}, \text{inc}_{it}, \text{size}_{it}, \text{work}_{it})' \quad \text{and} \quad x_{ijt} = \text{price}_{ijt};$$

RS is the base alternative. Börsch-Supan (1990) specified the related effect as δ_i, not δ_{ij}, and mentioned that δ_i can be an individual characteristic (for example, claustrophobic, or not caring much for space).

Part of his table 2 is shown here in Table 5.3 ("pool-cross" is for using NT observations as if they were cross-section data; t-values in $(\cdot)$).

TABLE 5.3 Housing Choice Equation Estimation

	pool−cross	PML 77−79−81	PML all years
price	−0.182 (−5.91)	−0.097 (−1.39)	−0.130 (−1.95)
inc−RL	0.013 (0.78)	0.015 (0.66)	0.040 (1.72)
inc−OS	0.065 (4.86)	0.083 (2.83)	0.050 (1.85)
inc−OL	0.093 (7.17)	0.106 (3.52)	0.068 (2.53)
size−RL	0.453 (3.87)	0.446 (2.16)	0.742 (3.28)
size−OS	0.472 (4.58)	0.815 (2.90)	1.081 (3.69)
size−OL	0.638 (6.64)	1.260 (4.33)	1.437 (5.21)
work−RL	−0.651 (−1.67)	−0.444 (−0.88)	−0.497 (−1.01)
work−OS	−0.459 (−1.37)	2.036 (1.83)	3.828 (2.87)
work−OL	−0.263 (−0.83)	2.444 (2.14)	3.859 (2.91)

Using all years, PML becomes more efficient, but not by as much as one would expect. The effect of price is much smaller in PMLs, compared with pool-cross. The significant estimates for inc are not much different across the all estimators, whereas the estimates for size-OS and size-OL differ by twice between pool-cross and PMLs. The biggest difference between pool-cross and PMLs is seen in work-OS and work-OL.

Moreover, although omitted in Table 5.3, age and age^2 are mostly significant with opposite signs across pool-cross and PMLs. The utility or satisfaction from age for pool-cross gives the ordering RS > OL $\cong$ OS > RL for ages 55 to 65, which is perverse. The implied utility from age for PML 77-79-81 gives the intuitively correct ordering OL > OS > RL > RS, whereas PML for all years yields OL > OS > RS $\cong$ RL.

5.7 AN EMPIRICAL EXAMPLE FOR COUNT RESPONSE

This section presents an empirical example for count response using the data set in Cincera (1997) on patents and R&D expenditure.

The relationship between patents and R&D has been a subject of interest in economics. A U-pattern in the effects of the current and lagged R&D's on patent has been found: the effect of the current and the last lagged R&D are positive and significant whereas the middle ones are not. But once a firm-specific effect was allowed for or the lag-truncation bias was accounted for, the U-pattern disappeared leaving only significant effect from the current R&D; see Hausman *et al.* (1984), Hall *et al.* (1986), Griliches (1995), and the references therein.

Cincera (1997) analyzed the effect of the log of R&D expenditure and the log of spill-overs on patent applications; the spill-over is the manufacturing sector-based R&D minus the firm's own R&D. The data has $N = 181$ firms over 9 years (1983–1991). Other than R&D and spillover, which are time variant, some time-invariant variables are used; time invariants are of no concern to us, however, for only the coefficients of time variants are identified in our first-difference type estimators. In line with Cincera (1997), year dummies are not used in the following discussion.

Denoting the R&D and spillover as k_{it} and s_{it}, respectively, Cincera used as regressors

$$k_{i,t-j}, \quad s_{i,t-j}, \quad for \ j = 0, 1, 2, 3, 4,$$

which means that the first wave is 1987 and there are five waves ($T = 5$). Although the details of the data can be found in Cincera, in the pooled sample, the sample mean (standard deviation) is, respectively

$$y_{it} : 60.8 \, (121.6), \quad \ln(k_{it}) : 5.3 \, (1.3), \quad \ln(s_{it}) : 9.5 \, (0.9).$$

The biggest problem with the data is multicollinearity: the minimum correlation between $\ln(k_{it})$ and $\ln(k_{i\tau})$, $t \neq \tau$, is 0.95. This makes detecting the pattern of the effects of the current and past R&Ds on patents difficult. Unless otherwise mentioned, we will use only the "raw" regressors, not their transformations, as instruments to keep the dimension of instruments low. Even with the raw regressors, the dimension of instruments can easily reach 50, which means estimating a 50×50 weighting matrix with only $181 \times 5 = 905$ total observations.

Table 5.4 shows two sets of estimates with t-values in ($\cdot$). The first is CPOI (or quasi-MLE (QMLE)) and the second is CW. For the former, two sets of t-values are given, one for CPOI and the other for QMLE. The big differences between the two sets of t-values indicate that the CPOI assumptions are violated; we will interpret only the QMLE t-values.

In computation, whereas the QMLE converged straightforwardly regardless of the starting values, this was not the case for GMM: GMM depended heavily on how the iteration was implemented. We tried three iterations: (4.6), the diagonal weighting with the diagonal components of the weighting matrix, and the identity weighting. For each algorithm, we tried two initial values, QMLE and zero's, to arrive at the same estimate for the two starting values. But across the three algorithms, the estimates were all different, with the one based on (4.6) being the best. Table 5.4 presents the estimates using (4.6).

The results for QMLE and CW are quite different. No U-pattern in the effects of R&D is visible in Table 5.4, and there is no significant R&D effect according to QMLE, although there are some (current and once lagged) according to CW. Overall, however, the effects vary in terms of signs and significance so much that it is hard to find any common ground between QMLE and CW; this difficulty seems to stem from the aforementioned multicollinearity problem. Despite this, the estimates for the total effects ("sumk" which is the sum for the k_t estimates and "sums" which is the sum for the s_t estimates) are similar: with t-values in (·),

sumk: QMLE is 0.35 (1.31) and CW is 0.42 (1.78)

sums: QMLE is 1.46 (4.58) and CW is 1.23 (3.58).

This shows a significant effect from the current or past spill-overs while an insignificant effect from the current and past R&D's on patents.

The CW-GMM over-id test fails to reject the CW model assumptions. The Wald test for QMLE = CW is rejected with ease. Because CW requires a PRE type assumption whereas QMLE requires EXO, the test result means the failure of EXO. But this should be taken with some caution, for there is a chance that the CW estimate at hand may not be a good one. That is, had we tried other algorithms, initial values, or had searched better, we might have obtained better estimates. This computational problem is, of course, not unique to this particular GMM.

TABLE 5.4 Patents and R&D

	CPOI (QMLE)			CW-GMM	
	b_N	tv-CPOI	tv-QMLE	b_N	tv
$\ln(k_t)$	0.292	(16.6)	(1.61)	0.369	(2.92)
$\ln(k_{t-1})$	0.062	(2.36)	(0.80)	0.359	(3.67)
$\ln(k_{t-2})$	0.069	(3.57)	(0.49)	−0.087	(−0.78)
$\ln(k_{t-3})$	−0.179	(−6.84)	(−1.29)	−0.055	(−0.59)
$\ln(k_{t-4})$	0.105	(5.29)	(0.77)	−0.163	(−1.90)
sumk	0.35	(21.9)	(1.31)	0.42	(1.78)
$\ln(s_t)$	1.269	(31.6)	(2.88)	−0.145	(−0.41)
$\ln(s_{t-1})$	−0.107	(−1.56)	(−0.26)	0.066	(0.24)
$\ln(s_{t-2})$	0.810	(10.7)	(2.78)	0.664	(2.43)
$\ln(s_{t-3})$	−0.740	(−11.5)	(−2.32)	0.117	(0.53)
$\ln(s_{t-4})$	0.224	(4.93)	(0.78)	0.527	(2.11)
sums	1.46	(42.9)	(4.58)	1.23	(3.58)

log-like (no constant): −100932.135

GMM over-id test stat. 49.96 (p-value: 0.32)

Test stat. for QMLE = CW: 43.34 (p-value: 0.00)

ρ (t-value) for BGW with b_N = CW: −0.1 (−0.89);

Using BGW for a specification test for CW, we fixed β at CW and grid-searched for ρ, over $[-0.8, 0.8]$ at increment 0.1. The best estimate turned out to be −0.1, with the t-value −0.89. Thus, CW is not rejected, not at least by BGW. We also tried to estimate BGW fully (both ρ and β), but there were many problems on convergence depending on the value of ρ.

In summary, the data used in this application does not seem to shed much light on patent and R&D relationship, although there are some effects of spillovers on patents. One real possibility that would undermine the patent and R&D relationship as economists see it is that a patent may be applied for in advance to preempt the research area, and R&D is done later following the patent application. This would reverse the causal direction.

6

PANEL DATA AND SAMPLE SELECTION MODELS

6.1 INTRODUCTION

In surveys, sometimes the respondent chooses not to answer certain questions; for example, in income surveys, the respondent may not answer if his or her income is too big (or too small). If the respondent does not answer only some questions in the survey, then this is called "item nonresponse"; if the respondent does not answer at all, then this is called "unit nonresponse." Obviously, the former poses less of a problem, for we may use the respondents' answered items to fill in the nonresponses.

An easy solution to the nonresponse problem is to use only the respondents with complete answers, but this can cause a bias. For example, if we are interested in the population mean income, the sample mean without the high income group will be biased downward. This, sampling from a special subpopulation and consequently incurring a bias in estimating the (whole) population parameter, is known as a "sample selection problem." A better expression could be a "biased sampling problem," but then we would have to specify what the sample is biased for. In the income example, the sample is biased for the population mean, but it may not be biased for the population mode.

In panel data, the subject may not participate in one wave but then come back for the next wave; or, the subject may never come back and be lost for good. The latter is called "attrition (dropout)"; sometimes, however, the former is also called attrition. In panel data, sample selection can mean item nonresponse in a wave, or unit nonresponse in a wave which then has the two subcases of comeback and attrition. As in cross-section data, one may use only the observations with complete answers for all items and waves ("square panel" or "rectangular panel"), which can, however, lead to a bias ("selection bias" or "attrition bias").

In the real world, the sample-selection problem seems to be the rule rather than the exception. The very fact that the subject ever entered the panel (and remained there for a while) reflects a collection of individual decisions over time. In a long panel such as the Panel Study of Income Dynamics (PSID) spanning a couple of decades, the remaining group are made up of special people: for one thing, they are patient because they have routinely filled out the questionnaires period after period; for another, they are healthy because they have survived the decades. Thus they may not be representative of the entire population that we are interested in. Learning about the population using selected and possibly nonrepresentative samples is our goal.

Sample selection is a big issue, and there is no way we could cover this topic fully in one chapter. Instead, we will look at what can be done for the following three common forms of panel selection:

(a) the usual (binary-) selection

(b) censored (tobit-type) selection

(c) attrition which may be called "truncated selection"

These classifications will be made clear in Sections 6.2 and 6.3. The first two topics will be discussed in detail; for the last topic, we will just show when attrition does not cause a bias for the least squares estimator (LSE) applied to the panel data that is trimmed (to create a balanced panel) and first-differenced (to remove the time-invariant error). Building specific models allowing for attrition is not easy in the selection framework when T is greater than, say, three; this is because nonattrition is a multiperiod decision, meaning a multivariate integration for estimation.

In a cross-section selection model, at least two equations appear: one for describing the selection decision and the other for the response variable of the main interest. In the income example, the binary decision to answer can be modeled as a binary response, whereas the income equation is the equation of the main interest. In a panel selection model, because a selection decision may be made each period anew, more than two equations may be required.

In a typical sample selection model, the selection equation is a binary response model, whereas the main ("outcome") equation has a continuous response variable; there, the binary response for the selection equation is of secondary importance. The notations for the binary response models in the preceding chapters were designed for when the binary response was of primary interest. Hence, notations in this chapter may not be comparable to those in the preceding chapters. As in the preceding chapters, this chapter will focus on "related-effect" (or fixed-effect) models where the time-invariant error δ_i is allowed to be related to regressors.

The rest of this chapter is organized as follows. Section 6.2 reviews sample selection models for cross-section data and examine two well-known estimators: Heckman's (1979) two-stage estimator and an estimator that resulted from the research of Powell (1987) and Newey *et al.* (1990). Section 6.3 presents the aforementioned three panel sample selection models, and Wooldridge's (1995) panel extension of Heckman (1979) is introduced for panel binary and censored selection; the models and notations in this section will be used in the other remaining sections. Section 6.4 examines two $\sqrt{N}$-consistent semiparametric methods for panel censored selection in Lee (2001) and Honoré and Kyriazidou (2000a). Section 6.5 examines a root-Nh consistent semiparametric estimator developed by Kyriazidou (1997) for panel binary selection. Finally, Section 6.6, drawing heavily on Lee and Cho (2002), presents conditions under which LSE is valid for trimmed and differenced panel data due to attrition. As we have done many times already, we will focus on two-period panels.

The estimators introduced in this chapter are fairly new except those for cross-section data, and we could not find good empirical examples in the literature; instead, illustrative examples will be provided throughout mostly to show that the new estimators yield "reasonable" results compared to the existing ones.

6.2 CROSS-SECTION SAMPLE SELECTION MODELS AND TWO ESTIMATORS

In this section, as a preparation for panel sample selection, we review cross-section sample selection models. Subsection 6.2.1 introduces selection models and selection bias. Subsections 6.2.2 and 6.2.3 review Heckman's (1979) two-stage estimator (TSE) and the semiparametric estimator developed by Powell (1987) and Newey *et al.* (1990); panel versions for the former will be presented later. Subsection 6.2.4 provides a brief empirical example on wage.

6.2.1 Three Sample Selection Models

Consider a typical cross-section sample selection model:

$$d_i^* = w_i'\alpha + \varepsilon_i, \quad d_i = 1[d_i^* > 0], \qquad (2.1)$$
$$y_i = x_i'\beta + u_i, \quad w_i = (x_i', c_i')', \quad E(\varepsilon|w_i) = E(u|w_i) = 0,$$
$$\alpha_c, \text{ the coefficient of } c_i \text{ in } w_i'\alpha, \text{ is not a zero vector,}$$
$$(d_i, w_i', d_i y_i)' \text{ observed, } i = 1, ..., N, \text{ iid,}$$

where w_i is a regressor vector with its first component 1, $1[A] = 1$ if A holds and 0 otherwise, ε_i and u_i are error terms, and α and β are conformable parameter vectors. The d-equation is the selection equation determining the selection (decision), and the y-equation is the outcome equation observed only when $d_i = 1$. Equation (2.1) includes an (inclusion and) exclusion restriction that c is (included in the selection equation while) excluded from the outcome equation.

An example for (2.1) is as follows: y is wage, $d = 1$ if working and 0 otherwise, x is a vector of explanatory variables relevant for wage and work decision, and c is an explanatory variable relevant for the work decision but not for the wage (for example, c is the parents' education levels); wage is observed only for those who choose to work. Another example is y is export volume, $d = 1$ if deciding to export, x is a vector of regressors for the export decision and volume, and c is an explanatory variable relevant for the export decision but not for the export volume (for example, an export barrier not related to export volume).

In (2.1), w is fully observed regardless d; that is, w, not dw, is observed. If (2.1) had

$$(d_i, d_i w_i', d_i y_i)' \text{ observed}, \quad i = 1, ..., N, \quad \text{iid}, \tag{2.2}$$

then (2.1) would be called a "truncated selection" model, which is harder to deal with because the observability is more limited than in (2.1). On the other hand, if (2.1) had

$$(d_i^* d_i, w_i', d_i y_i)' \text{ observed}, \quad i =, 1..., N, \quad \text{iid}, \tag{2.3}$$

then (2.1) would be called a "censored selection or tobit-type selection" model. Censored selection is easier to handle because d_i^* (not just d_i) is observed when $d_i^* > 0$.

Many estimators are available for censored selection; see Lee (1994), Chen (1997), Lee $et\ al.$ (2000), Honoré and Kyriazidou (2000a), and the references therein. Because censored selection is relatively rare (and easy to deal with), and because estimators good for binary selection are applicable also for censored selection, the rest of this section focuses on (binary-) selection cases.

The LSE of dy on dx is inconsistent for β, because in general,

$$E(y|w, d = 1) = x'\beta + E(u|w, d = 1) = x'\beta + E(u|w, \varepsilon > -w'\alpha) \neq x'\beta. \tag{2.4}$$

$E(u|w, \varepsilon > -w'\alpha)$ is called the "selection bias," which is zero if ε and u are independent given w:

$$E(u|w, \varepsilon > -w'\alpha) = E(u|w) = 0.$$

Because the LSE ignores the selection bias, the selection bias becomes part of the error term and causes an omitted variable bias for the LSE, because $E(u|w, \varepsilon > -w'\alpha)$, a function of w, is correlated with x in general. This shows also that the selection bias can be easily mistaken for a regression function misspecification (or the other way around). Note that sometimes the LSE omitted variable bias, not $E(u|w, \varepsilon > -w'\alpha)$, is called the "selection bias."

To see the form of the selection bias better, denote the joint density for $(\varepsilon = a, u = b)|w$ as $f(a, b|w) = f_{\varepsilon, u|w}(a, b)$ and the marginal density for $(\varepsilon = a)|w$ as $f(a|w) = f_{\varepsilon|w}(a)$. Assume that $\varepsilon|w$ has unbounded support for almost every (a.e.) w. Then the selection bias is (the integration ranges are omitted if they are ∞ or $-\infty$)

$$E(u|w, \varepsilon > -w'\alpha)$$

$$= \int\int_{-w'\alpha} u \cdot f(\varepsilon, u|w)d\varepsilon du \Big/ \int\int_{-w'\alpha} f(\varepsilon, u|w)d\varepsilon du \qquad (2.5)$$

$$= \int\int_{-w'\alpha} u \cdot f(u|\varepsilon, w) \cdot f(\varepsilon|w)d\varepsilon du \Big/ \int_{-w'\alpha} f(\varepsilon|w)d\varepsilon$$

$$= \int_{-w'\alpha} E(u|\varepsilon, w) \cdot f(\varepsilon|w)d\varepsilon \Big/ \int_{-w'\alpha} f(\varepsilon|w)d\varepsilon. \qquad (2.6)$$

Furthermore, with $\sigma_{\varepsilon u} \equiv COV(\varepsilon, u)$, $\sigma_\varepsilon^2 \equiv V(\varepsilon)$ and $\sigma_u^2 \equiv V(u)$, if

$$E(u|\varepsilon, w) = (\sigma_{\varepsilon u}/\sigma_\varepsilon^2) \cdot \varepsilon, \qquad (2.7)$$

then the selection bias becomes

$$(\sigma_{\varepsilon u}/\sigma_\varepsilon^2) \cdot \int_{-w'\alpha} \varepsilon \cdot f(\varepsilon|w)d\varepsilon \Big/ \int_{-w'\alpha} f(\varepsilon|w)d\varepsilon$$

$$= (\sigma_{\varepsilon u}/\sigma_\varepsilon^2) \cdot E(\varepsilon|w, \varepsilon > -w'\alpha)$$

$$= (\sigma_{\varepsilon u}/\sigma_\varepsilon^2) \cdot \sigma_\varepsilon E(\varepsilon/\sigma_\varepsilon|w, \varepsilon/\sigma_\varepsilon > -w'\alpha/\sigma_\varepsilon)$$

$$= \rho\sigma_u \cdot E(\varepsilon/\sigma_\varepsilon|w, \varepsilon/\sigma_\varepsilon > -w'\alpha/\sigma_\varepsilon), \qquad (2.8)$$

where $\rho \equiv COR(\varepsilon, u)$. In addition, if $\varepsilon \sim N(0, \sigma_\varepsilon^2)$ independently of w, then the selection bias becomes

$$\rho\sigma_u \cdot \phi(w'\alpha/\sigma_\varepsilon)/\Phi(w'\alpha/\sigma_\varepsilon), \qquad (2.9)$$

where ϕ and Φ are, respectively, the $N(0, 1)$ density and distribution function. If $\rho = 0$ ($\Leftrightarrow \sigma_{\varepsilon u} = 0$), then the selection bias is zero.

6.2.2 Heckman's Two-Stage Estimator

Assume for a while

    (a) independence of ε from w, and ε follows $N(0, \sigma_\varepsilon^2)$

    (b) linear regression of u on ε in (2.7)   (2.10)

(2.9) holds under this as shown in the preceding subsection, and Heckman's (1979) TSE, which accounts for the selection bias explicitly, proceeds as follows.

First, apply probit to the selection equation to estimate $\alpha/\sigma_\varepsilon$, and replace the part of the selection bias other than $\rho\sigma_u$ in (2.9)

$$\lambda(w_i'\alpha/\sigma_\varepsilon) \equiv \phi(w_i'\alpha/\sigma_\varepsilon)/\Phi(w_i'\alpha/\sigma_\varepsilon) \qquad (2.11)$$

with $\lambda_{Ni} \equiv \lambda(w_i'a_N)$ where a_N is the probit for $\alpha/\sigma_\varepsilon$. Second, the LSE g_N of $d_i y_i$ on

$$d_i \cdot z_{Ni} \equiv d_i \cdot (x_i', \lambda_{Ni})' \qquad (2.12)$$

is obtained for the parameter

$$\gamma \equiv (\beta', \rho\sigma_u)'.$$

Equation (2.11) is sometimes called the "selection correction term."

Despite the selection problem, β is estimated consistently so long as (2.10) holds and the regression function is correctly specified. The selection bias can be tested with $H_o : \rho\sigma_u = 0$ in the second stage LSE, if desired. But there is a complicating factor: the first stage estimation error $a_N - (\alpha/\sigma_\varepsilon)$ affects the asymptotic variance of the second stage LSE, which is derived in the following.

Denote $\{E(\cdot)\}^{-1}$ as $E^{-1}(\cdot)$, and define the probit score function as S_i and its influence function as η_i so that

$$\sqrt{N}(a_N - (\alpha/\sigma_\varepsilon)) = (1/\sqrt{N}) \sum_i \eta_i + o_p(1),$$

$$\{\eta_i\}_{i=1}^N \text{ iid}, \ E(\eta) = 0, \text{ and } E(\eta\eta') < \infty$$

where

$$\eta_i \equiv E^{-1}(SS') \cdot S_i = E^{-1}(SS') \cdot w_i(d_i - \Phi_i)\phi_i/\{\Phi_i(1 - \Phi_i)\}, \qquad (2.13)$$

$\phi_i \equiv \phi(w_i'\alpha/\sigma_\varepsilon)$ and $\Phi_i \equiv \Phi(w_i'\alpha/\sigma_\varepsilon)$; $E^{-1}(SS')$ should be replaced by $\{(1/N)\sum_i S_i S_i'\}^{-1}$ and $\alpha/\sigma_\varepsilon$ should be replaced by a_N in practice. Define a "link matrix" L such that

$$L = -\rho\sigma_u \cdot E\{d \cdot \lambda'(w'\alpha/\sigma_\varepsilon) \cdot zw'\}, \qquad (2.14)$$

where λ' is the first derivative of λ :

$$\lambda'(a) = -a\lambda(a) - \lambda(a)^2 \quad \text{and} \quad z_i \equiv (x_i', \lambda(w_i'\alpha/\sigma_\varepsilon))'.$$

Also define the "reduced form" error and its residual as, respectively,

$$v_i \equiv y_i - z_i'\gamma \quad \text{and} \quad v_{Ni} \equiv y_i - z_{Ni}'g_N.$$

Then

$$\sqrt{N}(g_N - \gamma) \Rightarrow N(0, \ E^{-1}(dzz') \cdot E\{(dvz + L\eta)(dvz + L\eta)'\} \cdot E^{-1}(dzz')). \qquad (2.15)$$

The asymptotic variance can be estimated consistently by replacing $E(\cdot)$ with $(1/N)\sum_i(\cdot)$ and the other unknowns by consistent estimates. Under $H_o : \rho\sigma_u = 0$, one may set $L\eta = 0$ in the asymptotic variance, which means there is no need to bother with the correction due to $a_N - \alpha/\sigma_\varepsilon$ as far as testing the H_o goes.

In principle, Heckman's TSE does not need an exclusion restriction (recall c_i in (2.1)) if the regression function is correctly specified. If the regression function is misspecified and no exclusion restriction is available, however, then one may falsely accept selection bias even if the bias is not present as noted already. Hence in practice, usually an exclusion restriction is imposed on Heckman's TSE to tell the genuine selection bias from a regression function misspecification

6.2.3 A Semiparametric Estimator

Although Heckman's TSE is easy to apply, the form of the selection correction term has to be (2.11) exactly. In this subsection, we examine a semiparametric estimator relaxing some restrictive assumptions in Heckman's TSE at the cost of an exclusion restriction; the estimator gets rid of the selection bias, rather than accounting for it explicitly.

Adding and subtracting $d \cdot E(u|w'\alpha, d = 1)$, rewrite $dy = dx'\beta + du$ as

$$
\begin{aligned}
dy &= dx'\beta + dE(u|w'\alpha, d = 1) + d\{u - E(u|w'\alpha, d = 1)\} \quad (2.16) \\
&= dx'\beta + d\lambda(w'\alpha) + d\{u - E(u|w'\alpha, d = 1)\},
\end{aligned}
$$

where

$$
\lambda(w'\alpha) \equiv E(u|w'\alpha, d = 1) = E(u|w'\alpha, \varepsilon > -w'\alpha);
$$

the definition of $\lambda(w'\alpha)$ here is slightly different from that in Heckman's TSE. Observe that, considering the two cases with $d = 0$ and 1,

$$
E(du|w'\alpha, d) = d \cdot E(u|w'\alpha, d) = d \cdot E(u|w'\alpha, d = 1).
$$

Take $E(\cdot|w'\alpha, d)$ on the dy equation (2.16) to get rid of the error term and then obtain

$$
d \cdot E(y|w'\alpha, d = 1) = d \cdot E(x|w'\alpha, d = 1)'\beta + d \cdot \lambda(w'\alpha). \quad (2.17)
$$

Subtract (2.17) from (2.16) to get the main equation:

$$
d\{y - E(y|w'\alpha, d = 1)\} = d\{\tilde{x} - E(\tilde{x}|w'\alpha, d = 1)\}'\tilde{\beta} + d\{u - E(u|w'\alpha, d = 1)\} \quad (2.18)
$$

where $\tilde{\beta}$ is the slope parameter (and $\bar{\beta}$ is the intercept) defined by,

$$
x = (1, \tilde{x}')' \quad \text{and} \quad \beta = (\bar{\beta}, \tilde{\beta}')'.
$$

In the subtraction, the intercept gets lost along with $\lambda(w'\alpha)$.

Suppose

$$
E(u|w, d = 1) = E(u|w'\alpha, d = 1),
$$

which holds, for example, if u is independent of w; the condition is an "index sufficiency" that the mean of $u|w$ depends on w only through the index $w'\alpha$.

In (2.18), following the Robinson's (1988) idea, it is conceivable to estimate $\tilde{\beta}$ by the LSE of

$$d\{y - E(y|w'\alpha, d = 1)\} \quad \text{on} \quad d\{\tilde{x} - E(\tilde{x}|w'\alpha, d = 1)\},$$

for the regressor has zero correlation with the error term:

$$E[d \cdot \{\tilde{x} - E(\tilde{x}|w'\alpha, d = 1)\} \cdot \{u - E(u|w'\alpha, d = 1)\}] \qquad (2.19)$$
$$= E[d \cdot E[\{\tilde{x} - E(\tilde{x}|w'\alpha, d = 1)\} \cdot \{u - E(u|w'\alpha, d = 1)\}|w, d = 1]]$$
$$= E[d \cdot \{\tilde{x} - E(\tilde{x}|w'\alpha, d = 1)\} \cdot E[\{u - E(u|w'\alpha, d = 1)\}|w, d = 1]] = 0.$$

For the LSE to work, the matrix

$$E[d \cdot \{\tilde{x} - E(\tilde{x}|w'\alpha, d = 1)\} \cdot \{\tilde{x} - E(\tilde{x}|w'\alpha, d = 1)\}']$$

should be invertible, for which we need an inclusion/exclusion restriction that c should be in the d-equation but not in the y-equation. Otherwise, if $w = x$, then with $\alpha = (\bar{\alpha}, \tilde{\alpha}')'$, where $\bar{\alpha}$ is the intercept and $\tilde{\alpha}$ is the slope parameters,

$$\{\tilde{x} - E(\tilde{x}|x'\alpha, d = 1)\}'\tilde{\alpha} = \tilde{x}'\tilde{\alpha} - E(\tilde{x}'\tilde{\alpha}|x'\alpha, d = 1) = \tilde{x}'\tilde{\alpha} - \tilde{x}'\tilde{\alpha} = 0;$$

the columns of $\tilde{x} - E(\tilde{x}|x'\alpha, d = 1)$ are linearly dependent.

Newey et al. (1990) also presented an empirical application on work hours where the estimation result of Heckman's TSE does not much differ from theirs; they allow an endogenous regressor (wage rate) and use an instrument for the regressor. Instrumental variable estimator (IVE) with an instrument vector q can be accommodated simply by replacing $\tilde{x}$ in (2.19) with q:

$$E[d \cdot \{q - E(q|w'\alpha, d = 1)\} \cdot \{u - E(u|w'\alpha, d = 1)\}]$$
$$= E[d \cdot E[\{q - E(q|w'\alpha, d = 1)\} \cdot \{u - E(u|w'\alpha, d = 1)\}|q, d = 1]] = 0$$

under the assumption $E(u|q, d = 1) = E(u|w'\alpha, d = 1)$.

Newey et al. (1990) showed only the idea (2.18) and (2.19) that originates in Powell (1987). In the following discussion, we present the actual estimation procedures and its asymptotic distribution; the reader may want to skip this discussion and move on to the next subsection. The regularity conditions and proofs for the following discussion are analogous to those in Lee et al. (2000).

First, estimate α $\sqrt{N}$-consistently by a_N, such as in Han (1987) and Sherman's (1993) estimator, Klein and Spady (1993), or Ichimura (1993); probit may be used if (2.10)(a) is assumed, which is what we will do for our empirical example later.

Second, estimate $E(y|w_i'\alpha, d_i = 1)$ and $E(\tilde{x}|w_i'\alpha, d_i = 1)$ nonparametrically with $E_N(y|w_i'a_N, d_i = 1)$ and $E_N(\tilde{x}|w_i'a_N, d_i = 1)$, respectively:

$$E_N(y|w_i'a_N, d_i = 1)$$
$$\equiv \{(N - 1)h\}^{-1} \sum_{j, j \neq i} K((w_j'a_N - w_i'a_N)/h)d_j y_j \qquad (2.20)$$
$$/\{(N - 1)h\}^{-1} \sum_{j, j \neq i} K((w_j'a_N - w_i'a_N)/h)d_j,$$

where K is a kernel, h is a bandwidth, and $E_N(\tilde{x}|w_i'a_N, d_i = 1)$ can be obtained analogously by replacing y_j with $\tilde{x}_j$ in $E_N(y|w_i'a_N, d_i = 1)$.

Third, do the LSE of $d\{y - E_N(y|w'a_N, d = 1)\}$ on $d\{\tilde{x} - E_N(\tilde{x}|w'a_N, d = 1)\}$ for $\tilde{\beta}$; denote this LSE as $\tilde{b}_N$.

For the asymptotic distribution, rewrite $y - E_N(y|w'a_N, d = 1)$ as

$$x'\beta + u - E_N(x'\beta + u|w'a_N, d = 1)$$
$$= \{\tilde{x} - E_N(\tilde{x}|w'a_N, d = 1)\}'\tilde{\beta} + u - E_N(u|w'a_N, d = 1). \quad (2.21)$$

Using this, we get

$$\sqrt{N}(\tilde{b}_N - \tilde{\beta})$$
$$= [(1/N)\sum_i d_i\{\tilde{x}_i - E_N(\tilde{x}|w_i'a_N, d_i = 1)\}\{\tilde{x}_i - E_N(\tilde{x}|w_i'a_N, d_i = 1)\}']^{-1}$$
$$\cdot (1/\sqrt{N})\sum_i d_i\{\tilde{x}_i - E_N(\tilde{x}|w_i'a_N, d_i = 1)\}\{u_i - E_N(u|w_i'a_N, d_i = 1)\}.$$

Let η_i denote an influence function for a_N (η_i depends on the choice of a_N in the first step), and define

$$H \equiv E[d \cdot \{\tilde{x} - E(\tilde{x}|w'\alpha, d = 1)\}\{\tilde{x} - E(\tilde{x}|w'\alpha, d = 1)\}'] \quad (2.22)$$
$$L \equiv E[d \cdot \{\tilde{x} - E(\tilde{x}|w'\alpha, d = 1)\}w' \cdot \nabla E(u|w'\alpha, d = 1)],$$

where $\nabla E(u|w'\alpha, d = 1) = dE(u|t, d = 1)/dt|_{t=w'\alpha}$. Then,

$$\sqrt{N}(\tilde{b}_N - \tilde{\beta}) \overset{p}{=} H^{-1} \cdot (1/\sqrt{N})\sum_i \xi_i \Rightarrow N(0, H^{-1}E(\xi\xi')H^{-1}); \quad (2.23)$$
$$\xi_i \equiv d_i\{\tilde{x}_i - E(\tilde{x}|w_i'\alpha, d_i = 1)\}\{u_i - E(u|w_i'\alpha, d_i = 1) - L\eta_i\}.$$

The error $a_N - \alpha$ influences the asymptotic variance through w in $w'\alpha$, which in turn affects $E(u|w'\alpha, d = 1)$; this is why $w'\nabla E(u|w'\alpha, d = 1)$ appears in L.

Consistent estimators for H and $E(\xi\xi')$ are, respectively,

$$H_N \equiv (1/N)\sum_i d_i\{\tilde{x}_i - E_N(\tilde{x}|w_i'a_N, d_i = 1)\}$$
$$\{\tilde{x}_i - E_N(\tilde{x}|w_i'a_N, d_i = 1)\}', \quad (2.24)$$
$$A_N \equiv (1/N)\sum_i \xi_{Ni}\xi_{Ni}' \quad (2.25)$$

where (recall (2.21))

$$
\begin{aligned}
\xi_{Ni} &\equiv d_i\{\tilde{x}_i - E_N(\tilde{x}|w_i'a_N, d_i = 1)\{y_i - E_N(y|w_i'a_N, d_i = 1) \\
&\quad -(\tilde{x}_i - E_N(\tilde{x}|w_i'a_N, d_i = 1))'\tilde{b}_N\} - L_N\eta_{Ni}, \\
L_N &\equiv (1/N)\sum_i d_i\{\tilde{x}_i - E_N(\tilde{x}|w_i'a_N, d_i = 1)\}w_i'\nabla_N E(u|w_i'a_N, d_i = 1),
\end{aligned}
$$

$$
\begin{aligned}
&\nabla_N E(u|w_i'a_N, d_i = 1) \\
&\equiv [\{(N-1)h\}^{-1}\sum_{j,j\neq i} K((w_j'a_N - w_i'a_N)/h)d_j]^{-1} \\
&\quad \cdot[-\{(N-1)h^2\}^{-1}\sum_{j,j\neq i} K'((w_j'a_N - w_i'a_N)/h)d_j(y_j - \tilde{x}_j'\tilde{b}_N) \\
&\quad +E_N(y - \tilde{x}'\tilde{b}_N|w_i'a_N, d_i = 1) \\
&\quad \cdot\{(N-1)h^2\}^{-1}\sum_{j,j\neq i} K'((w_j'a_N - w_i'a_N)/h)d_j],
\end{aligned}
$$

K' is the derivative of K, and η_{Ni} is a consistent estimator for η_i. As for $\nabla_N E(u|w_i'a_N, d_i = 1)$, it is the derivative of $E_N(y - \tilde{x}'\tilde{b}_N|w_i'a_N, d_i = 1)$ with respect to (wrt) $w_i'a_N$; although $E_N(y - \tilde{x}'\tilde{b}_N|w_i'a_N, d_i = 1)$ is consistent for $\bar{\beta} + E(u|w_i'\alpha, d_i = 1)$, $\bar{\beta}$ drops out in the differentiation.

6.2.4 An Empirical Example on Wage

Mroz (1987) used the PSID data for 1975 (the survey was done in 1976) to check the sensitivity of selection models to various assumptions. In the following illustration, we use the same data to illustrate Heckman's TSE and the semiparametric LSE; see Mroz (1987) for details about the data.

The selection equation is for working/nonworking decision and the outcome equation is for the working hours per month of wives; $N = 753$ with 54.3% working. We use the following variables for w: 1, age (age in years), edu (education in years), exper (job experience in years), pkid (number of pre-school children of age less than 6), skid (number of schooling children of age between 6 and 18), ump (local unemployment rate percentage in the county of residence), edumom (education in years of the mother), and edudad (education in years of the father). Edumom and edudad are excluded from the outcome equation.

For the semiparametric LSE, the "quaratic (or bi-weight)" kernel is used:

$$
K(t) = (15/16)\cdot(1 - t^2)^2\cdot 1[|t| \leq 1].
$$

The bandwidth is chosen by "cross-validation" minimizing

$$
(1/N)\sum_i d_i\{y_i - E_N(y|w_i'a_N, d_i = 1)\}^2
$$

with respect to c_o where the bandwidth is $c_o SD(w'a_N)N^{-1/5}$; the optimal value for c_o turns out to be 1.4. The same bandwidth is used also for $\nabla_N E(u|w_i'a_N,$

$d_i = 1$), although this is unlikely to be an optimal choice. We present the estimates and t-values in Table 6.1.

TABLE 6.1 Working Hour Equation under Selection

	Heckman TSE estimate	t−value	Semiparametric LSE estimate	t−value	tv−boot
1	30.634	1.066			
age	0.795	0.683	0.475	0.350	0.349
age^2	−0.010	−0.650	−0.012	−0.457	−0.648
edu	−1.010	−1.446	0.103	0.036	0.076
exper	0.179	0.450	0.867	0.458	1.028
pkid	−0.302	−0.053	−7.899	−0.366	−0.786
skid	−1.671	−2.543	−1.490	−1.643	−1.712
ump	−0.280	−1.175	−0.388	−0.841	−1.264
λ	−11.331	−1.066			

Probit is used for a_N in the first stage. The last column, "tv-boot," is a bootstrap t-value (see, for instance, Horowitz (2001) and the references therein): 500 (pseudo) random samples with the same sample size are drawn from the data with replacement, from which 500 bootstrap estimates are obtained; tv-boot is obtained by dividing the estimate column in Table 6.1 by the standard deviations from the bootstrap estimates. In the bootstrap, the bandwidth is fixed with $c_o = 1.4$. There is no proof that the tv-boot is consistent; tv-boot is computed only for the sake of comparison, for the other t-value is somewhat cumbersome to obtain.

Comparing the two column estimates, only skid is (nearly) significant. The insignificant estimates for edu, exper, and pkid are quite different between Heckman's TSE and the semiparametric LSE. In Heckman's TSE, education seems to have the wrong sign, whereas pkid's magnitude is too small compared with skid; in the semiparametric LSE, the magnitude of pkid is much bigger than that of skid, which makes sense. The selection correction term λ in Heckman's TSE is insignificant with negative sign. In the semiparametric LSE, the tv-boot does not differ too much from the asymptotic t-value, although there are a couple of instances where the tv-boot is almost twice greater.

6.3 PANEL SAMPLE SELECTION MODELS AND HECKMAN'S TWO-STAGE ANALOGS

In the preceding section, we reviewed three cross-section sample selection models and two better known estimators. In this section, we present panel analogs for the three sample selection models in Subsection 6.3.1, two censored-selection estimators in Subsection 6.3.2, a binary-selection estimator in Subsection 6.3.3, and an empirical example for binary selection in Subsection 6.3.4 with the same health data that have been used a couple of times already. Given the popularity of Heckman's two-stage estimator, the reader may find Subsections 6.3.3 and 6.3.4 on binary selection useful.

6.3.1 Three Panel Sample Selection Models

Consider, for $i = 1, \ldots, N$ and $t = 1, 2$,

$$d_{it}^* = x_{it}'\alpha + \psi_i + \varepsilon_{it}, \quad y_{it} = x_{it}'\beta + \delta_i + u_{it}, \qquad (3.1)$$

x_{it} is a regressor vector, ε_{it} and u_{it} are time-variant error terms,

y_{it} is observed only when $d_{it}^* > 0$,

where ψ_i and δ_i are time-invariant errors possibly related to components of x_{it}, which includes both time-invariant and variant regressors.

Define

$$d_{it} \equiv 1[d_{it}^* > 0], \ d_i \equiv d_{i1}d_{i2}, \ d_i^* \equiv (d_{i1}^*, d_{i2}^*)', \ x_i \equiv (x_{i1}', x_{i2}')', \qquad (3.2)$$

$$y_i \equiv (y_{i1}, y_{i2})', \ u_i \equiv (u_{i1}, u_{i2})', \ \varepsilon_i \equiv (\varepsilon_{i1}, \varepsilon_{i2})',$$

$$\Delta y_i \equiv y_{i2} - y_{i1}, \ \Delta x_i \equiv x_{i2} - x_{i1}, \ \Delta u_i \equiv u_{i2} - u_{i1}, \ \Delta\varepsilon_i \equiv \varepsilon_{i2} - \varepsilon_{i1},$$

$$x_{it} \equiv (\bar{x}_i', \tilde{x}_{it}')', \ \alpha \equiv (\bar{\alpha}', \tilde{\alpha}')', \ \beta \equiv (\bar{\beta}', \tilde{\beta}')',$$

where $\bar{x}_i$ contains the time invariants in x_{it}, $\tilde{x}_{it}$ contains the time variants, and $(\bar{\alpha}', \bar{\beta}')$ and $(\tilde{\alpha}', \tilde{\beta}')$ are conformably defined parameters for $\bar{x}_i$ and $\tilde{x}_{it}$, respectively. Note that d_i is not defined as $(d_{i1}, d_{i2})'$, but this will cause hardly any confusion, for $d_i = 1$ means $d_{i1} = 1$ and $d_{i2} = 1$. Unlike the cross-section selection models, exclusion restrictions are not necessary, in general, for panel data, because $\tilde{x}_{i1}$ is excluded from $t = 2$, whereas $\tilde{x}_{i2}$ is excluded from $t = 1$; an exception to this occurs, however, if Δy_i and Δx_i are used as in cross-section selection models for $T = 2$.

For panel data, although many more cases can be thought of, consider the following three cases of observability (with iid assumed across i as usual):

    (a) (binary-) selection: $(d_{i1}, d_{i2}, x_i', d_{i1}y_{i1}, d_{i2}y_{i2})'$

    (b) censored-selection: $(d_{i1}^*d_{i1}, d_{i2}^*d_{i2}, x_i', d_{i1}y_{i1}, d_{i2}y_{i2})' \qquad (3.3)$

    (c) attrition: $(d_{i1}, d_i, d_{i1}x_{i1}', d_i x_{i2}', d_{i1}y_{i1}, d_i y_{i2})'$

These three panel models are reminiscent of the cross-section (binary-) selection, censored-selection, and truncated selection, respectively, in (2.1), (2.3), and (2.2).

An example of censored selection is as follows: d_{it}^* is hours worked and y_{it} is wage: when a person works, we may observe not only the wage but also the hours worked. An example of binary selection is as follows: $d_{it} = 1$ if the subject joins a labor union and y_{it} is the union wage; here the subject makes the binary decision of joining the union or not anew every period. Another example already mentioned for binary selection is item nonresponse where the item y_{it} is not observed for some periods.

In the rest of this section, we will review Wooldridge's (1995) extension of Heckman's TSE for panel related-effect selection models; more parametric approaches on panel selection and attrition can be seen in Nijman and Verbeek (1992), Rochina-Barrachina (1999), Verbeek and Nijman (1992), Vella and Verbeek (1999), and the references therein.

6.3.2 Two Censored-Selection Estimators

Wooldridge (1995) extended Heckman's TSE to panel data by imposing a marginal normality on ε_{it}, and by assuming some mean independence and linear conditional means on the outcome equation. Wooldridge suggested various selection bias tests and estimators. Here and in the following subsection, we present what seems to be his main contribution with $T = 2$. We present two estimators for censored selection in this subsection and one estimator for binary selection in the next subsection.

Recall the latent selection equation, but with its error term denoted as e_{it}, not ε_{it}: $d_{it}^* = x_{it}'\alpha + \psi_i + e_{it}$. Rewrite this as

$$d_{it}^* = x_{it}'\alpha + E(\psi_i|x_i) + \psi_i - E(\psi_i|x_i) + e_{it}. \tag{3.4}$$

Assume that, for all t,

(a) $E(\psi_i|x_i) = $ a linear function of x_i,

(b) $\psi_i - E(\psi_i|x_i) + e_{it}$ follows $N(0, \sigma_t^2)$ independently of x_i,

$$\tag{3.5}$$

where σ_t is an unknown constant. Then, for some conformably defined parameter vectors $\bar{\alpha}_t$, $\tilde{\alpha}_{1t}$ and $\tilde{\alpha}_{2t}$,

$$d_{it}^* = \bar{x}_i'\bar{\alpha}_t + \tilde{x}_{i1}'\tilde{\alpha}_{1t} + \tilde{x}_{i2}'\tilde{\alpha}_{2t} + \varepsilon_{it} = w_i'\alpha_t + \varepsilon_{it}, \tag{3.6}$$

$$\varepsilon_{it} \equiv \psi_i - E(\psi_i|x_i) + e_{it} \sim N(0, \sigma_t^2) \text{ independently of } x_i, t = 1, 2,$$

where $\bar{\alpha}_t$, $\tilde{\alpha}_{1t}$ and $\tilde{\alpha}_{2t}$ are functions of components of α and the parameters in (3.5)(a), and

$$w_i \equiv (\bar{x}_i', \tilde{x}_{i1}', \tilde{x}_{i2}')', \quad \alpha_t \equiv (\bar{\alpha}_t', \tilde{\alpha}_{1t}', \tilde{\alpha}_{2t}')', \quad \text{for} \quad t = 1, 2.$$

As for the outcome equation, assume

$$E(u_{it}|\psi_i, \delta_i, x_i, \varepsilon_i) = E(u_{it}|\psi_i, \delta_i, \varepsilon_{it}) = \rho(\psi_i, \delta_i) + \rho_u \varepsilon_{it}, \quad t = 1, 2, \tag{3.7}$$

where $\rho(\cdot, \cdot)$ is an unknown function and ρ_u is an unknown scalar. The first equality is that u_{it} is mean-independent of x_i and $\varepsilon_{i\tau}$, $\tau \neq t$, conditional on $(\psi_i, \delta_i, \varepsilon_{it})$. Then

$$E(y_{it}|\psi_i, \delta_i, x_i, \varepsilon_i) = x_{it}'\beta + \delta_i + \rho(\psi_i, \delta_i) + \rho_u \varepsilon_{it}.$$

Rewrite the y_{it} equation as

$$y_{it} = x'_{it}\beta + \delta_i + \rho(\psi_i, \delta_i) + \rho_u \varepsilon_{it} + v_{it}, \qquad v_{it} \equiv u_{it} - \rho(\psi_i, \delta_i) - \rho_u \varepsilon_{it}.$$
(3.8)

First-difference (3.8) to get

$$\Delta y_i = \Delta x'_i \beta + \rho_u \Delta \varepsilon_i + \Delta v_i.$$
(3.9)

Do tobit for $\max(d_{it}^*, 0)$, $t = 1, 2$; this yields two residuals $\hat{\varepsilon}_{i1}$ and $\hat{\varepsilon}_{i2}$ for the data with $d_i = 1$. Then, do the LSE of $d_i \Delta y_i$ on $d_i \Delta x_i$ and $d_i \Delta \hat{\varepsilon}_i = d_i(\hat{\varepsilon}_{i2} - \hat{\varepsilon}_{i1})$; this is the first estimator for censored selection, with the second estimator shown following the brief review on tobit below.

In (3.9), $\Delta \varepsilon_i$ controls for the endogeneity that is the source of the selection problem. The asymptotic distribution of the LSE for (3.9) can be derived analogously to the asymptotic distribution of Heckman's TSE for cross-section data; we will, however, show the derivation only for the (binary-) selection estimator in the next subsection. As in cross-section Heckman's TSE, the first-stage estimation error $\Delta \hat{\varepsilon}_i - \Delta \varepsilon_i$ complicates the asymptotic distribution of the two-stage LSE. A simpler approach is to ignore the first-stage error and use the LSE asymptotic variance, which does not pose a problem as far as testing $H_o : \rho_u = 0$ goes.

Consider a cross-section censored regression model:

(a) $y_i^* = x'_i \beta + u_i$, $\quad y_i = \max(y_i^*, 0)$

(b) $(x'_i, y_i)'$ observed, $i = 1, ..., N$, iid

(c) u_i follows $N(0, \sigma^2)$ independently of x_i

Note that (a) and (b) together form a censored model (censoring below at zero) and adding (c) renders "tobit." The log-likelihood function is

$$Q_N(b, s) = (1/N) \sum_i [(1 - 1_i) \cdot \ln \Phi(-x'_i b/s) + 1_i \ln\{s^{-1}\phi((y_i - x'_i b)/s)\}],$$

which is to be maximized over b and s where $1_i \equiv 1[y_i > 0]$. Defining $\phi_i = \phi(x'_i b/s)$ and $\Phi_i = \Phi(x'_i b/s)$, the gradient is

$$\partial Q_N / \partial b = (1/N) \sum_i [-(1 - 1_i)\phi_i x_i/\{s(1 - \Phi_i)\} + 1_i(1/s^2)(y_i - x'_i b)x_i],$$

$$\partial Q_N / \partial s = (1/N) \sum_i [(1 - 1_i)x'_i b \cdot \phi_i/\{s^2(1 - \Phi_i)\}$$

$$-1_i/s + 1_i(y_i - x'_i b)^2/s^3].$$

Tobit is used, for example, for female labor supply and household expenditure studies.

In (3.9), δ_i was removed by differencing. Another way to deal with δ_i is to specify $E(\delta_i|x_i)$ as a linear function of x_i as in (3.5)(a). Assume (3.5) and (instead of (3.7)),

$$E(u_{it}|x_i, \varepsilon_{it}) \quad = \quad E(u_{it}|\varepsilon_{it}) = \rho_u \varepsilon_{it}, \qquad (3.10)$$

$$E(\delta_i|x_i, \varepsilon_{it}) \quad = \quad \bar{x}_i'\bar{\theta} + \tilde{x}_{i1}'\tilde{\theta}_1 + \tilde{x}_{i2}'\tilde{\theta}_2 + \rho_\delta \varepsilon_{it}, \qquad (3.11)$$

where $\rho_u, \bar{\theta}, \tilde{\theta}_1, \tilde{\theta}_2$, and ρ_δ are unknown parameters; here, ρ_u is not necessarily the same as the ρ_u in (3.7). Equation (3.10) is the mean independence of u_{it} from x_i given ε_{it}. Note that ε_{it}, not ε_i, is in the conditioning set in (3.10).

Use (3.10) to rewrite the outcome equation as

$$\begin{aligned}
y_{it} \quad = \quad & x_{it}'\beta + E(\delta_i|x_i, \varepsilon_{it}) + E(u_{it}|x_i, \varepsilon_{it}) \\
& + \delta_i - E(\delta_i|x_i, \varepsilon_{it}) + u_{it} - E(u_{it}|x_i, \varepsilon_{it}) \\
y_{it} \quad = \quad & x_{it}'\beta + \bar{x}_i'\bar{\theta} + \tilde{x}_{i1}'\tilde{\theta}_1 + \tilde{x}_{i2}'\tilde{\theta}_2 + \rho_\delta \varepsilon_{it} + \rho_u \varepsilon_{it} \\
& + \delta_i - E(\delta_i|x_i, \varepsilon_{it}) + u_{it} - E(u_{it}|x_i, \varepsilon_{it}) \\
= \quad & \bar{x}_i'(\bar{\beta} + \bar{\theta}) + \tilde{x}_{it}'(\tilde{\beta} + \tilde{\theta}_t) + \tilde{x}_{i\tau}'\tilde{\theta}_\tau + \rho \varepsilon_{it} + v_{it}, \\
& \tau \neq t, \quad t = 1, 2, \qquad (3.12)
\end{aligned}$$

where

$$\rho \equiv \rho_\delta + \rho_u \quad \text{and} \quad v_{it} \equiv \delta_i - E(\delta_i|x_i, \varepsilon_{it}) + u_{it} - E(u_{it}|x_i, \varepsilon_{it}). \quad (3.13)$$

LSE of y_{it} on $\bar{x}_i, \tilde{x}_{i1}, \tilde{x}_{i2}$ and ε_{it} can be done with ε_{it} replaced by the tobit residual, because the moment condition for the LSE holds:

$$E\{(x_i', \varepsilon_{it}) \cdot v_{it}\} = E\{(x_i', \varepsilon_{it}) \cdot E(v_{it}|x_i, \varepsilon_{it})\} = 0.$$

6.3.3 A Binary-Selection Estimator

Recall (3.10) to (3.13) for censored selection. For (binary-) selection, we need $E(y_{it}|x_i, d_{it} = 1)$, which is obtained by integrating

$$E(y_{it}|x_i, \varepsilon_{it}) = \bar{x}_i'(\bar{\beta} + \bar{\theta}) + \tilde{x}_{it}'(\tilde{\beta} + \tilde{\theta}_t) + \tilde{x}_{i\tau}'\tilde{\theta}_\tau + \rho \varepsilon_{it}, \quad \tau \neq t, \quad (3.14)$$

over $\varepsilon_{it} > -w_i'\alpha_t$ (recall (3.6)) to get

$$E(y_{it}|x_i, d_{it} = 1) = \bar{x}_i'(\bar{\beta} + \bar{\theta}) + \tilde{x}_{it}'(\tilde{\beta} + \tilde{\theta}_t) + \tilde{x}_{i\tau}'\tilde{\theta}_\tau + \rho\sigma_t \cdot \lambda(w_i'\alpha_t/\sigma_t)$$

where $\lambda(\cdot) \equiv \phi(\cdot)/\Phi(\cdot)$ and

$$E(\varepsilon_{it}|x_i, d_{it} = 1) = \sigma_t \cdot \lambda(w_i'\alpha_t/\sigma_t), \quad t = 1, 2. \quad (3.15)$$

$\lambda(\cdot)$ can be estimated by probit at each t, and the rest of the steps can be done by LSE for each wave and then by minimum distance estimation (MDE) to impose cross-equation restrictions as shown in the following example. Note that ρ in (3.14) is defined in (3.13), which is not $COR(u_{it}, \varepsilon_{it})$.

Suppose $T = 2$. Let a_{Nt} denote the probit for α_t/σ_t, and let η_{it} denote the corresponding influence function for a_{Nt}:

$$\eta_{it} \equiv E^{-1}(S_t S_t') \cdot S_{it} = E^{-1}(S_t S_t') \cdot w_i(d_{it} - \Phi_{it})\phi_{it}/\{\Phi_{it}(1 - \Phi_{it})\},$$

where $\Phi_{it} \equiv \Phi(w_i'\alpha_t/\sigma_t)$ and $\phi_{it} \equiv \phi(w_i'\alpha_t/\sigma_t)$. Define

$$z_{i1} \equiv (w_i', \lambda(w_i'\alpha_1/\sigma_1))', \quad z_{i2} \equiv (w_i', \lambda(w_i'\alpha_2/\sigma_2))',$$
$$z_{Ni1} \equiv (w_i', \lambda(w_i'a_{N1}))', \quad z_{Ni2} \equiv (w_i', \lambda(w_i'a_{N2}))',$$

and the second-stage LSE g_{Nt}, $t = 1, 2$, for their parameters, respectively,

$$\gamma_1 \equiv ((\bar{\beta}+\bar{\theta})', (\tilde{\beta}+\tilde{\theta}_1)', \tilde{\theta}_2', \rho\sigma_1)' \quad \text{and} \quad \gamma_2 \equiv ((\bar{\beta}+\bar{\theta})', \tilde{\theta}_1', (\tilde{\beta}+\tilde{\theta}_2)', \rho\sigma_2)'.$$

Further define L_t such that

$$L_t = -\rho\sigma_t \cdot E\{d_t \cdot \lambda'(w'\alpha_t/\sigma_t) \cdot z_t w_t'\}, \quad \text{where } \lambda'(a) = -a\lambda(a) - \lambda(a)^2,$$

and the "reduced form" error term and its residual, respectively, as

$$v_{it} \equiv y_{it} - z_{it}'\gamma_t \quad \text{and} \quad v_{Nit} \equiv y_{it} - z_{Nit}'g_{Nt}.$$

Then $\sqrt{N}(g_{Nt} - \gamma_t) \Rightarrow N(0, C_t)$ where

$$C_t \equiv E^{-1}(d_t z_t z_t') \cdot E\{(d_t v_t z_t + L_t \eta_t)(d_t v_t z_t + L_t \eta_t)'\} \cdot E^{-1}(d_t z_t z_t').$$

An influence function ζ_{it} for $\sqrt{N}(g_{Nt} - \gamma_t)$ is

$$\zeta_{it} = E^{-1}(d_t z_t z_t') \cdot (d_{it} v_{it} z_{it} + L_t \eta_{it}); \tag{3.16}$$

to estimate ζ_{it}, the unknown entities in ζ_{it} are to be replaced by consistent estimates, and $E(\cdot)$ by $(1/N)\sum_i(\cdot)$. The influence functions are needed for MDE as shown next.

The estimators g_{N1} and g_{N2} ignore the restrictions in γ_1 and γ_2 : $\bar{x}_i$ shares the same parameter, and $\tilde{x}_{i1}$ and $\tilde{x}_{i2}$ yield four sets of estimates in the two waves whereas there are only three sets of parameters: $\tilde{\beta}, \tilde{\theta}_1$ and $\tilde{\theta}_2$. To take advantage of these restrictions, we do MDE. Define

$$\gamma \equiv ((\bar{\beta} + \bar{\theta})', \tilde{\beta}', \tilde{\theta}_1', \tilde{\theta}_2', \rho\sigma_1, \rho\sigma_2)'.$$

Let $\bar{\beta}$ $(\tilde{\beta})$ be a $k_c \times 1$ $(k_v \times 1)$ vector. The MDE uses $(\gamma_1', \gamma_2')' = R\gamma$, where R is

$$\begin{bmatrix}
I_{k_c} & 0_{k_c \times k_v} & 0_{k_c \times k_v} & 0_{k_c \times k_v} & 0_{k_c \times 2} \\
0_{k_v \times k_c} & I_{k_v} & I_{k_v} & 0_{k_v \times k_v} & 0_{k_v \times 2} \\
0_{k_v \times k_c} & 0_{k_v \times k_v} & 0_{k_v \times k_v} & I_{k_v} & 0_{k_v \times 2} \\
0_{1 \times k_c} & 0_{1 \times k_v} & 0_{1 \times k_v} & 0_{1 \times k_v} & 1, 0 \\
I_{k_c} & 0_{k_c \times k_v} & 0_{k_c \times k_v} & 0_{k_c \times k_v} & 0_{k_c \times 2} \\
0_{k_v \times k_c} & 0_{k_v \times k_v} & I_{k_v} & 0_{k_v \times k_v} & 0_{k_v \times 2} \\
0_{k_v \times k_c} & I_{k_v} & 0_{k_v \times k_v} & I_{k_v} & 0_{k_v \times 2} \\
0_{1 \times k_c} & 0_{1 \times k_v} & 0_{1 \times k_v} & 0_{1 \times k_v} & 0, 1
\end{bmatrix},$$

which has dimension $\{2(k_c + 2k_v + 1)\} \times (k_c + 3k_v + 2)$. We then have

$$g_{mde} = (R'W_N^{-1}R)^{-1}R'W_N^{-1} \cdot (g_{N1}', g_{N2}')', \qquad (3.17)$$
$$\sqrt{N}(g_{mde} - \gamma) \Rightarrow N(0, (R'W_N^{-1}R)^{-1}),$$
$$N \cdot \{(g_{N1}', g_{N2}')' - Rg_{mde}\}'W_N^{-1}\{(g_{N1}', g_{N2}')' - Rg_{mde}\} \Rightarrow \chi^2_{k_c + k_v}$$

where

$$W_N \equiv (1/N)\sum_i \zeta_i \zeta_i' \quad \text{and} \quad \zeta_i \equiv (\zeta_{i1}', \zeta_{i2}')'.$$

6.3.4 An Empirical Example on Wage for Binary-Selection

Recall the Health and Retirement Study data. Let $d_{it} = 1$ if i works at t and 0 otherwise, and let $y_{it} = \ln(\text{wage}_{it})$. The list of regressors is as follows:

time-invariant: 1, age (in years), education (in years), man $(0,1)$;

time-variant: married $(0,1)$, medicare $(0,1)$, medicaid $(0,1)$, blue-hmo $(0,1)$, physical health, mental health;

physical and mental health are measured in 1-5 with 1 being the best. Age should be treated as time invariant for it changes only in the deterministic fashion. Eight time-invariant regional dummies are also used but their estimates are not shown.

The empirical results are presented in two sets: before MDE and after MDE. Before MDE, we get g_{N1} and g_{N2}, which are provided in Table 6.2. The first two starred columns are supposed to be close to each other, for they are for the same parameters $\bar{\beta} + \bar{\theta}$. The second two starred columns are also supposed to be close for they are both for $\tilde{\beta}$: $\tilde{\beta}$ is estimated as $(\tilde{\beta} + \tilde{\theta}_1$ from wave 1) minus $(\tilde{\theta}_1$ from wave 2) in $\tilde{b}_N$ (1), and as $(\tilde{\beta} + \tilde{\theta}_2$ from wave 2) minus $(\tilde{\theta}_2$ from wave 1) in $\tilde{b}_N$ (2).

The coefficient for $\lambda(\cdot)$ indicates a significant selection problem only for wave 1. Among the estimates for the time invariants, those for 1, education and man are not much different across the two waves. The estimates for edu are 8.4% and 9.1%, which are the sum of β_{edu} in the wage equation and $\bar{\theta}_{\text{edu}}$ in the $E(\delta_i|\cdot)$ equation; of course, if we assume $\bar{\theta}_{\text{edu}} = 0$, then β_{edu} is estimated as 8.4% or 9.1%. As for man, $\bar{\beta}_{\text{man}} + \bar{\theta}_{\text{man}}$ is about 15%; again our interest would be in $\bar{\beta}_{\text{man}}$. In the estimates for the time variants, other than married, the other estimates look different across the two waves. This may be due to the endogeneity problem that the health insurance dummies and the two health variables may be endogenous to wage; of course, there are many other things that can go wrong in the model.

Table 6.2 Ln(wage) Equation Estimation without MDE

	Wave 1		Wave 2			
	g_{N1}	t−value	g_{N2}	t−value	$\tilde{b}_N$ (1)	$\tilde{b}_N$ (2)
$\lambda(\cdot)$	0.470	1.99	0.182	0.65		
one	9.136*	54.17	9.592*	33.54		
age	−0.005*	−1.13	−0.012*	−1.65		
edu	0.084*	20.12	0.091*	18.91		
man	0.150*	2.51	0.159*	2.11		
married$_1$	0.471	7.35	0.959	8.99	−0.488*	
medicare$_1$	−0.179	−1.24	−0.185	−1.33	0.006*	
medicaid$_1$	−0.485	−1.92	−0.129	−0.56	−0.356*	
blue−hmo$_1$	0.385	5.91	0.252	2.97	0.133*	
phy−health$_1$	−0.065	−3.01	−0.071	−2.70	0.006*	
psy−health$_1$	−0.026	−2.06	−0.010	−0.60	−0.015*	
married$_2$	0.146	3.16	−0.258	−2.45		−0.405*
medicare$_2$	−0.173	−1.69	−0.033	−0.21		0.141*
medicaid$_2$	−0.486	−3.33	−0.252	−1.19		0.234*
blue−hmo$_2$	0.182	3.80	0.172	3.32		−0.010*
phy−health$_2$	−0.060	−3.53	−0.075	−2.92		−0.015*
psy−health$_2$	0.002	0.15	0.017	1.04		0.015*
Second−stage LSE R^2: 0.296			0.218			

After MDE, we get the following result shown in Table 6.3.

TABLE 6.3 Ln(wage) Equation Estimation with MDE

	g_{mde}	t−value		g_{mde}	t−value
$\lambda_1(\cdot)$	0.121	0.79	married$_1$	0.924	9.39
$\lambda_2(\cdot)$	0.080	0.60	medicare$_1$	−0.157	−1.56
one	9.156	60.64	medicaid$_1$	−0.205	−1.11
age	−0.002	−0.50	blue−hmo$_1$	0.270	4.34
edu	0.086	24.08	phy−health$_1$	−0.050	−2.65
man	0.083	2.04	psy−health$_1$	−0.029	−2.04
married	−0.406	−3.65	married$_2$	0.160	3.53
medicare	0.082	0.70	medicare$_2$	−0.059	−0.76
medicaid	0.088	0.40	medicaid$_2$	−0.384	−3.06
blue−hmo	0.002	0.03	blue−hmo$_2$	0.137	3.18
phy−health	0.011	0.45	phy−health$_2$	−0.061	−3.99
psy−health	0.006	0.34	psy−health$_2$	−0.001	−0.11
MDE over−id test stat. (p−value): 62.291 (0.000)					

There is now no evidence for selection bias. The estimate for edu is about the same as before, whereas that for man is much subdued. Only marriage and man are significant in the wage equation, whereas the other time variants are not significant. In the $E(\delta_i|\cdot)$ equation with $\tilde{\theta}_1$ and $\tilde{\theta}_2$, many time variants are significant. Unfortunately, the MDE over-id test easily rejects the parameter restrictions used for the MDE.

Because $\tilde{\beta}$, $\tilde{\theta}_1$, and $\tilde{\theta}_2$ are identified, we can separate the effects of a time variant on wage$_{it}$ and δ_i; call the former the short-run effect, whereas the latter is the long-term association. Although the short-term effect of marriage is significantly negative (if one gets newly wed, some wage may be lost), the long-term association is significantly positive; unfortunately, the long-term associations are too different across the two waves to be plausible. The long-term associations of medicare and medicaid are negative, whereas those of blue-hmo are positive. The long-term associations of health indicators are positive (recall small, not large, numbers for indicators mean good health).

6.4 TWO FIRST-DIFFERENCE ESTIMATORS FOR CENSORED SELECTION

This section presents two semiparametric $\sqrt{N}$-consistent first-difference (or error-differencing) estimators for the censored-selection model: Lee (2001) and Honoré and Kyriazidou (2000a, HK in this section); also, a simple empirical example is provided. Neither estimator requires exclusion restrictions. Recall the censored-selection model in (3.1) to (3.3).

Lee (2001) imposed the following four assumptions, none of which is parametric; also unknown forms of heteroskedasticity are allowed. First,

$$E(u_{it}|x_i, \varepsilon_i) = h(x_i) + E(u_{it}|\varepsilon_i), \quad t = 1, 2, \tag{4.1}$$

where $h(x_i)$ is an unknown function exchangeable in x_{i1} and x_{i2}: $h(x_{i1}, x_{i2}) = h(x_{i2}, x_{i1})$; (4.1) allows $h(\cdot) = 0$, with which (4.1) becomes the mean-independence of u_{it} from x_i given ε_i. Second, for unknown parameters ρ_{t1} and ρ_{t2},

$$E(u_{it}|\varepsilon_i) = \rho_{t1}\varepsilon_{i1} + \rho_{t2}\varepsilon_{i2}, \quad t = 1, 2. \tag{4.2}$$

Third,

$$\rho_{11} = \rho_{22} \equiv \rho_0 \quad \text{and} \quad \rho_{12} = \rho_{21} \equiv \rho_1. \tag{4.3}$$

A sufficient condition for (4.3) is the (joint) "exchangeability": with $f(\cdot)$ denoting a density for $(\varepsilon_{i1}, \varepsilon_{i2}, u_{i1}, u_{i2})|x_i$, for a.e. x_i,

$$f(\varepsilon_{i1}, \varepsilon_{i2}, u_{i1}, u_{i2}|x_i) = f(\varepsilon_{i2}, \varepsilon_{i1}, u_{i2}, u_{i1}|x_i); \tag{4.4}$$

the sufficiency holds because (4.4) implies the same marginal distribution and equivalence of looking forward to looking backward. Fourth, $(\varepsilon_{i1}, \varepsilon_{i2})|(\psi_i, x_i)$ is exchangeable, which is also implied by (4.4).

Using (4.1) and (4.2), we get

$$E(y_{it}|x_i, \varepsilon_i) = x'_{it}\beta + E(\delta_i|x_i, \varepsilon_i) + h(x_i) + \rho_{t1}\varepsilon_{i1} + \rho_{t2}\varepsilon_{i2}, \quad t = 1, 2. \quad (4.5)$$

Rewrite the y_{it} equation as

$$y_{it} = x'_{it}\beta + \delta_i + h(x_i) + \rho_{t1}\varepsilon_{i1} + \rho_{t2}\varepsilon_{i2} + v_{it}, \quad (4.6)$$

where

$$v_{it} \equiv u_{it} - h(x_i) - \rho_{t1}\varepsilon_{i1} - \rho_{t2}\varepsilon_{i2}, \quad t = 1, 2. \quad (4.7)$$

First-difference (4.6) to get, with $\Delta v_i \equiv v_{i2} - v_{i1}$ and (4.3),

$$\begin{aligned} \Delta y_i &= \Delta x'_i\beta + \rho_{21}\varepsilon_{i1} + \rho_{22}\varepsilon_{i2} - \rho_{11}\varepsilon_{i1} - \rho_{12}\varepsilon_{i2} + \Delta v_i \quad (4.8) \\ &= \Delta x'_i\beta + \rho\Delta\varepsilon_i + \Delta v_i, \quad where \ \rho \equiv \rho_0 - \rho_1. \quad (4.9) \end{aligned}$$

If $\Delta\varepsilon_i$ were observable, then LSE would be applicable to (4.9), for (recall (4.1))

$$E(\Delta v_i|x_i, \varepsilon_i) = E(v_{i2}|x_i, \varepsilon_i) - E(v_{i1}|x_i, \varepsilon_i) = 0 - 0 = 0. \quad (4.10)$$

A $\sqrt{N}$-consistent estimator for $\Delta\varepsilon_i$ can be obtained using the fourth estimator, say a_N, in Honoré (1992, the LSE version for a panel censored model); this estimator was introduced in the preceding chapter. But, because the notations in this chapter are different from those in the preceding chapter, we present the estimator again: with $d^c_{it} \equiv \max(d^*_{it}, 0)$, the estimator is obtained by minimizing, wrt a,

$$(1/N) \sum_i [\{\max(d^c_{i2}, \Delta x'_i a) - \max(d^c_{i1}, -\Delta x'_i a) - \Delta x'_i a\}^2$$

$$-2 \cdot 1[d^c_{i2} < \Delta x'_i a](d^c_{i2} - \Delta x'_i a)d^c_{i1} - 2 \cdot 1[d^c_{i1} < -\Delta x'_i a](d^c_{i1} + \Delta x'_i a)d^c_{i2}].$$

Denoting the estimator for $\Delta\varepsilon_i$ as $\Delta\hat{\varepsilon}_i \equiv \Delta d^c_i - \Delta x'_i a_N$, rewrite (4.9) as

$$\Delta y_i = \Delta x'_i\beta + \rho \cdot \Delta\varepsilon_i + \Delta v_i = \Delta x'_i\beta + \rho \cdot \Delta\hat{\varepsilon}_i + \{\Delta v_i - \rho \cdot (\Delta\hat{\varepsilon}_i - \Delta\varepsilon_i)\}. \quad (4.11)$$

Using only the observations with $d_i = 1$, LSE for this with $\{\cdot\}$ as the error term is Lee's (2001) estimator.

As for the asymptotic distribution, define

$$\hat{z}_i \equiv (d_i\Delta x'_i, d_i\Delta\hat{\varepsilon}_i)' \quad and \quad z_i \equiv (d_i\Delta x'_i, d_i\Delta\varepsilon_i)'.$$

Let η_i denote an influence function for Honoré's estimator a_N:

$$\sqrt{N}(a_N - \alpha) = (1/\sqrt{N}) \sum_i \eta_i + o_p(1),$$

$$\eta_i \equiv \{E(1[-d^c_{i1} < \Delta x'_i\alpha < d^c_{i2}] \cdot \Delta x_i\Delta x'_i)\}^{-1} \cdot \{(\Delta d^c_i - \Delta x'_i\alpha)$$
$$\cdot 1[-d^c_{i1} < \Delta x'_i\alpha < d^c_{i2}] - d^c_{i1}1[d^c_{i2} < \Delta x'_i\alpha] + d^c_{i2}1[-d^c_{i1} > \Delta x'_i\alpha]\}.$$

The LSE g_N for $\gamma \equiv (\beta', \rho)'$ is

$$g_N = \{(1/N) \sum_i \hat{z}_i \hat{z}_i'\}^{-1} (1/N) \sum_i \hat{z}_i \Delta y_i, \tag{4.12}$$

and

$$\sqrt{N}(g_N - \gamma) \Rightarrow N(0, \{E(zz')\}^{-1} \cdot \Omega \cdot \{E(zz')\}^{-1}), \tag{4.13}$$

where

$$\Omega \equiv E[\{z\Delta v + \rho E(z\Delta x')\eta\} \cdot \{z\Delta v + \rho E(z\Delta x')\eta\}'];$$

Ω can be consistently estimated replacing $E(\cdot)$ by its sample version; η_i can be also consistently estimated replacing α with a_N.

Turning to HK, let $\zeta_i \equiv (\psi_i, \delta_i, x_i')'$. HK assume

$$P((\varepsilon_{i1}, \varepsilon_{i2}, u_{i1}, u_{i2}) \le \tau | \zeta_i) = P((\varepsilon_{i2}, \varepsilon_{i1}, u_{i2}, u_{i1}) \le \tau | \zeta_i), \tag{4.14}$$

which is analogous to (4.4). HK estimate β by minimizing

$$\sum_i (\Delta y_i - \Delta x_i' b)^2 \cdot 1[d_{i1}^c > \max(0, -\Delta x_i' a_N), d_{i2}^c > \max(0, \Delta x_i' a_N)] \tag{4.15}$$

for b; HK propose a number of estimators, and (4.15) is only one of them that is computationally convenient.

The idea for (4.15) rests on the equivalence of the event in $1[\cdot]$ to

$$\varepsilon_{i1} > \max(-x_{i1}'\alpha - \psi_i, -x_{i2}'\alpha - \psi_i), \quad \varepsilon_{i2} > \max(-x_{i1}'\alpha - \psi_i, -x_{i2}'\alpha - \psi_i) : \tag{4.16}$$

under (4.14), conditional on this event and ζ_i, $\Delta y_i - \Delta x_i'\beta$ is symmetrically distributed around zero, which then leads to the LSE expression in (4.15). This estimator is certainly reminiscent of Honoré (1992). HK do not provide the asymptotic distribution for their estimator, although it does not seem to be too difficult to get.

HK do not need any linear regression assumptions for error terms as in (4.2), whereas Lee's (2001) estimator and Wooldridge's (1995) estimators do. On the other hand, HK require exchangeability involving four errors, whereas Wooldridge (1995) needs a marginal normality and Lee (2001) needs a weaker form of exchangeability. Because Lee's estimator requires only a LSE after Honoré's (1992) estimator is obtained, it is easier to obtain than HK. Thus, it also can be used as an initial estimate for HK's numerical optimization; the empirical example that follows demonstrates that this is a sensible thing to do, for the two estimators are quite close.

With exchangeability invoked several times, one may wonder how plausible the exchangeability is. For two random variables (v_1, v_2) with a density function $f(v_1, v_2)$, exchangeability is the symmetry about the 45-degree line on the (v_1, v_2) plane; a necessary condition is that the marginal distributions are identical. If (v_1, v_2) is jointly normal with the same marginal distribution, then

TABLE 6.4 Ln(income) Equation under Censored Selection

	Lee	Honoré−Kyriazidou	MEAN	SD
$\Delta\varepsilon$	0.003 (2.091)			
1	0.035 (2.874)	0.036 (2.888)	55.31	5.49
married	0.756 (6.954)	0.757 (6.935)	0.83	
medicare	−0.152 (−2.014)	−0.172 (−2.103)	0.058	
medicaid	0.084 (0.581)	0.079 (0.500)	0.031	
blue−hmo	0.076 (1.266)	0.069 (1.126)	0.722	
phy. condition	0.009 (0.613)	0.008 (0.562)	2.438	1.141
psy. condition	−0.025 (−1.819)	−0.029 (−2.069)	2.473	1.047
Managerial	0.385 (3.160)	0.396 (1.638)	0.102	
Prof.tech.support	0.413 (3.525)	0.404 (1.818)	0.111	
Sales	0.547 (4.107)	0.554 (2.308)	0.073	
Clerical,adm.	0.392 (3.372)	0.399 (1.688)	0.112	
Bldg.service	0.450 (2.217)	0.413 (1.397)	0.011	
Protect.service	0.164 (0.658)	0.114 (0.371)	0.011	
Food prep.	0.271 (1.758)	0.303 (1.152)	0.020	
Health serv.	0.102 (0.501)	0.091 (0.310)	0.016	
Personal sev.	0.497 (2.830)	0.533 (1.786)	0.045	
Farm.fishing	0.496 (2.717)	0.463 (1.542)	0.021	
Mechanics,repair	0.299 (1.183)	0.287 (0.867)	0.025	
Const.,extract.	0.442 (2.698)	0.443 (1.671)	0.025	
Precision prod.	0.296 (1.472)	0.278 (0.951)	0.024	
Machine oper.	0.463 (2.487)	0.431 (1.570)	0.046	
Transp. oper.	0.311 (1.516)	0.284 (0.966)	0.034	
Oper., handler	0.402 (2.966)	0.382 (1.551)	0.016	

(v_1, v_2) is exchangeable for $f(v_1, v_2) = f(v_2, v_1)$. In general, in view of the necessary condition, exchangeability seems plausible in stationary environments where looking back is the same as looking forward; in practice, if the time difference between two waves is small, exchangeability will have a better chance of holding.

To illustrate how the two estimators may work in practice, we applied the two estimators to the Health Retirement Study data. The outcome equation is for ln(income) and the censored selection is for hours worked. Because time-invariants are not identified, they are dropped and 16 job category dummy variables are added; other than these, we use four time-variant regressors: married, medicare, physical condition, and psychological condition. The last two variables take five ordered values 1 to 5, with 1 being the best. The job dummies could not be used for the (binary-) selection estimator developed by Wooldridge (1995), which was presented in the previous section, due to numerical problems.

Because HK do not provide the asymptotic distribution, the t-values in $(\cdot)$ in Table 6.4 are obtained using the first two numerical derivatives of the HK's estimator maximand, which ignores the first-stage error $a_N - \alpha$. Overall, two sets of estimates are quite close. The only notable difference is that the t-values of Lee's estimator tend to be larger than those of HK, which confirms the finding in Lee's (2001) simulation that Lee's estimator tends to be the more efficient; this is, however, subject to the caveat that the t-values for HK are ad hoc. Judging from ρ in Lee, there is a significant selection problem. The estimates for the time variants do not seem to make much sense possibly due to endogeneity problems between the time variants and wage.

The estimates are quite different from the estimates of Wooldridge (1995) for panel (binary-) selection in Table 6.3. Recall that, for panel binary response, there was also much difference between conditional logit and panel probit; the former is an error-differencing estimator, whereas the latter is an error-specifying estimator. The two estimators in this section are error differencing, whereas Wooldridge's estimator (1995) is error specifying. If the endogeneity problems operate mainly through time invariants, then error-differencing estimators are preferred in general. Otherwise, if the endogeneity problems are due to time variants, then error-specifying estimators seem to be better choices. Recall the discussion between the within group estimator and the between group estimator in Chapter 2; there, we noted that the within group estimator, which is error-differencing, can work poorly if there are errors-in-variable problems in time-variants, which are endogeneity problems.

6.5   A ROOT-Nh CONSISTENT ESTIMATOR FOR BINARY SELECTION

In this section, we review Kyriazidou's (1997) root-Nh consistent semiparametric estimator for (binary-) selection models. Because the estimator requires an exclusion restriction, replace x_{it} in the selection equation (3.1) with $w_{it} = (x_{it}', c_{it}')'$ to get

$$d_{it}^* = w_{it}'\alpha + \psi_i + \varepsilon_{it}, \quad d_{it} = 1[d_{it}^* > 0],$$
$$y_{it} = x_{it}'\beta + \delta_i + u_{it}, \quad t = 1, 2, \quad d_i \equiv d_{i1}d_{i2};$$
$$(d_{i1}, d_{i2}, x_{i1}', x_{i2}', d_{i1}y_{i1}, d_{i2}y_{i2}) \text{ observed}, i = 1, ..., N, iid.$$

Other than c_{it}, the notations in Section 6.3 apply. The time-invariant regressors are absorbed into ψ_i and δ_i.

Compared with Wooldridge (1995), Kyriazidou (1997) relaxed the assumption that the selection equation error term follows a normal distribution independently of the regressors, and the assumption that the selection and outcome equation error terms satisfy linear regression assumptions as in (3.5), (3.10) and (3.11). But this comes at the cost of (a) imposing an exclusion restriction, (b) slowing down the convergence rate below the usual $\sqrt{N}$-rate, (c) requiring exchangeability on the error terms as shown shortly, and (d) not being able to identify time-invariant regressors' coefficients.

The estimation scheme proceeds in two steps. In the first step, α is estimated by a panel version of the smoothed maximum score estimator as explained in

Chapter 4. In the second step, Kyriazidou (1997) adopts Ahn and Powell's (1993) approach for cross-section selection models: individuals with $w'_{i1}\alpha = w'_{i2}\alpha$ are selected, and the LSE is applied to the first-differenced outcome equation. The condition $w'_{i1}\alpha = w'_{i2}\alpha$, the same selection equation index, implies that the selection bias terms in the two periods are the same and thus cancel each other under the (joint) exchangeability for $(\varepsilon_{i1}, \varepsilon_{i2}, u_{i1}, u_{i2})$ given $(\psi_i, \delta_i, w_{i1}, w_{i2})$; this key idea is shown in the following discussion.

Denote a density of $u|v$ evaluated at $u = a$ and $v = b$ as $f_{u|v=b}(a)$. Omit "$|(\psi, \delta, w_1, w_2)$." In terms of densities, the exchangeability is

$$f_{\varepsilon_1,\varepsilon_2,u_1,u_2}(a_1, a_2, b_1, b_2) = f_{\varepsilon_1,\varepsilon_2,u_1,u_2}(a_2, a_1, b_2, b_1). \tag{5.1}$$

This means that having $(\varepsilon_1 = a_1, \varepsilon_2 = a_2, u_1 = b_1, u_2 = b_2)$ is the same as having $(\varepsilon_1 = a_2, \varepsilon_2 = a_1, u_1 = b_2, u_2 = b_1)$, which is a "time reversal." Integrating out (b_1, b_2), it holds that

$$f_{\varepsilon_1,\varepsilon_2}(a_1, a_2) = f_{\varepsilon_1,\varepsilon_2}(a_2, a_1). \tag{5.2}$$

Divide (5.1) by (5.2), and integrate out b_2 to get

$$f_{u_1|(\varepsilon_1=a_1,\varepsilon_2=a_2)}(b_1) = f_{u_2|(\varepsilon_1=a_2,\varepsilon_2=a_1)}(b_1). \tag{5.3}$$

Now consider $E(u_1|\varepsilon_1 > -\mu_1, \varepsilon_2 > -\mu_2)$ with μ_1 and μ_2 fixed, which is for the first period selection bias: omitting the range of integration if it is ∞ or $-\infty$,

$$E(u_1|\varepsilon_1 > -\mu_1, \varepsilon_2 > -\mu_2)$$

$$= \iint_{-\mu_2} \int_{-\mu_1} b_1 f_{u_1|(\varepsilon_1=a_1,\varepsilon_2=a_2)}(b_1) \cdot da_1 da_2 \cdot db_1$$

$$/ \iint_{-\mu_2} \int_{-\mu_1} f_{u_1|(\varepsilon_1=a_1,\varepsilon_2=a_2)}(b_1) \cdot da_1 da_2 \cdot db_1 \tag{5.4}$$

$$= \iint_{-\mu_2} \int_{-\mu_1} b_1 f_{u_2|(\varepsilon_1=a_2,\varepsilon_2=a_1)}(b_1) \cdot da_1 da_2 \cdot db_1$$

$$/ \iint_{-\mu_2} \int_{-\mu_1} f_{u_2|(\varepsilon_1=a_2,\varepsilon_2=a_1)}(b_1) \cdot da_1 da_2 \cdot db_1. \tag{5.5}$$

As for the second period selection bias,

$$E(u_2|\varepsilon_1 > -\mu_1, \varepsilon_2 > -\mu_2)$$

$$= \iint_{-\mu_1} \int_{-\mu_2} b_1 f_{u_2|(\varepsilon_1=a_2,\varepsilon_2=a_1)}(b_1) \cdot da_1 da_2 \cdot db_1$$

$$/ \iint_{-\mu_1} \int_{-\mu_2} f_{u_2|(\varepsilon_1=a_2,\varepsilon_2=a_1)}(b_1) \cdot da_1 da_2 \cdot db_1. \tag{5.6}$$

If $\mu_1 = \mu_2$, then (5.5) = (5.6): the two selection bias terms agree if the two selection function indices μ_1 and μ_2 do.

Let a_N denote the first-stage panel smoothed maximum score estimator; it is $(Nh_1)^{1/2}$-consistent, where h_1 is a bandwidth. Thus depending on h_1, the convergence rate varies. Suppose that the convergence rate of a_N is faster than $N^{2/5}$, which is feasible at the second stage. Under this, the first-stage estimation error does not affect the second stage, for the convergence rate at the first stage is faster than that at the second stage.

Define

$$\Delta w_i = w_{i2} - w_{i1}. \tag{5.7}$$

The second stage estimator is

$$
\begin{aligned}
\tilde{b}_N &= \{(1/N)\sum_i h_2^{-1} K(\Delta w_i' a_N / h_2) \cdot d_i \Delta x_i \Delta x_i'\}^{-1} \tag{5.8}\\
&\quad \cdot\{(1/N)\sum_i h_2^{-1} K(\Delta w_i' a_N / h_2) \cdot d_i \Delta x_i \Delta y_i\},
\end{aligned}
$$

where K is a kernel and h_2 is a bandwidth; $\tilde{b}_N$ is consistent for the slope parameter β as $N \to \infty$. The second stage needs another bandwidth h_2 in addition to the bandwidth(s) h_1 for the first-stage estimator.

The inverted matrix in $\tilde{b}_N$ converges in probability to

$$H \equiv E(d \cdot \Delta x \Delta x' | \Delta w' \alpha = 0) \cdot f_{\Delta w' \alpha}(0), \tag{5.9}$$

where $f_{\Delta w' \alpha}$ is the density function of $\Delta w' \alpha$. H shows that an exclusion restriction is necessary; otherwise $\Delta x | (\Delta w' \alpha = 0)$ becomes linearly dependent. Also, the appearance of $f_{\Delta w' \alpha}(0)$ suggests choosing h_2 such that the choice of h_2 gives a smooth estimate for $f_{\Delta w' \alpha}$ around $\Delta w' \alpha = 0$.

The asymptotic normality follows from

$$(Nh_2)^{-1/2} \sum_i h_2^{-1} K(\Delta w_i' \alpha / h_2) \cdot d_i \Delta x_i \Delta u_i \Rightarrow N(0, C), \tag{5.10}$$

where

$$C \equiv E\{\Delta x \Delta x' \cdot (\Delta v)^2 d | \Delta w' \alpha = 0\} \cdot f_{\Delta w' \alpha}(0) \cdot \int K(z)^2 dz,$$

$$v_{it} \equiv u_{it} - E(u_{it}|d_i = 1, \psi_i, \delta_i, w_{i1}, w_{i2}), \quad \Delta v_i \equiv v_{i2} - v_{i1} = \Delta u_i.$$

Combine (5.9) and (5.10) to get

$$(Nh_2)^{1/2}(\tilde{b}_N - \beta) \Rightarrow N(0, H^{-1}CH^{-1}). \tag{5.11}$$

A consistent estimator for H is the inverted matrix in $\tilde{b}_N$, and C can be estimated consistently by

$$\int K(z)^2 dz \cdot (1/N) \sum_i h_2^{-1} K(\Delta w_i' a_N / h_2) \cdot d_i (\Delta y_i - \Delta x_i' \tilde{b}_N)^2 \cdot \Delta x_i \Delta x_i'. \tag{5.12}$$

Instead of using the smoothed maximum score estimator in the first stage, one may use Lee's (1999) $\sqrt{N}$-consistent estimator, if the requisite assumptions for Lee (1999) hold. The resulting TSE would follow the same asymptotic distribution as that of Kyriazidou (1997), while it would depend on only one bandwidth, not two.

6.6   LSE ON TRIMMED AND DIFFERENCED PANEL DUE TO ATTRITION

Attrition is a problem plaguing most panel data. For instance, the Panel Study of Income Dynamics has about a 50% attrition rate as of 1989 since its inception in 1968 (Fitzgerald *et al.*, 1998). Other panel data even with a short history often suffer from attrition, because much of attrition usually takes place in the first couple of periods.

Recall (3.1), (3.2), and (3.3)(c), with the error term in the outcome equation satisfying

$$E(u_{it}|x_{i1}, x_{i2}) = 0, \quad t = 1, 2. \tag{6.1}$$

The initial period sample selection problem can occur due to d_{i1} attached to x_{i1} and y_{i1}, whereas the attrition problem is due to $d_i \equiv d_{i1}d_{i2}$ attached to x_{i2} and y_{i2} (that is, a subject is observed at period 2 only when observed in both periods).

Our use of the term "attrition" is only for the observability as in (3.3)(c): *first, there is no comeback after dropout, and second, x_{it} is not observed when y_{it} is not observed*. About the former, comeback in a two-wave panel is having $(d_{i2}x'_{i2}, d_{i2}y_{i2})$ instead of $(d_{i1}d_{i2}x'_{i2}, d_{i1}d_{i2}y_{i2})$. As for the latter, in a sample-selection framework, we have "truncated selection", not the usual selection. When we discuss the literature on attrition later, however, attrition will be interpreted broadly ("the broad-sense attrition") including comebacks and the cases where x_{it} is observed always.

In the simulations of Verbeek and Nijman (1992) and Lee (2001), despite various sample selection problems, first-difference estimators performed well with almost no bias, because *differencing can remove not only the related effect but also the selection bias*. If this is true for attrition as well, it will be a big relief, for attrition is hard to deal with. Rectangular panels with only complete-record subjects are often used, and it is important to know when trimming the data and using the LSE on the differenced model is innocuous, which is the goal of this section.

In the following, we review some broad-sense attrition models, which differ in how the d_{it}-equation is modeled, and then present three conditions that justify the LSE. In passing, we note that Verbeek and Nijman (1992) suggested simple tests for selection/attrition bias: get funcions of d_{it}'s such as $\sum_{t=1}^{T} d_{it}$ or $\prod_{t=1}^{T} d_{it}$, and see if they are significant as regressors in the unbalanced panel. If the answer is yes, this is an evidence that selection/attrition matters.

Differently from (3.3)(c), the typical observability assumption in the attrition literature has been that

$$(d_{i2}, \; x'_{i1}, x'_{i2}, \; y_{i1}, d_{i2}y_{i2})' \text{ is observed:} \tag{6.2}$$

x_{it}'s are observed always; also the initial selection problem with d_{i1} is assumed away. Under (6.2), Hausman and Wise (1979) specified

$$d_{it} = 1[x'_{it}\alpha_x + \nu_i + \varepsilon_{it} > 0] \tag{6.3}$$

where α_x is a parameter vector and ν_i is an *unrelated* effect (that is, ν_i is a time-invariant error unrelated to the regressors). Because Hausman and Wise had a two-wave panel with (6.2), there was no need to consider comebacks.

Let $T \geq 2$ for a while. Suppose

$$(d_{i2}, ..., d_{iT}, \; x'_{i1}, ..., x'_{iT}, \; y_{i1}, d_{i2}y_{i2}, ..., d_{iT}y_{iT})' \text{ observed.} \tag{6.4}$$

Ridder (1990) generalized (6.3) into

$$d_{it} = 1[x'_{it}\alpha_x + \alpha_1 d_{i,t-1} + \cdots + \alpha_{t-1}d_{i,1} + \alpha_D D_{it} + \nu_i + \varepsilon_{it} > 0], \tag{6.5}$$

where D_{it} is the length of the current spell of participation with comebacks allowed, and $\alpha_1, ..., \alpha_{t-1}$ and α_D are parameters.

Zabel's (1998) model for d_{it} is

$$d_{it} = 1[x'_{it}\alpha_x + g'_{it}\alpha_d + \nu_i + \varepsilon_{it} > 0], \tag{6.6}$$

where g_{it} is the $T \times 1$ time dummy vector, and α_d is a parameter vector. Because no comeback is allowed in Zabel's data,

$$(d_{i2}, ..., d_{iT}, \; x'_{i1}, d_{i2}x'_{i2}, ..., \prod_{s=2}^{T} d_{is} \cdot x'_{iT}, \tag{6.7}$$

$$y_{i1}, d_{i2}y_{i2}, ..., \prod_{s=2}^{T} d_{is} \cdot y_{iT}) \text{ is observed.}$$

But Zabel adopted

$$(d_{i2}, ..., d_{iT}, \; x'_{i1}, d_{i2}x'_{i2}, ..., d_{iT}x'_{iT}, \; y_{i1}, d_{i2}y_{i2}, ..., d_{iT}y_{iT}), \tag{6.8}$$

which is not tenable, however, for this allows comebacks.

To avoid the truncated selection problem, Zabel used lagged time variants instead of the current versions in the d_{it}-equation, which was also done in Ziliak and Kniesner (1998) and Lillard and Panis (1998). But this is ill-advised, because attrition can be due to $\Delta x_i \neq 0$, which certainly requires the current time variants in the d_{it}-equation.

So far, shortcomings in the broad-sense attrition literature have been pointed out: (a) inadequate treatment of truncated selection, (b) neglecting the initial selection, and (c) inappropriate use of observability. In addition to these, (d) few papers allow a related-effect for d_{it}, and (e) the literature is heavily parametric. In the following discussion, we show three conditions out of five in Lee and Cho (2002) that justify the LSE for trimmed and differenced panel data while avoiding these shortcomings.

First-difference the outcome equation and multiply by d_i to get

$$d_i \Delta y_i = d_i \Delta x'_i \beta + d_i \Delta u_i. \tag{6.9}$$

For the LSE to this equation to be consistent, one needs (assume $P(d_i = 1) > 0$)

$$0 = E(d_i \Delta x_i \Delta u_i) = E(\Delta x_i \Delta u_i | d_i = 1) \cdot P(d_i = 1). \tag{6.10}$$

This depends on what determines d_i. For example, we have been assuming so far

d_i is determined only by x_i, ψ_i, and ε_i;

because $d_{it} = 1[x'_{it}\alpha + \psi_i + \varepsilon_{it} > 0]$ and $d_i = d_{i1}d_{i2}$.

Turning to the first condition justifying the LSE, denote the time-invariant regressors as $\bar{x}_i$ and suppose

d_i is determined only by $\bar{x}_i$ and ψ_i, $\qquad$ (C1)

which is dubbed "*only time-invariants for d_i*." Rewrite (6.10) as

$$0 = E[d_i \Delta x_i \cdot E\{E(u_{i2} - u_{i1} | \Delta x_i, \bar{x}_i, \psi_i) | \Delta x_i, d_i = 1\}]; \tag{6.11}$$

$(\Delta x_i, \bar{x}_i, \psi_i)$ is a more "refined" conditioning set than $(\Delta x_i, d_i = 1)$ owing to C1. Then (6.10) follows from

$$E(u_{i2} | \Delta x_i, \bar{x}_i, \psi_i) = E(u_{i1} | \Delta x_i, \bar{x}_i, \psi_i). \tag{M1}$$

M1 is implied by the *stationarity of $u_i | (x_i, \psi_i)$*. This kind of conditions appear in Manski (1987) and Honoré and Kyriazidou (2000a).

The second condition is "*selection on observables*":

u_i being independent of d_i given x_i. $\qquad$ (C2)

This establishes (6.10) with

$$E(u_{i2} | x_i, d_i = 1) - E(u_{i1} | x_i, d_i = 1) = E(u_{i2} | x_i) - E(u_{i1} | x_i) = 0 - 0 = 0 \tag{M2}$$

as (6.10) can be written as

$$0 = E[d_i \Delta x_i \cdot E\{E(u_{i2} - u_{i1} | x_i, d_i = 1) | \Delta x_i, d_i = 1\}]. \tag{6.12}$$

C2 requires $\psi_i + \varepsilon_{it}$ to be independent of u_{it} given $x_i, t = 1, 2$. Differently from C1, C2 allows both ψ_i and ε_i to affect d_{it}. M2 seems an "overkill" in the sense that the two terms in M2 do not have to be 0 for (6.10) to hold: it is enough if the two terms are equal as in M1.

The third condition is *"selection on observables and related effect"*:

$$\text{(i) } u_i \text{ is independent of } \varepsilon_i \text{ given } (x_i, \psi_i); \qquad \text{(C3)}$$
$$\text{(ii) } E(u_{i1}|x_i, \psi_i) = E(u_{i2}|x_i, \psi_i).$$

This implies

$$E(u_{i2}|x_i, \psi_i, d_i = 1) - E(u_{i1}|x_i, \psi_i, d_i = 1)$$
$$= E(u_{i2}|x_i, \psi_i) - E(u_{i1}|x_i, \psi_i) = 0, \qquad \text{(M3)}$$

that is enough for (6.10). As in C2, C3 allows ψ_i and ε_i to affect d_{it}.

In C3(i), u_i *can be related to* ε_i *through* ψ_i *given* x_i; this is an improvement over selection on observables, which rules out a relationship between u_i and ε_i given x_i; this improvement is possible only for panel data, not for cross-section data. But this comes with a restriction involving $E(u_{it}|x_i, \psi_i)$ in C3(ii). For example, if ψ_i affects $E(u_{it}|\cdot)$ differently for $t = 1, 2$, then C3(ii) may not hold; this point applies also to M1. Note that C3(ii) can be strengthened to

$$E(u_{it}|x_i, \psi_i) = 0, \quad t = 1, 2, \qquad (6.13)$$

which implies (6.1). As M1 does, C3(ii) follows from the stationarity of $u_i|(x_i, \psi_i)$. In summary, (C3) seems to be an attractive condition to justify the LSE for trimmed and differenced panel data to avoid attrition biases.

DATA AND GAUSS PROGRAMS

This appendix is for the data and GAUSS programs (for the empirical examples used in the main text). The programs and data are provided for the benefit of the reader. Any reader who uses them is expected to acknowledge the source as a matter of academic honesty and courtesy.

Four data sets are provided:

1. linwage.dat: explained in Subsection 2.5.3.

2. union.dat: drawn from the *Journal of Applied Econometrics* data archives; explained in Vella and Verbeek (1998).

3. patent.dat: drawn from the *Journal of Applied Econometrics* data archives; explained in Cincera (1997).

4. health.dat: explained in Subsection 4.2.2; detailed explanations can be found in Lee and Kobayashi (2001).

Ten GAUSS programs are provided, covering linear models and nonlinear models (binary, ordered discrete response (ODR), censored, count, binary sample-selection, and censored sample-selection); collectively, most important models in panel limited dependent variables are covered. For those models, only the estimators that converge well (or at least better than others) in practice are chosen. Specifically, the following models have been selected:

1. linmme: for Subsection 2.5.3; linear model LSE, WIT, IVE, and GMM.

2. linmde: for Subsection 3.2.3; linear model wave-by-wave GMM and MDE.

3. biclog: for Section 4.7; conditional logit for waves 6, 7, 8, and MDE.

4. bipro: for Section 4.7; panel probit with waves 7, 8, and MDE.

5. odrclog3: for ODR with three categories, 2 waves, and MDE.

6. odrclog4: for ODR with four categories, 3 waves, and MDE.

7. odrclog5: for ODR with five categories, 2 waves, and MDE.

8. crgmm: for Section 5.7; count-data conditional QMLE and GMM.

9. bisel: for Subsection 6.3.4; Heckman's two-stage type estimation and MDE.

10. censel: for Section 6.4; censored-selection two-stage estimation; the first stage is Honoré (1992) and the second stage is Lee (2001).

In all iterations, Newton-Raphson type algorithms are used with the second-order derivative matrix replaced by the outer product of the first-order derivative. Analytic first-order derivatives are used mostly, but in (10) censel, numerical derivatives are used. In general, numerical derivatives can be used whenever the analytic versions are cumbersome to get. The price one will pay for this choice, however, is that the numerical derivatives slow down the algorithm somewhat.

MDE appears in many places, and the time spent on learning it will not be wasted. The ODR programs transform ODR into a number of binary responses, and then use conditional logit and MDE; the programs can be easily adapted for more than five categories or for more than two (or three) waves. Nonlinear GMM appears in (8) crgmm for count responses; it goes without saying that the nonlinear GMM there can be adapted for other problems. As noted in (10) censel, Honoré's (1992) estimator is used which is explained in Section 5.5; in (10), Lee's (2001) estimator is chosen because it takes only one LSE step from Honoré's estimator.

REFERENCES

ECA: *Econometrica*,
JAE: *Journal of Applied Econometrics*,
JBES: *Journal of Business and Economic Statistics*,
JOE: *Journal of Econometrics*.

Abrevaya, J. (2000). Rank estimation of a generalized fixed-effects regression model. *JOE* **95**, 1–23.

Ahn, D. H., and Gao, B. (1999). A parametric nonlinear model of term structure dynamics. *Rev. Financial Stud.* **12**, 721–762.

Ahn, H. T., and Powell, J. L. (1993). Semiparametric estimation of censored selection models with a nonparametric selection mechanism. *JOE* **58**, 3–29.

Ahn, S. C., and Schmidt, P. (1995). Efficient estimation of models for dynamic panel data. *JOE* **68**, 5–27.

Ahn, S. C., and Schmidt, P. (1997). Efficient estimation of dynamic panel data models: Alternative assumptions and simplified estimation. *JOE* **76**, 309–321.

Alzaid, A. A., and Al-Osh, M. A. (1990). Integer-valued pth order autoregressive structure (INAR(p)) process. *J. Applied Probability* **27**, 314–324.

Amemiya, T., and MaCurdy, T. E. (1986). Instrumental variable estimation of an error-components model. *ECA* **54**, 869–881.

Anderson, E. B. (1970). Asymptotic properties of conditional maximum likelihood estimators. *J. Royal Statistical Society, Series B*, **32**, 283–301.

Anderson, T. W., and Hsiao, C. (1981). Estimation of dynamic models with error components. *J. Amer. Statistical Assn.* **81**, 598–606.

Anderson, T. W., and Hsiao, C. (1982). Formulation and estimation of dynamic models using panel data. *JOE* **18**, 47–82.

Andrews, D. W. K. (1987). Asymptotic results for generalized Wald tests. *ET* **3**, 348–358.

Angrist, J., Imbens, G. W., and Krueger, A. B. (1999). Jackknife instrumental variables estimation. *JAE* **14**, 57–67.

Angrist, J. and Krueger, A. B. (1991). Does compulsory school attendance affect schooling and earnings? *Quarterly J. Econ.* **106**, 979–1014.

Angrist, J. and Krueger, A. B. (1995). Split-sample instrumental variables estimates of the return to schooling. *JBES* **13**, 225–235.

Anselin, L. (1988). *Spatial Econometrics: Methods and Models.* Kluwer Academic Publishers, Dordrecht.

Anselin, L., and Bera, A. K. (1998). Spatial dependence in linear regression models with an introduction to spatial econometrics. In *Handbook of Applied Economic Statistics* (A. Ullah and D. E. A. Giles, eds.). Marcel Dekker, New York.

Arellano, M., and Bond, S. (1991). Some tests of specification for panel data: Monte Carlo evidence and an application to employment equations. *Rev. Econ. Stud.* **58**, 277–297.

Arellano, M., and Bover, O. (1995). Another look at the instrumental variable estimation of error-components models. *JOE* **68**, 29–51.

Arellano, M., and Carrasco, R. (1999). Binary choice panel data models with predetermined variables. Unpublished paper, CEMFI, Spain.

Arellano, M., and Honoré, B. (2001). Panel data models: Some recent developments. In *Handbook of Econometrics V*, (J. J. Heckman and E. E. Leamer, eds.). North-Holland, Amsterdam.

Ashenfelter, O., and Krueger, A. B. (1994). Estimates of the economic return to schooling from a new sample of twins. *Amer. Econ. Rev.* **84**, 1157–1173.

Avery, R. B., Hansen, L. P., and Hotz, V. J. (1983). Multiperiod probit models and orthogonality condition estimation. *Intl. Econ. Rev.* **24**, 21–35.

Baltagi, B. H. (1995). *Econometric Analysis of Panel Data.* Wiley, New York.

Baltagi, B. H., and Griffin, J. M. (1984). Short and long run effects in pooled models. *Intl. Econ. Rev.* **25**, 631–645.

Baltagi, B. H., Griffin, J. M., and Xiong, W. (2000). To pool or not to pool: Homogenous versus heterogeneous estimators applied to cigarette demand. *Rev. Econ. and Statistics* **82**, 117–126.

Baltagi, B. H., and Khanti-Akom, S. (1990). On efficient estimation with panel data. *JAE* **5**, 401–406.

Behrman, J. R., and Wolfe, B. L. (1989). Does more schooling make women better nourished and healthier? Adult sibling random and fixed-effects estimates for Nicaragua. *J. Human Resources* **24**, 644–663.

Bell, K. P., and Bockstael, N. E. (2000). Applying the generalized-moments estimation approach to spatial problems involving microlevel data. *Rev. Econ. and Statistics* **82**, 72–82.

Bertschek, I., and Lechner, M. (1998). Convenient estimators for the panel probit model. *JOE* **87**, 329–371.

Bickel, P. J., Klaassen, C. A. J., Ritov, Y., and Wellner, J. A. (1993). *Efficient and adaptive estimation for semiparametric models.* Johns Hopkins University Press.

Blundell, R., Griffith, R., and Windmeijer, F. (2002). Individual effects and dynamics in count data models. *JOE*, forthcoming.

Börsch-Supan, A. (1990). Panel data analysis of housing choices, *Regional Sci. and Urban Econ.* **20**, 65–82.

Breusch, T. S., Mizon, G. E., and Schmidt, P. (1989). Efficient estimation using panel data. *ECA* **57**, 695–700.

Cameron, A. C., and Trivedi, P. K. (1998). *Regression analysis of count data,* Cambridge University Press.

Card, D. (1999). The causal effect of education on earnings. In *Handbook of Labor Economics 3*, (O. Ashenfelter and D. Card, eds.), p. 1801–1863. North-Holland, Amsterdam.

Cavanagh, C., and Sherman, R. P. (1998). Rank estimators for monotonic index models. *JOE* **84**, 351–381.

Chamberlain, G. (1980). Analysis of covariance with qualitative data. *Rev. Econ. Studies* **47**, 225–238.

Chamberlain, G. (1982). Multivariate regression models for panel data. *JOE* **18**, 5–46.

Chamberlain, G. (1984). Panel data. In *Handbook of Econometrics II*, (Z. Griliches and M. Intrilligator, eds.). North Holland, Amsterdam.

Chamberlain, G. (1985). Heterogeneity, omitted variable bias and duration dependence. In *Longitudinal Analyses of Labor Market Data* (J. Heckman and B. Singer, eds.). Academic Press, San Diego.

Chamberlain, G. (1987). Asymptotic efficiency in estimation with conditional moment restrictions. *JOE* **34**, 305–334.

Chamberlain, G. (1992). Comment: Sequential moment restrictions in panel data. *JBES* **10**, 20–26.

Charlier, E., Melenberg, B., and van Soest, A. (1995). A smoothed maximum score estimator for the binary choice panel data model with an application to labor force participation. *Statistica Neerlandica* **49**, 324–343.

Chen, S. (1997). Semiparametric estimation of the type 3 Tobit model. *JOE* **80**, 1–34.

Chintagunta, P., Kyriazidou, E., and Perktold, J. (2001). Panel data analysis of household brand choices. *JOE* **103**, 111–153.

Cincera, M. (1997). Patents, R&D, and technological spillovers at the firm level: Some evidence from econometric count models for panel data. *JAE* **12**, 265–280.

Collado, M. D. (1997). Estimating dynamic models from time series of independent cross-section. *JOE* **82**, 37–62.

Corcoran, M., and Hill, M. S. (1985). Reoccurence of unemployment among young adult men. *J. Human Resources* **20**, 165–183.

Cornwell, C., and Ruppert, P. (1988). Efficient estimation with panel data: An empirical comparison of instrumental variables estimators. *JAE* **3**, 149–155.

Cornwell, C., and Trumbull, W. N. (1994). Estimating the economic model of crime with panel data. *Rev. Econ. and Statistics* **76**, 360–6.

Deaton, A. (1985). Panel data from time series of cross-sections. *JOE* **30**, 109–126.

Deaton, A. (1995). Data and econometric tools for development analysis. In *Handbook of Development Economics III* (J. Behrman and T. N. Srinivasan, eds.). North-Holland, Amsterdam.

Erdem, T. and Sun, B. (2001). Testing for choice dynamics in panel data. *JBES* **19**, 142–152.

Fitzgerald, J., Gottschalk, P., and Moffitt, R. (1998). An analysis of sample attrition in panel data. *J. Human Resources* **33**, 251–299.

Frees, E. W. (1995). Assessing cross-section correlation in panel data. *JOE* **69**, 393–414.

Gerfin, M. (1996). Parametric and semiparametric estimation of the binary response model of labor market participataion. *JAE* **11**, 321–339.

Granger, C. W. J. (1969). Investigating causal relations by econometric models and cross-spectral methods. *ECA* **37**, 424–438.

Granger, C. W. J. (1980). Testing for causality: A personal viewpoint. *J. Econ. Dynamics and Control* **2**, 329–352.

Greenwood, P. E., and Nikulin, M. S. (1996). *A Guide to Chi-squared Testing*, New York, John Wiley & Sons.

Griliches, Z. (1995). R&D and productivity: Econometric results and measurement issues. In *Handbook of the Economics of Innovation and Technological Change* (P. Stoneman, ed.). Blackwells, Oxford.

Griliches, Z., and Hausman, J. (1986). Errors in variables in panel data. *JOE* **31**, 93–118.

Griliches, Z., and Mairesse, J. (1998). Production functions: The search for identification. In *Econometrics and Economic Theory in the 20th Century* (Steinar Strom, ed.). Cambridge University Press, Cambridge.

Hall, A. R., Rudebusch, G. D., and Wilcox, D. W. (1996). Judging instrument relevance in instrumental variables estimation. *Intl. Econ. Rev.* **37**, 283–298.

Hall, B. H., Griliches, Z., and Hausman, J. (1986). Patents and R&D: Is there a lag? *Intl. Econ. Rev.* **27**, 265–283.

Han, A. (1987). Nonparametric analysis of a generalized regression model. *JOE* **35**, 303–316.

Hansen, L. P. (1982). Large sample properties of generalized method of moments estimators. *ECA* **50**, 1029–1054.

Hansen, L. P., Heaton, J., and Yaron, A. (1996). Finite sample properties of some alternative GMM estimators. *JBES* **14**, 262–280.

Härdle, W. (1990). *Applied Nonparametric Regression*, Cambridge University Press.

Hausman, J. A. (1978). Specification tests in econometrics. *ECA* **46**, 1251–1272.

Hausman, J. A., Hall, B. H., and Griliches, Z. (1984). Econometric models for count data with an application to the patents-R&D relationship. *ECA* **52**, 909–938.

Hausman, J. A., and Taylor, W. E. (1981). Panel data and unobservable individual effects. *ECA* **49**, 1377–1398.

Hausman, J. A. and Wise, D. A. (1979). Attrition bias in experimental and panel data: The Gary income maintenance experiment. *ECA* **47**, 455–473.

Heckman, J. J. (1979). Sample selection bias as a specification error. *ECA* **47**, 153–161.

Heckman, J. J. (1981). Statistical models for discrete panel data. In *Structural Analysis of Discrete Data with Econometric Applications* (C. F. Manski and D. McFadden, eds.). MIT Press, Cambridge.

Hettmansperger, T. P. (1984). *Statistical Inference Based on Ranks*. Wiley, New York.

Hochguertel, S. (1998). *Households' Portfolio Choices*. Center for Economic Research, Dissertation Series 39, Tilburg University, The Netherlands.

Holtz-Eakin, D., Newey, W., and Rosen, H. S. (1988). Estimating vector autoregressions with panel data. *ECA* **56**, 1371–1395.

Holtz-Eakin, D., Newey, W., and Rosen, H. S. (1989). The Revenue-expenditure nexus: Evidence from local government data. *Intl. Econ. Rev.* **30**, 415–429.

Honoré, B. E. (1992). Trimmed LAD and LSE of truncated and censored regression models with fixed effects. *ECA* **60**, 533–565.

Honoré, B. E. (1993). Orthogonality conditions for Tobit models with fixed-effects and laged dependent variables. *JOE* **59**, 35–61.

Honoré, B. E. and Kyriazidou, E. (2000a). Estimation of tobit-type models with individual specific effects. *Econometric Rev.* **19**, 341–366.

Honoré, B. E. and Kyriazidou, E. (2000b). Panel data discrete choice models with lagged dependent variables. *ECA* **68**, 839–874.

Honoré, B. E., and Lewbel, A. (2002). Semiparametric binary choice panel data models without strictly exogeneous regressors. *ECA*, forthcoming.

Hoogstrate, A. J., Palm, F. C., and Pfann, G. A. (2000). Pooling in dynamic panel-data models: An application to forecasting GDP growth rates. *JBES* **18**, 274–283.

Horowitz, J. L. (1992). A smoothed maximum score estimator for the binary response model. *ECA* **60**, 505–531.

Horowitz, J. L. (1993). Semiparametric estimation of a work-trip mode choice model. *JOE* **58**, 49–70.

Horowitz, J. L. (2001). The bootstrap. In *Handbook of Econometrics V*, (J. J. Heckman and E. E. Leamer, eds.). North-Holland, Amsterdam.

Hsiao, C. (1986). *Analysis of Panel Data*, Cambridge University Press.

Ichimura, H. (1993). Semiparametric least squares (SLS) and weighted SLS estimation of single index models. *JOE* **58**, 71–120.

Imbens, G. W. (1997). One-step estimators for over-identified generalized method of moment models. *Rev. Econ. Stud.* **64**, 359–383.

Jakubson, G. (1988). The sensitivity of labor-supply parameter estimates to unobserved individual effects: Fixed- and random-effects estimates in a nonlinear model using panel data. *J. Labor Econ.* **6**, 302–329.

Keane, M. P. (1997). Modeling heterogeneity and state dependence in consumer choice behavior. *JBES* **15**, 310–327.

Keane, M. P. and Runkle, D. E. (1992). On the estimation of panel-data models with serial correlation when instruments are not strictly exogenous, *JBES* **10**, 1–9.

Kerkhofs, M., Lindeboom, M., and Theeuwes, J. (1999). Retirement, financial incentives and health. *Labor Econ.* **6**, 203–227.

Kim, J. K. and Pollard, D. (1990). Cube-root asymptotics, *Annals of Statistics* **18**, 191–219.

Klein, R. W. and Spady, R. H. (1993). An efficient semiparametric estimator for binary response models. *ECA* **61**, 387–421.

Koenker, R., Machado, J. A. F., Skeels, C. L., and Welsh, A. H. (1994). Momentary lapses: Moment expansions and the robustness of minimum distance estimation. *Econometric Theory* **10**, 172–197.

Kyriazidou, E. (1997). Estimation of a panel data sample selection model. *ECA* **65**, 1335–1364.

Lechner, M. (1995). Some specification tests for probit models estimated on panel data. *JBES* **13**, 475–488.

Lee, L. F. (1992). Amemiya's generalized least squares and tests of overidentification in simultaneous equation models with qualitative or limited dependent variables. *Econometric Rev.* **11**, 319–328.

Lee, L. F. (1994). Semiparametric two-stage estimation of sample selecion models subject to Tobit-type selection rules. *JOE* **61**, 305–344.

Lee, M. J. (1996). *Methods of Moments and Semiparametric Econometrics for Limited Dependent Variable Models*. New York, Springer-Verlag.

Lee, M. J. (1998). Two-stage procedures for some semiparametric estimators in discrete and censored response models. Dept. Economics, Sungkyunkwan University. Unpublished paper.

Lee, M. J. (1999). A Root-N consistent semiparametric estimator for related-effect binary response panel data. *ECA* **67**, 427–434.

Lee, M. J. (2001). First-difference estimator for panel censored-selection models. *Econ. Letters* **70**, 43–49.

Lee, M. J., and Cho, M. H. (2002). Validity of LSE for trimmed and differenced panel data due to absorbing attrition. *Econ. Letters* **74**, 251–256.

Lee, M. J., and Kobayashi, S. (2001). Proportional treatment effects for count response panel data: Effects of binary exercise on health care demand. *Health Econ.* **10**, 411–428.

Lee, M. J., Vella, F., and Wooldridge, J. (2000). Semiparametric estimation of the type 3 tobit model under a mean independence condition. Dept. Economics, Sungkyunkwan University. Unpublished paper.

Lillard, L. A., and Panis, C. W. A. (1998). Panel attrition from the panel study of income dynamics. *J. Human Resources 33*, 437–457.

Maddala, G. S. (1987). Limited dependent variable models using panel data. *J. Human Resources 22*, 307–338.

Manski, C. F. (1985). Semiparametric analysis of discrete response. *JOE* **27**, 313–333.

Manski, C. F. (1987). Semiparametric analysis of random effects linear models from binary panel data. *ECA* **55**, 357–362.

Mátyás, L., and Sevestre, P. (1992). *The Econometrics of Panel Data: Handbook of theory and applications*. Kluwer Academic Publishers, Dordrecht.

Melenberg, B. and Van Soest, A. (1996). Measuring the costs of children: Parametric and semiparametric estimators. *Statistica Neerlandica* **50**, 171–192.

Mroz, T.A. (1987). The sensitivity of an empirical model of married womens' hours of work to economic and statistical assumptions. *ECA* **5**, 765–799.

Newey, W. (1993). Efficient estimation of models with conditional moment restrictions. In *Handbook of Statistics 11* (G. S. Maddala, C. R. Rao and H. D. Vinod, eds.). North-Holland, Amsterdam.

Newey, W. (1994). The asymptotic variance of semiparametric estimators. *ECA* 1349–1382.

Newey, W. and McFadden, D. L. (1994). *Large sample estimation and hypothesis testing, in Handbook of Econometrics IV*, edited by R. F. Engle and D. L. McFadden, Amsterdam, North-Holland.

Newey, W., Powell, J. L., and Walker, J. R. (1990). Semiparametric estimation of selection models: Some empirical results. *Amer. Econ. Rev., Papers and Proceedings* **80**, 324–328.

Nijman, T., and Verbeek, M. (1992). Nonresponse in panel data: The impact on estimates of a life cycle consumption function. *JAE* **7**, 243–257.

Owen, A. B. (2001). Empirical likelihood, Boca Raton, Chapman & Hall/CRC.

Pirotte, A. (1999). Convergence of the static estimation toward the long-run effects of dynamic panel data models. *Econ. Letters* **63**, 151–158.

Pohlmeier, W., and Ulrich, V. (1995). An econometric model of the two-part decision making process in the demand for health care. *J. Human Resources* **30**, 339–361.

Powell, J. L. (1987). Semiparametric estimation of bivariate latent variable models. SSRI 8704, Dept. Economics, U. Wisconsin-Madison.

Powell, J. L. (1994). Estimation of semiparametric models. In *Handbook of Econometrics IV* (R. F. Engle and D. L. McFadden, eds.). North-Holland, Amsterdam.

Qin, J. and Lawless, J. (1994). Empirical likelihood and general estimating equations. *Annals of Statistics* **22**, 300–325.

Rasch, G. (1961). On general law and the meaning of measurement in psychology. *Proceedings of the Fourth Berkeley Symposium on Mathematical Statistics and Probability* **4**, 321–333.

Rice, N., and Jones, A. (1997). Multilevel models and health economics. *Health Econ.* **6**, 561–575.

Ridder, G. (1990). Attrition in multi-wave panel data. In *Panel Data and Labor Market Studies*, (J. Hartog, G. Ridder, and J. Theeuwes, eds.). North-Holland, Amsterdam.

Robinson, P. M. (1988). Root-N consistent semiparametric regression, *ECA* **56**, 931–954.

Rochina-Barrachina, M. E. (1999). A new estimator for panel data sample selection models. *Annales D'Économie et De Statistique* **55-56**, 153–181.

Schmidt, P., Ahn, S. C., and Wyhowski, D. (1992). Comment, *JBES* **10**, 10–14.

Shea, J. (1997). Instrumental relevance in mutivariate linear models: A simple measure. *Rev. Econ. and Statistics* **79**, 348–352.

Sherman, R. (1993). The limiting distribution of the maximum rank correlation estimator. *ECA* **61**, 123–137.

Stock, J. H., and Wright, J. H. (2000). GMM with weak identification. *ECA* **68**, 1055–1096.

Staiger, D., and Stock, J. H. (1997). Instrumental variables regression with weak instruments. *ECA* **65**, 557–586.

Udry, C. (1995). Risk and savings in Northern Nigeria. *Amer. Econ. Rev.* **85**, 1287–1300.

Urdy, C. (1996). Gender, agricultural production and the theory of the household. *J. Political Econ.* **104**, 1010–1046.

Vella, F., and Verbeek, M. (1998). Whose wages do unions raise? A dynamic model of unionism and wage determination for young men. *JAE* **13**, 163–183.

Vella, F., and Verbeek, M. (1999). Two-step estimation of panel data models with censored endogenous variables and selection bias. *JOE* **90**, 239–263.

Verbeek, M., and Nijman, T. (1992). Incomplete panels and selection bias. In *The Econometrics of Panel Data* (L. Mátyás and P. Sevestre, eds.). Dordrecht, Kluwer Academic Publishers.

Wang, J. and Zivot, E. (1998). Inference on structurual parameters in instrumental variables regression with weak instruments. *ECA* **66**, 1389–1404.

Wooldridge, J. M. (1995). Selection corrections for panel data models under conditional mean independence assumptions. *JOE* **68**, 115–132.

Wooldridge, J. M. (1997). Multiplicative panel data models without the strict exogeneity assumption. *Econometric Theory* **13**, 667–678.

Wooldridge, J. M. (1999). Distribution-free estimation of some nonlinear panel data models. *JOE* **90**, 77–97.

Zabel, J. E. (1998). An analysis of attrition in the panel study of income dynamics and the survey of income and program participation with an application to a model of labor market behavior. *J. Human Resources* **33**, 479–506.

Ziliak, J. P. (1997). Efficient estimation with panel data when instruments are predetermined: An empirical comparison of moment-condition estimators. *JBES* **15**, 419–431.

Ziliak, J. P. and Kniesner, T. J. (1998). The importance of sample attrition in life-cycle labor supply estimation. *J. Human Resources* **33**, 507–530.

INDEX